T0313887

I TATTI STUDIES IN
ITALIAN RENAISSANCE HISTORY

Published in collaboration with I Tatti
The Harvard University Center for Italian Renaissance Studies
Florence, Italy

GENERAL EDITOR
Kate Lowe

NICCOLÒ DI LORENZO DELLA MAGNA

and the Social World of Florentine Printing,

ca. 1470–1493

LORENZ BÖNINGER

Harvard University Press

Cambridge, Massachusetts

London, England

2021

Copyright © 2021 by the President and Fellows of Harvard College

All rights reserved

Printed in the United States of America

First printing

Library of Congress Cataloging-in-Publication Data

Names: Böninger, Lorenz, author.
Title: Niccolò di Lorenzo della Magna and the social world of Florentine
    printing, ca. 1470–1493 / Lorenz Böninger.
Other titles: I Tatti studies in Italian Renaissance history.
Description: Cambridge, Massachusetts : Harvard University Press, 2021. |
    Series: I Tatti studies in Italian renaissance history | Includes bibliographical
    references and index. |
Identifiers: LCCN 2020041889 | ISBN 9780674251137 (cloth)
Subjects: LCSH: Laurentii, Nicolaus, active 1475–1486. | Printers—Italy—Florence—
    History—15th century. | Publishers and publishing—Italy—History—
    15th century. | Florence (Italy)—Civilization.
Classification: LCC Z156.F5 B66 2021 | DDC 686.20945/511—dc23
LC record available at https://lccn.loc.gov/2020041889

CONTENTS

NICCOLÒ DI LORENZO
DELLA MAGNA
AND THE SOCIAL WORLD *of*
FLORENTINE PRINTING,
ca. 1470–1493

Introduction

*I*n Italy, the printing revolution arrived step by step. Attention for the unknown art grew slowly in the 1460s, when increasing numbers of books produced in Western and Southern Germany arrived on the peninsula.[1] Simultaneously, a young generation of printers spread out from there in search of new opportunities.[2] Some of them settled in Subiaco and thereafter in Rome, where their presses began working in the middle of the decade. Elsewhere one had to wait until 1470–1472, when a sudden frenzy overcame important centers like Bologna, Florence, Milan, or Venice. In the dynamic and geographically mobile society of the time, now even more individuals from different backgrounds sought to learn this promising craft from experienced printers. As must be stressed, the complex typographical process could not be improvised or reinvented without the expertise of these "masters." Such miraculous "reinventions" were nevertheless more than once propagated, for instance, by the mysterious priest Clemente da Padova, who twice—in 1470 and 1472—offered himself to introduce printing in the town of Lucca.[3]

From the very beginning, printing was "a meeting point of economic forces," as Brian Richardson formulated, and Renaissance Florence was no exception to this.[4] Regarding these forces, Richard Goldthwaite added that the Florentine printing industry "was the one business that, unlike any other in Florence outside the textile industry, was oriented to production for foreign markets." Not very much is known about the functioning of these markets. With respect to serial manuscript production, the example of the famous bookseller and writer Vespasiano da Bisticci demonstrates how easily the whole of the Italian Peninsula could be reached with his handwritten products. The mechanisms of the early printed book trade have, on the other hand, only in the last decades become a matter of historiographical interest. If thus, as Goldthwaite put it, "for the most part the history of [*Florentine*] printers is that of ventures that hobbled along, from one contract to another, until the Giunti appeared on the scene at the end of the [*fifteenth*] century," this requires further explanation.[5]

Already in the fourteenth century, Florentine citizens prided themselves on one of the highest rates of literacy in Europe and propagated their ethical and cultural values derived—as they claimed—from ancient and modern literature. Reading was a fundamental element of this culture. Florence's internal market for printed books was therefore potentially richer than that of other civic centers. The natural question arises as to why, then, printing turned out to be so difficult and risky in Florence, if on the other hand one of the traditional characteristics of its economic culture was its vocation to long-distance trade and if its merchants were omnipresent on the principal fairs and markets of the time. Could it really be that at a certain point the Florentine printers realized that they were "not able to produce for export" and that they thus limited their efforts on the—however rich—local markets, publishing their books predominantly for the nearby towns of Siena, Pisa or Bologna, as Paolo Trovato maintained?[6]

Comparing the Florentine output of incunabula with that of the three most dynamic printing centers in Italy (i.e., Milan, Rome, and Venice), Brian Richardson found that on the Arno River fewer legal or theological volumes in Latin were produced because of the relatively modest size of the Florentine university, the Studium Generale, which in 1473 had been transferred to Pisa.[7] Florentine vernacular editions suffered, on the other hand, from an "inward-looking and insular" attitude. Another reason for the rather modest local production lay in the

Florentines' reticence to invest in the new industry: whereas in Venice printing "had the support of many leading statesmen, academics and clerics," in Florence "the works printed were often more ephemeral and printing itself did not attract the sort of patronage which helped to launch Jenson's career."[8] This last point has also been stressed by other scholars, such as Neil Harris and Martin Lowry, who recorded the mental "predisposition" of Venetian publishers to economic risks and their eagerness to invest risk capital.[9]

Although one of the most important scholars in this field, Roberto Ridolfi, went so far as to define the study of the economical factors of printing as the "philosophy of the history of the book," these problems have never been dealt with in a more than impressionistic manner.[10] Of course, many other factors contributed to the growth of the new business as well—for example, social and cultural aspects and, more generally, the legal, political, and economical conditions. For this study the considerations of all these aspects must be considered as fundamental.

The richness of Florence's libraries and archives has always stimulated scholarly research on its civic, literary, and artistic culture, as well as on a multitude of other, sometimes even neglected, aspects. With the help of hitherto unknown archival material, these pages will reflect on the life and work of the most prolific Florentine printer in the 1470s and early 1480s, Niccolò di Lorenzo della Magna, and on printing in Renaissance Florence in general. Before doing so, this introduction will present the institutional framework in which local typographers operated, the problems regarding the distribution of their works, and the wider economic context. This will be followed by a brief presentation of how this text is organized and the archival sources on which it is based.

A striking aspect of early printing in Renaissance Florence seems to be the fact that the publishers only exceptionally indicated their investments as part of their professional activities. As will be shown, many of them were quite young, in their twenties, and were described in their tax returns to the Catasto as without any profession ("senza exercizio," "non fa nulla"). Sometimes investments in printing seem to have been made by the wealthier scions of Florentine society shortly after their weddings, and in these cases one might suspect that parts of the dowry funds were used for them, turning even their spouses into possibly unaware but certainly legitimate owners of the finished volumes. The printers, booksellers, and stationers (*cartolai*), just like the painters and haberdashers or mercers (*merciai*), were, unlike the publishers, subject to the guild of doctors of medicine and apothecaries commonly known as the Arte dei medici e speziali (or *aromatai*).[11] The reason for this was that the main substance used by the stationers, paper, was originally listed among the merchandise traded exclusively by the apothecaries.[12] Although doctors, apothecaries, and sometimes even stationers played an important role in Florentine political and social life, their guild was dominated by a handful of patrician families, as the rather repetitive lists of names in the lists of its "consuls" prove.[13] As it seems, apothecaries were only represented in the larger, general council meetings.[14] No painters, stationers, or printers seem to have reached high positions in the guild.

Unlike the local painters who regularly met in their religious confraternity of Saint Luke or the stationers in other towns like Milan or Genoa, Florentine stationers and printers had no such confraternity of their own in the fifteenth century.[15] They were subject to the exclusive jurisdiction of the guild of doctors and apothecaries and could not pursue their debtors from the guild in a secular or ecclesiastical court.[16] Unfortunately, the loss of all of the guild's internal records does not allow any further considerations. Neither is there a list of the members of the guild (*matricola*) for the crucial years of our interest. Many Florentine and foreign printers, whose presence or activity before 1490 can only be guessed at, remain therefore nameless. In compensation there is a member list of the surrounding territory (*contado*) and four matriculation lists regarding the city of Florence for the period after 1490 which have been studied by Gustavo Bertoli.[17]

The guild of doctors and apothecaries occasionally sold both manuscripts and printed books. Although this was probably no organized trade, one might consider the hypothesis that these books had been confiscated from its members in order to balance their debts.[18] This corporation was furthermore, as has been seen, the first judicial instance in disputes between stationers or printers and their business partners. Naturally, the guild also decided all questions between fabric merchants and local paper producers (*cartai*).[19] Again, no documents regarding these cases have survived. Sometimes, however, we can gain a glimpse on how the corporation worked. The partially known history of a dispute between the notary, publisher, and book dealer Piero Pacini and the typographer Francesco di Dino in the 1480s on the printing of three different books shows, for example, that the guild tribunal arrived at a first sentence in 1484, but that in order to conclude his plea successfully, Pacini had to turn to the court of the Mercanzia and finally to that of the Podestà, who eventually forced the printer to give in by imprisoning him.[20]

Albinia de la Mare has described how the Florentine stationers and scribes adapted to the new situation created by the printing industry.[21] The expansion of the increasingly dynamic book market caused a stronger competition and, as an unwelcome "by-product," a rising number of conflicts between different professional categories working in printing and selling which—as elsewhere—sometimes turned even violent. One of the most obvious changes the printing press brought to Florence was the considerable increase not only of local stationers but also of ambulant booksellers. These worked in two different ways, as salaried salesmen for other printers or on their own, on a more modest level as peddlers, *cerretani* or *circulatores,* as they were called in Genoa.[22]

Few sources have fueled the interest in this professional category more than the so-called diary of the Florentine convent of San Iacopo di Ripoli (1476–1484), in which many of these middlemen appear with their qualifications and names.[23] As one of the most important sources for the study of early printing, this account book has been studied from various points of view ever since it was discovered in the eighteenth century. One of the lessons to be learned from it is that "the printer's ability to locate suitable distributors for his products—energetic and shrewd judges of an audience's actual and potential tastes—and his ability to create and maintain stable relations with them, may have been as important to his success as his choice of text or type."[24] As various examples show, this counted also for the local stationers.

In Venice and not in Florence, the merchants Girolamo Strozzi and Giambattista Ridolfi organized in 1476 for the printing of three important volumes, the Florentine histories of Leonardo Bruni and Poggio Bracciolini, and Cristoforo Landino's *volgare* translation of Pliny's *Historia naturale.* The finished volumes were then sent to Florence to be sold by a group of competing stationers. The reasons given for this procedure were quite interesting. Strozzi knew "by experience that it is unwise to allow the booksellers to have more than two or three copies at a time and that it is very difficult to get them to reimburse him for the copies sold." He therefore advised his Florentine agent "not to furnish any more copies until those already disposed of have been paid for and further advises him to make a tour of all the shops every fortnight, checking to see that unsold copies are still in evidence because of the tendency of the book- sellers to lend them to those who would probably purchase copies if un- able to borrow them."[25]

The role of both "stationary" and ambulant booksellers was consid- ered so crucial that at times it was mentioned as an integral part of a new printing enterprise—as, for example, in Pavia (1474).[26] A recent three- volume dictionary on the Italian book market between the fifteenth and seventeenth centuries has justly given much space to this profes- sional category.[27] And even the following discussion of Niccolò di Lo- renzo della Magna's career will include short biographical portraits of those individuals—Antonio di Mariano *speziale*, Domenico di Benedetto Doni—who were presumably involved with the distribution of his works.

This matter has to be considered in the more general economic con- text. A recent survey on the production of a typographer in the Swiss town of Basel, Michel Wenssler, has stressed that his activity was "capital- intensive and marked by a very long return on investment. Indeed, a considerable amount of time would pass between the initial investments in infrastructure, raw material and labour force, and the moment the first books were sold. Finally, for early publishers it was almost impos- sible to make predictions about market expectations. Local markets nor- mally were quite restricted, whereas trans-regional markets were hard to read; moreover, it was necessary to travel to fairs in order to promote the product."[28] The question of whether these aspects can already be dis- cussed in a "protocapitalistic" perspective today seems to have lost much of its appeal. It leads, however, to another crucial point: that of debt capital in joint ventures between publishers and printers.[29] From the court acts in Basel it has been demonstrated that printers like Wens- sler ran their business from the very beginning on debt capital. This was, for example, needed for assembling the press, the purchase of paper, or other services: "With all due respect towards quantitative analysis, there is strong evidence that debts shaped both the late medieval urban economy as well as everyday life. In this sense, Michel Wenssler and his steady presence in court are representative of the late medieval urban economy and particularly telling for how the debt economy is essential in understanding how he ran his printing workshop."[30] As has convincingly been concluded, debt economy was in this sense the "underlying financial structure for the [printing] industry as a whole."[31]

The present study is organized into three parts, covering roughly (and mostly chronologically) two decades—that is, from around 1470/1471 until 1493, when Niccolò di Lorenzo della Magna's name was mentioned for the last time. Beginning rather conventionally with the presumed "inventor" of typography in Florence, Bernardo Cennini, it will become clear that there was at least one other professional colleague, Giovanni di Piero da Magonza, and presumably a third one, the as yet nameless "Printer of Terentius, Pr. 6748," who all gave proof of their skills in the years around 1471. Part I will end with the hitherto overlooked relationship between wool merchants and printers, which is a perfect example of the debt economy as described above. For wool merchants the investment in printing was considered a natural, if not instinctive way of selling cloth, especially the so-called *panni di garbo,* in an "alternative" way and in a saturated home market that was characterized by overproduction of exactly this sort of wool. On a larger scale, these transactions confirm the results of Paul McLean and Neha Gondal's research on the "credit network" in Renaissance Florence.[32]

Niccolò di Lorenzo della Magna's career, his typographical production and his frequent legal struggles between 1475 and 1486, stand at the center of Parts II and III. Leaving a modest position in the court of the Mercanzia, Niccolò received his professional formation after 1474, probably from his "master," Giovanni di Piero da Magonza, before entering into a partnership with the Florentine citizen Cappone di Bartolomeo Capponi. This company secured him economic stability for five years, during which, according to the partnership rules, single commissions for works could be accepted from other citizens or institutions like religious convents. Whenever such a direct commission could be reasonably argued, the text will investigate the circumstances and biographies of the single publishers involved with them.

Niccolò di Lorenzo had no permanent business partner after 1480/1481, when he ventured to become an independent printer. Many of his best-known books date from these years, like Cristoforo Landino's commented and partly illustrated edition of Dante Alighieri's *Divina*

Commedia, Francesco Berlinghieri's *Geographia,* and Leon Battista Alberti's *De re aedificatoria.* All of these works derived from single commissions, just like his last—disastrous—enterprise of Saint Gregory's *Morali* (1483–1486). As in Part I, biographical data will help to illustrate the lives of the individuals known to have been involved with either Niccolò's printing press or the distribution of its works. Unfortunately, most of the craftsmen in his workshop—in which after 1480 up to four presses were simultaneously used, employing probably no less than ten craftsmen—remain for now anonymous, despite all the research. Probably Niccolò di Lorenzo was employing itinerant and therefore "nameless" printers from central Europe, but the historical sources on this matter remain disappointingly silent.[33] As will be demonstrated, he still relied on the direct or indirect support of other citizens, foremost the humanist Cristoforo Landino. Especially from this side, he continued to receive his necessary share of "vertical solidarity," as this characteristic feature of late medieval society has been called by Francis William Kent.[34]

Following the long and complicated legal battle over the printing of Saint Gregory's *Morali,* the epilogue will finally address a central matter in all early book printing—that is, the question of paper supply. Although no final conclusions can be reached on the specific role that paper prices and paper trade played in early Tuscan book production, their crucial importance for printing, not only in Florence, will become evident. Another fundamental question, that of the selling prices of books, will only be touched upon in a nonsystematic and "impressionistic" way, i.e., supplying information on prices every time the sources permit this.

These pages concentrate therefore on the typographer's professional career and not so much on the bibliographical analysis of his products. A detailed and satisfying account in this sense could only be offered by book historians and bibliographers with a special interest in early printing. The complex analytical methods derived from the study of Johannes Gutenberg's products or Shakespeare's *First Folio* have set standards that cannot be met here. Certainly this study would have greatly benefited from a collaboration regarding the physical aspects, the printing practices, print or state variants, and similar problems in Niccolò di Lorenzo's books. Albeit, such an undertaking would imply viewing the highest possible numbers of extant copies; as these are spread around the globe, at times in large numbers and at others in just a few or single copies, the project would have become very demanding. For all bibliographical aspects this text will therefore mostly rely on Victor Scholderer's 1930 catalog of books from the fifteenth century in the British Library and Dennis Rhodes's *Annali* from 1988, just as much as on the online repertories of the *Incunabula Short Title Catalogue at the British Library (ISTC)*, and the *Gesamtkatalog der Wiegendrucke (GW)*, usually with the reference number of the single editions.

In a few exceptional cases, however, bibliographical questions will be addressed from a historical point of view. The German writer and philosopher Walter Benjamin once quoted Anatole France: "The only exact knowledge there is is the knowledge of the date of publication and the format of books." Alas, this knowledge remains often incomplete if not contradictory, and especially in Florence, where many of the earliest prints appeared without any indication regarding these crucial matters, *sine notis*.[35] In more fortunate cases printers presented themselves with their signatures (colophons), but even this information at times raises doubts.[36] This counts also for Niccolò di Lorenzo's books. For instance, not always can the dates derived from his colophons be harmonized with the historical documents at hand, as the example of his edition of Fra Cherubino da Spoleto's *Della vita spirituale* will show.

A last instruction on the archival sources used and the methodology followed here must be given. In general, historical sources on early typography in Florence are very scarce and often difficult to interpret. This is due to the fact that here, as in the rest of the Italian Peninsula, the foreign printers normally arrived with little more than their technical knowledge and very little or no capital. Typically they belonged to the lower strata of society and only exceptionally married, set up households, and became fiscal subjects, depending on their personal economic situation or outlook. As a direct consequence, modern historical research has to focus on sources other than those traditionally studied by Florentine historians and art historians, such as notarial and fiscal records (the Catasto), private and public account books and *ricordanze* (recollections), letters, and the like.

For the study of early printing, the more than twenty thousand registers of the Florentine notarial archive, the *Notarile antecosimiano*, have traditionally presented the richest grounds. For Niccolò di Lorenzo's biography, they have mostly been exploited.[37] As a consequence, few if any relevant new documents can still be unearthed in them. As must be remembered, however, interpreting notarial acts in a "complete" way often requires additional archival research, especially if they are related to economic or legal conflicts. Compromises as results of private arbitrations were often recorded by notaries and sometimes arrived after earlier, fruitless legal action taken in court; often the court officials themselves ordered such arbitrations (*lodi*).[38] In the opposite scenario, one of the two parties went to court after a private arbitration had failed. In both cases, however, the pertinent court documents need to be unearthed. Special attention has furthermore to be paid to the legal witnesses named in these documents. Generally, it has to be borne in mind that the testimonies listed in notarial acts often indicate the formal or informal "guarantees" of a contract or the members of a network who in this particular moment were all defending their own financial interests. Whenever possible, some light will be thrown on these "bystanders." It is hoped that the resulting, sometimes very detailed studies on individuals who have so far eluded historical interest will not bore the reader, result in a "flat narrative," or become, even worse, an example of the "tunnel vision, (to) an unwillingness to look beyond the immediate object of study to search for contexts and connections," so typical for much of the research on late medieval and Renaissance Florence.[39]

As a direct consequence of this approach, the following pages draw heavily on the documentation of the judicial court reserved for the resolution of financial and economic disputes, the so-called Mercanzia. For the more than two decades in question, the acts of this court have been studied systematically, not only in their three main series ("Atti ordinari," "Atti straordinari," and "Sentenze"), but also in the other, less numerous and thus more "accessible" ones.[40] To a minor degree, other legal records—for instance, those from the tribunal of the Podestà—have been studied as well, despite their incompleteness. Due to their formal character, the information to be gathered from court acts is usually limited to the names of the two or more disputants and the amount(s) of sum(s) requested by the supposed creditor(s). Only in very rare cases is the nature or origin of the debt stated other than in general terms.

In at least one important case, the immense files of the court of the Podestà have contributed to our knowledge on Niccolò di Lorenzo's activity as well. From these registers came, for instance, the copy of the printing contract regarding the publication of Landino's commentary on Dante's *Divina Commedia* (24 December 1480). The first informal exchanges on the correct interpretation of this document grew into the project of a conference, jointly organized in November 2014 in Florence by the Società Dantesca Italiana and Villa I Tatti, the Harvard University Center for Italian Renaissance Studies.[41] Some of the problems raised on this occasion regarded both Niccolò di Lorenzo's printing practices and the financial aspects of his business. Concentrating only on the latter, I realized that they had to be reconsidered. The result of these reflections is the present study.

In the course of this project I have contracted several debts. The deepest is certainly with Neil Harris with whom I discussed it some time after the 2014 conference. He then followed the earliest stages of this manuscript in "real time" and corrected and commented on its very first version, without dismissing it altogether (to my surprise). My second thanks go to Kate Lowe who has a been a true friend while accompanying the work to publication with Harvard University Press. I would furthermore like to thank the three anonymous peer readers who dedicated their time and energy on examining the manuscript and making it more readable. Oliver Duntze from the GW in Berlin, explained to me in detail how and why the GW's measures of Niccolò di Lorenzo's characters sometimes differ from those of Victor Scholderer for the *Catalogue of Books Printed in the XVth Century Now in the British Museum* in 1930. My thanks go also to some friends with whom I could always exchange views and who helped with advice and archival sources: Robert D. Black, Luca Boschetto, Philippa Jackson, Paolo Procaccioli, and Karl Schlebusch. Obviously, all errors contained in this book are only mine. This book is dedicated to my family, especially our two daughters, Bhakti and Muskan, who suffered in the long months of the "lockdown" when everything—school, tools of learning—turned digital. But, please, don't forget the printed books!

Part I

The Introduction of Printing
in Florence

1

Bernardo Cennini and His Family Enterprise, 1471–1472

$\mathscr{I}$n the fifteenth century there were no "typical" careers of book printers. As could be seen with the inventor of the new art, Johannes Gutenberg, a solid preparation as a gold- or silversmith, preferably in a mint, was an ideal basis for cutting the punches of printing types.[1] Among the earliest Italian printers with such skills were, to name but just a few, Filippo Cavagni in Milan, the Frenchman Nicolas Jenson in Venice, and Pietro Paolo Pòrro in Turin.[2]

It was, however, in Florence where the intimate relationship between these activities and printing became most evident. One of the first printed books in Florence, Maurus Servius Honoratus's *Commentarii in Vergilii opera*, was completed after more than a year of work on 7 October 1472.[3] The volume contained for its three parts, Servius's comments on the *Bucolics,* the *Georgics,* and the *Aeneid,* three different colophons, the first dating 7 November 1471, the second 9 January 1471 (i.e., 1472 according to the modern calendar), and the third 7 October 1472. In public libraries around the globe, today one can find thirteen copies of the Cenninis' *Commentarii in Vergilii opera.* In the first of its three colophons it was proudly stated that the book was produced using cast metal types made from iron punches ("chalybs"), and that this work—including the editing—had been easy because nothing was difficult for Florentine minds ("Florentinis ingeniis nil ardui est").[4] The beautiful volume was actually the result of a family cooperation between the Florentine gold- and silversmith Bernardo Cennini and his two sons.[5] Whereas the eldest, Piero, was a humanist scribe and notary who claimed to have edited the Latin text on the basis of "old and various" manuscripts ("cum antiquissimis autem multis exemplaribus contulit"), the younger son, Domenico, followed in the professional footsteps of his father.[6]

The choice of this text was not incidental. In the Florentine university, the Studium Generale, Servius's commentary on Virgil was then widely studied. This accounted, for example, for the classes of Cristoforo Landino, who taught his first course on Virgil in 1462 / 1463, and the circle of the humanist Bartolomeo Fonzio, of whom Piero Cennini was a close friend.[7] In 1466 another student, Lorenzo Guidetti, had valued his own "corrected" copy of Servius at no less than ten gold florins.[8] But Servius's commentary on Virgil was also read by humanists all around Italy and thus responded to the needs of the whole academic world. Piero Cennini added to his—as far as possible critical—edition a grammatical text of his own, *De natura syllabarum*, which he had dedicated to Bartolomeo Fonzio in 1468.[9]

As a direct result of their far from unambiguous presentation, from the eighteenth century onward the Florentine invention of printing became a matter of civic pride.[10] On 24 June 1871 the Florentine typographers, goldsmiths, and representatives of "similar professions" celebrated the four hundredth anniversary of Bernardo Cennini's "invention" with various patriotic ceremonies and inscriptions, patriotic toasts, and the promise to erect a monument in his honor.[11] Although this dubious claim was already corrected by Giacomo Manzoni in 1882, it seems not to have lost any of its fascination.[12] In 2014 it was, for instance, purported that Cennini—who incidentally "might have heard of Gutenberg's invention"—"intuitively" developed both the idea and the technique of printing from his work in the Florentine mint.[13] This position, however, bears little account of the speed of technological transfer in the period; printed books were known in Florence and Rome from the early 1460s on, and Cennini was not even the only Florentine printer at his time.

Both the elegant form of the Cenninis' work and their concern to obtain a more accurate text than the two or three preceding print editions were clearly intended to set a standard for typographical culture as it was requested by the humanist elite.[14] Just like in Rome or Venice, this was a sensitive matter in Florence, where the contrast between popular printing and the still rather new field of humanist philology was deeply felt.[15] Already in 1473, for example, Alamanno Rinuccini asked the fellow humanist Gentile Becchi to acquire in Rome only those volumes that contained corrected texts and were produced with beautiful characters.[16]

Bernardo Cennini worked as a cutter of punches of coins in the Florentine mint, the *zecca,* from the 1460s until 19 January 1475, when he was replaced by his son Domenico.[17] Domenico initially served on the basis of annual contracts before reaching a stable position, whereas his father in 1475 assumed the post of one the two "judges" for the correct gold rate in the coined florins (*sententiator auri*).[18] This change guaranteed both of them a secure post with the modest monthly income of five *lire,* which they kept at least until late 1492.[19] It is quite possible that after the fall of the Medici in the winter of 1494 and in the course of the new organization of the mint they both lost their occupations.[20]

Much earlier in his career Bernardo Cennini had worked with Lorenzo Ghiberti during the making of the famous bronze doors for the Baptistery of San Giovanni.[21] In the years between 1460 and 1463 he had been the partner of a little-known silk manufacturer and goldsmith, Betto di Francesco di Duccio Betti.[22] Their cooperation proved to be a failure. For this very reason, in July 1465 Cennini was granted by the Florentine Signorìa *a* six-month immunity from being prosecuted by his creditors.[23] He was probably helped out by the goldsmith Piero di Bartolomeo "Meo" Sali, who had been his close long-term colleague in the mint. In the summer of 1468, Sali asked Cennini to repay him a sum of 150 gold florins, and on 10 May 1469 the court of the Mercanzia judged this charge to be fully legitimate.[24] As a direct consequence, Cennini was forced to sell some of his real estate property in order to repay his debts, as he declared in his tax declaration (*portata*) in 1469.[25]

Despite these misadventures he remained in close contact with the Medici family. This was probably due to both his professional expertise and local neighborhood links: when in 1466 his daughter Lisabetta married the architect and woodworker Francesco di Giovanni, known as Francione, the decision on the amount of the dowry was placed in the hands of Piero di Cosimo de' Medici.[26] On yet another occasion in 1477, Bernardo Cennini was recorded as a witness in Palazzo Medici.[27] He also continued to run his shop and work for the Florentine government; in 1480 he produced silver flatware for the Signorìa.[28]

Considering his critical economic situation in these years, one must assume that Cennini had other business partners when he decided to invest in printing. One of these could have been his neighbor, the *rigattiere* (secondhand dealer) Braccio di Filippo Braccesi, with whom he rented in late 1470 a house close to the priory of San Iacopo in Campo Corbolini—a house that presumably housed his typography.[29] Another business partner could have been a certain Zanobi di Zanobi del Cica, who in late 1473 sold no less than forty-four copies of Cennini's book for the considerable price of two ducats per copy.[30] Zanobi di Zanobi del Cica frequently held public office between 1434 and 1485 and was known as a book collector; from 1470 he also seems to have been in relations with the goldsmith Antonio del Pollaiuolo.[31]

The rather mysterious buyer of these books, the "alchemist" Agostino di Giovanni de' Cavalli from Trento, left his forty-four copies in deposit with a goldbeater named Alessandro di Giovanni Carucci before leaving Florence in January 1474.[32] Carucci seized these books legally in the second half of 1474; interestingly, the court of the Mercanzia now estimated the single copies at one gold florin.[33] As was gradually becoming clear to the Florentines, the prices of printed books were subject to the market laws and therefore varied a great deal. Naturally, the initial high price of the Cenninis' *Commentarii in Vergilii opera*—or its equivalent, two gold florins—could not be compared to that of the much cheaper books produced for large circulation and consumption, often printed in *volgare*.

2

Giorgio di Niccolò Baldesi,
Giovanni di Piero da Magonza, and Partners,
1470–1473

*B*ernardo Cennini and his sons were not the only typographers in Florence at their time. In the very same years the German Giovanni di Piero da Magonza printed for example the seven penitential psalms in *volgare* tercets (1471), a fifteenth-century translation which in later editions was sometimes attributed to no less than Dante Alighieri. His other three known prints are Giovanni Boccaccio's *Filocolo* (12 November 1472); Goro Dati's *Sfera* (1472?); and Petrarch's *Trionfi* (22 February [1473?]).[1]

All these publications are now extremely rare: of the *Sette salmi penitenziali* in quarto, dated 1471 in its colophon ("DEO.LAUS.HONOR:ET GLORIA//M.CCCC.LXXI."), only a single copy has survived in the Vatican Library, whereas there are six copies of the folio *Filocolo* and four of the Florentine poem in octaves known as *La Sfera* (also a folio). Despite their very different subjects, these rather short works had in common that they were "easy sellers." Giovanni di Piero's edition of the seven psalms could be used as much in the domestic devotional sphere as in the liturgy of religious confraternities; it was immediately reprinted in Venice and came out at least five times in the fifteenth century.[2] The following first edition of Boccaccio's prose romance *Filocolo* bore the proud colophon "master Hans Petri of Mainz wrote this work 12 November 1472."[3] Again, it was immediately followed by other Venetian editions, which added a short biography of Boccaccio by the humanist scholar Girolamo Squarciafico; at least nine editions were printed in the fifteenth century, of which four were Venetian.[4]

The poem known as *La Sfera*, variously attributed to Gregorio (Goro) Dati or his brother Leonardo, was the translation of an astrological and geographic text which had become very popular in fifteenth-century Florence, even before Giovanni di Piero da Magonza's *editio princeps*.[5] At least seventeen other editions were printed before 1500, most of them Florentine. Interestingly, at least seven earlier Florentine manuscripts contained the *Sfera* together with Petrarch's *Trionfi*, sometimes in direct sequence, despite no evident thematic relationship.[6] It might thus appear as a curious coincidence that Giovanni di Piero also printed the *Trionfi*. In the case of his quarto edition of this text, however, it was no *editio princeps*, but the first edition to contain only the *Trionfi*, without the *Canzoniere*.[7] Only four copies of this book have survived.

In comparison with other *incunabula, the* modest numbers in which Giovanni di Piero da Magonza's books have been conserved present no exception. Several years ago Neil Harris reported some of the results of a research on the London-based Incunabula Short Title Catalogue (*ISTC*). According to this, about sixty-eight hundred books from that age are conserved in only one copy, thirty-one hundred in two copies, two thousand in three, fifteen hundred in four, and twelve hundred in five.[8] The "chances of survival" of a book were directly linked to its success with contemporary readers: if today a certain *incunabulum* is known from only a few copies, this is not so much an indication of its hypothetical print run as it is more evident of the fact that the book was widely read. This is obviously true for the prints of Giovanni di Piero da Magonza, as well, which appealed not so much to the humanists as to the local Florentine readership in general.

Apart from the Florentine printers known by name, modern incunabulists like Piero Scapecchi and Dennis Rhodes have attributed to Florence three equally rare books produced by an anonymous "printer of Terentius, Pr. 6748" (Giovanni Boccaccio, *Decamerone; Epistolae et Evangelia* in *volgare;* Publius Terentius, *Comoediae*), all assigned to the years 1470–1471.[9]

This attribution opened up a fracture between the disciplines of bibliography and the history of the Italian language. On the basis of some linguistic "contaminations" in this edition of Boccaccio's masterwork, the Italian textual scholar Paolo Trovato has argued that it was printed in Naples, as must consequentially have been the other two; in the following discussion, even Rome has been proposed as the origin of these three books.[10] The question has become even more important because of the observation that the editor and/or compositor used—in the best Florentine tradition—more than one manuscript, one of which was Boccaccio's famous autograph which is kept today in the State Library in Berlin, the manuscript Hamilton 90.[11] The collation with another copy was necessary because some of its parts were already missing. Some signs on the margins of this manuscript actually seem to confirm that it was used as a printer's copy in a typography.[12] As far as we know, however, Boccaccio's autograph never left the town of Florence in the fifteenth century. For this and other reasons the problem of the "printer of Terentius, Pr. 6748" is still open to debate.

In the year 1472 more than twenty copies of Boccaccio's *Decamerone* were sold in Florence by the famous singer, maestro Antonio di Guido, and a certain Niccolò di Lorenzo della Magna, then still a modest employee (*donzello*) of the Mercanzia.[13] Antonio di Guido also sold his books on his own—for example, to the stationers Antonio di Bartolo di Fruosino and Giovanni di Domenico di Lorenzo.[14] If this *Decamerone* was indeed the edition cited above, then the "printer of the Terentius, Pr. 6748" must have been in close financial relations with Antonio di Guido and, possibly, even Niccolò di Lorenzo.[15] Building on this evidence, Piero Scapecchi went even one step further: in his entry for the printer Niccolò di Lorenzo della Magna for the "Dizionario biografico degli Italiani" and in his recent catalog of the incunabula owned by the National Central Library of Florence, he tentatively identified the "Printer of Terentius, Pr. 6748" as Niccolò di Lorenzo himself.[16] In this he was followed by other scholars—for example, Giorgio Montecchi.[17] As Part II will show, however, this hypothesis must be rejected for biographical reasons.

Bernardo Cennini's contemporary, Giovanni di Piero da Magonza, was quite an enigmatic figure.[18] He was living in Florence as early as 1470, if not before, in the parish of Sant'Ambrogio. On 2 September of that year he married Mona Lisabetta, daughter of a certain Consiglio di Paolo from the parish of San Pier Gattolini in Oltrarno who worked in the Florentine customs office ("istà in doghana").[19] Lisabetta was then sixteen years old; she was born on 24 September 1454 when her father was still working as a grocer (*pizzicagnolo*) in another part of Oltrarno, the parish of San Iacopo sopr'Arno.[20] One may note that among the witnesses present at the wedding ceremony was, interestingly, a stationer, Cione di Damiano di Matteo Fiordalisi, *cartolaio,* who in 1470 was still at the beginning of his career and later became a well-known dealer of printed books.[21] This circumstance almost certainly indicates that from the very beginning Giovanni di Piero da Magonza's profession of printer was respected among the Florentine booksellers.

It was, in any case, another Florentine stationer from the quarter of Oltrarno, Giorgio di Niccolò di Guido Baldesi, who assumed a crucial role in this new industry between 1470 and 1473.[22] Baldesi was a very experienced professional who before 1457 had owned a shop in the Piazza della Signorìa.[23] He was also trained in metal and wooden works. As the son of a woodworker (*legnaiuolo*), Baldesi became a member of his father's guild in 1465, and on this occasion was described as a stationer who had for some time produced pieces of jewelry ("maestro che faciea le buchole, chartolaio").[24] In early 1468 he was briefly employed as one of the secret "spies" of the mint to gather information on the circulation of false or forbidden coins (*commissarius et explorator zeche*).[25] In 1469 he was forty-nine years old and lived in a house on the street known as Costa di San Giorgio.[26] He was a member of several religious confraternities in *Oltrarno:* in Sant'Agnese he taught the boys singing the *laudi*,[27] and in the summer of 1473 was responsible, together with another colleague from the confraternity of the Annunciation and Saint Silvester known as the "compagnia dell'Orciuolo," for the realization of the Annunciation play in the church of San Felice in Piazza.[28]

From a court case in the Mercanzia from early 1472 we learn that the first Florentine printing company was set up as early as 20 October 1470. On this day four citizens from very different social backgrounds signed a contract for a partnership that was to last for ten months, until 1 September 1471. They were the stationer Giorgio Baldesi; the moderately wealthy silk merchant, Francesco di Niccolò Berlinghieri, from the quarter of Santa Croce; the banker Salvestro di Giuliano Ceffini; and the painter Piero del Massaio.[29] Berlinghieri, himself author of the geographical poem *Geographia* which was published more than a decade later, in 1470 was still at the beginning of his political career.[30] He was a friend of Lorenzo de' Medici and of humanists like Cristoforo Landino or Marsilio Ficino. He also seems to have been the driving force behind the enterprise.[31]

The society's capital consisted of the considerable sum of three hundred gold florins, and despite Baldesi's exemption from contributing to this, he had a right to one-fourth of the company's gains. This was his remuneration for using all his "intelligence" to secretely set up a workshop in which the new art of "formatting scriptures" would be able to flourish.[32] A central condition of the contract was the production of neat characters, so that the work would be appreciated by readers.[33] Both the terms *formare* and *gittare in forma* were traditionally attributed to mechanical reproduction from forms, like waxen images—as, for example, in the paragraph of the statutes of the guild of the Florentine doctors and apothecaries from 1349 which forbade its members the commission of devotional, reproducible "icons," especially ex-votos, to nonmembers.[34] In our context, however, to produce *le scripture formate* meant not only the production of characters but was considered identical to "printing."[35]

On 5 May 1471, the partners confirmed the initial terms that Baldesi should work all through summer. On 1 September, when a final balance had to be drawn up, however, the wind had changed. On behalf of Berlinghieri it was now decided that Baldesi had not operated to his partners' satisfaction, and that all the items in the workshop should be sold, as written in their initial contract ("artifici et masseritie").[36] Thus, on 10 September 1471, all the parties involved agreed to seek a compromise and lay their economic differences into the hands of two Florentine citizens.[37] As often was the case in such cases, no conclusion was reached. Therefore, several months later, on 22 February 1472, on the initiative of Francesco Berlinghieri and also in the name of Piero del Massaio, Giorgio Baldesi was summoned in the Mercanzia to repay a sum that was initially indicated as forty-five ducats and then as thirty-four gold florins and fifty lire.[38] The stationer responded to this claim on 28 February on very general terms, refusing to pay.[39] In yet another attempt to resolve their differences, the parties met again on 10 March 1472, but again to no avail.[40] Ten days later the Mercanzia officials thus accepted and validated Francesco Berlinghieri's account book, according to which he had lent Baldesi for the shop, in total and over time, thirty-two gold florins and more than sixty lire.[41] On the following day, the court gave its final sentence: after the conversion of the two different currencies into one, the debt amounted to the considerable sum of 150 lire. A final provision ruled that Baldesi was allowed to stay in his workshop—which lay outside the city walls—until the end of October 1472 without having to pay any rent.[42] Baldesi's general power of attorney from 25 November 1472 does not allow any conclusions but was shortly later used in the court of the Mercanzia.[43] From the document of 10 March it is known that this house lay in the parish of San Leonardo (di Arcetri), just outside the southern gate of Saint George, and thus close to the so-called Costa di San Giorgio, where Baldesi owned a house himself.

The end of this company invites us to draw some further conclusions. It shows, first, that the act of the partners' splitting up was not one of complete disarray. The workshop's rent had possibly been paid in advance. The choice of its location, far from the town's busy streets, was almost certainly due to the fact that Baldesi and his partners wanted to hide their business from curious eyes.[44] Second, it may be assumed that the workshop was then already printing or was close to printing books with which Baldesi's creditors trusted to be paid back before October 1472. If no progress whatsoever had been made, the society would probably have closed much earlier. In a similar case dating from 1471 in Milan, a would-be typographer had been sustained by a local partner, but when it turned out after a few months that he was neither a master nor even a simple worker in the new art, the partners separated immediately and without further ado.[45]

There is as yet no documentary proof that Giorgio Baldesi's first company collaborated with either the printer known as "Printer of Terentius, Pr. 6748" or with Giovanni di Piero da Magonza. As some documents show, however, Baldesi and Giovanni di Piero were indeed business partners from the fall of 1471 onward, that is, after the end of the company with Francesco Berlinghieri. On 28 January 1473 the printer's father-in-law, Consiglio di Paolo, deposited seven gold florins in the court of the Mercanzia in order to free him from a debt with Giorgio di Niccolò Baldesi and two wool producers (*lanaiuoli*), Francesco di Goccio di

Bartolomeo (called "Rosso") and Giovanni di messer Sallustio Buongug-lielmi.[46] For his part, the stationer explained that the first of these sums was due for the lease of a house which he had rented for the printer in the autumn of 1471—possibly Giovanni di Piero's workshop.[47] Soon later, on 1 November 1471, the printer had agreed on the terms of how to repay his debt.[48] Quite distinctively, Giorgio Baldesi himself was indebted to the two wool merchants for the price of cloth.[49] It seems that these two distinct legal procedures were intimately linked: both creditors had paid the necessary fees in the court of the Mercanzia to present their requests at the same time—fees known as *diritto*—and probably both credits had in some way to do with the printing enterprise itself.

In this unsatisfactory way the partnership between Giorgio Baldesi and Giovanni di Piero da Magonza, certainly begun in late 1471 and pos-sibly even before that, split up in January 1473. The date of the afore-mentioned edition of Petrarch's *Trionfi*, in which the colophon records only the day but not the year, is therefore open to doubt.[50] On the basis of the observation that the watermark of the paper used in it is the same as that found "in the greater part of the Boccaccio, *Filocolo*, of November, 1472," Victor Scholderer believed that the Petrarch was published after that (i.e., on 22 February 1473), but of course it could also be the other way around: Giovanni di Piero da Magonza initially printed Petrarch's *Trionfi* on 23 February 1472, and after that the *Filocolo*.[51]

Again the documents from the court of the Mercanzia contain bits of evidence that hint in this direction. A seizure of household goods be-longing to an otherwise unknown Florentine cloth worker, Giuliano di Niccolò *filatoiaio*, mentions in fact two books—which, given the rather modest overall value attributed to the cloth and domestic objects con-fiscated, were probably printed—"una Spera e Trionfi del Petrarcha" (27 October 1472).[52] These could well be two works of Giovanni di Piero da Magonza. And yet another Mercanzia act from October 1473 men-tions both titles together. This time the case originated from a cleric, the prior of San Iacopo in Campo Corbolini, Matteo di Agnolo Vagnucci da Cortona, from the order of the Knights of Saint John.[53] He asked the goldsmith Banco di Filippo Banchi to repay him a debt of five gold flo-rins in twenty days or else the books left with him as pawns would be sold.[54] Given the low price, most of these books could again have been printed, if not in Florence by Giovanni di Piero da Magonza, then in

Venice; yet, for the widely known theological text *Trenta gradi di San Girolamo*, no previous print edition is recorded.[55]

Just like Giorgio Baldesi, the goldsmith Banco di Filippo Banchi was a very experienced craftsman. Born around 1433, he was recorded in the 1457 *Catasto* as laboring in another workshop ("Bancho di Filippo istà a l'orafo, anni 24").[56] The many family members of his father and uncle, both already in their sixties, then lived in the street known as Borgo San Lorenzo, and only Banco and one of his brothers were working.

As his full name was Banco di Filippo di Simone di Banco Banchi, Latin sources sometimes referred to him as "Bancho Filippi Banchi." This name appears, for example, in the Mercanzia act from 1473 and in a later *bullettinum securitatis*, a document which guaranteed him immunity from being legally prosecuted, in May 1479.[57] In 1477 he sold his old family house in the Borgo San Lorenzo, then married the daughter of a notary and bought a farm; he also ran a central shop next to the Loggia dei Cavalcanti on today's Via Porta Rossa, right in front of that of Bernardo Cennini.[58] Today Banco is known primarily for having acted as a judge in an arbitration case in 1468 and for his work, together with two colleagues, on the fireworks wagon used in the religious procession and the civic festivities for Saint John the Baptist in June 1478.[59]

Although Banco's name cannot be linked to any of the activities in the mint, the cutting and casting of letters were certainly among his skills. In 1473 he asked the notary, ser Clemente Bellosi, to pay him the sum of nine lire and ten soldi for work, possibly the price for cutting a seal.[60] Naturally, he also sold more traditional religious objects, as, for example, in 1473 a silver tabernacle to a Florentine cleric for forty-four gold florins ("uno tabernaculo fornito d'ariento").[61] In 1475 he had a debt with his younger cousin Francesco di Michele Banchi, who was living in Venice. This power of attorney was interestingly drawn up in the workshop of the famous typographer Nicolas Jenson.[62] In 1481 Banco sold typographical material to the Ripoli press for seven lire, and a year later was recorded as the debtor of the bankrupt banker, Francesco di Bernardo Cambini, of more than fifteen gold florins.[63] After Banco's death, the famous publisher Piero Pacini charged his heirs one gold florin and more than fourteen lire, and again one could argue that their business relation was in some way linked to printing (4 August 1485).[64] It would thus not come as a surprise if already in the early 1470s Banco had fabricated types for Giovanni di Piero da Magonza and that in exchange he was partly paid with some of his publications.

Let us now briefly return to Giovanni di Piero da Magonza's official partner, the stationer Giorgio di Niccolò Baldesi. After his Florentine years he was sometimes described as living in Poggibonsi, on the southern borders of the Florentine state.[65] Why Poggibonsi? The response to this question is almost certainly linked to the most important economic question in early printing—that of paper supply.

In Poggibonsi, just as in nearby Colle Valdelsa, numerous mills had been built on the artificially created channels (*gore*) of the Elsa River. Traditionally located at a place named Poggiosecco, some of them almost certainly produced paper.[66] Two monasteries were particularly active in this business, the ancient abbey of Poggibonsi, San Michele Arcangelo di Marturi, and the monastery of Santa Brigida al Paradiso, close to Bagno a Ripoli. In 1445 these two had been united under the control of the Florentine Republic.[67] Even private citizens constructed mills on the Elsa's channels at Poggibonsi, causing at times damage to the neighboring ecclesiastical property. According to a document from 1476 regarding the donation of a chaplain of the Cardinal of Milan, Stefano Nardini, to a lay confraternity in the Augustinian convent of San Lorenzo in Poggibonsi, the stationer Giorgio Baldesi had received from the chaplain a considerable quantity of hemp (*accia*).[68] Hemp was then used, for example, in pillows, but also for paper production.[69]

Soon after their split in early 1473, Giovanni di Piero da Magonza's financial situation seems to have forced him out of business for some time. Maybe for this reason his wife Lisabetta in March 1475 brought a dispute to court, possibly that of the Podestà. The trial was probably directed against the father of the stationer Cione di Damiano, who, as we have seen, had been one of the witnesses at their wedding. The public document issued by the Florentine Signorìa, which had so far safeguarded Cione's father from imprisonment (*bullettinum securitatis*), was therefore revoked.[70]

It appears that the Florentine printing industry suffered an impasse in early 1473 or shortly thereafter, and there are no details known from the following months. As elsewhere, the inactivity of the printers on the Arno River was presumably due to the unwillingness of private investors to finance new enterprises. Even if one does not sustain the thesis of a general "crisis" that hit the Italian market for printed books—or at least that of Rome and Venice—around 1472 / 1473, the temporary coincidence with the shutting of many printing presses in other towns is striking.[71] It must therefore be considered surprising that the Florentines—"Florentinis ingeniis nil ardui est"—conceived no immediate strategies to overcome the standstill. For a new beginning of production the readers had to wait until the year 1474.

The false problem regarding the temporary precedence of printing in Florence is an expression of the "communalistic" spirit of the eighteenth and nineteenth centuries, which today has lost most of its attraction. Even excluding the question of the "Printer of Terentius, Pr. 6748," it has become evident that Bernardo Cennini and Giovanni di Piero della Magonza were laboring in both rivalry and practical exchange, although on two very different types of products. With even a superficial knowledge of the functioning of Florentine workshops, it is clear that they not only knew of each other but that technical expertise traveled between their houses, whether through workmen or other interested persons. It is therefore justified to conclude this debate with the wise words of another Florentine, Matteo Palmieri, who in his earlier Della vita civile had one of his fellow citizens pronounce the phrase "Who does not seek will not find, and once things have been found, everybody claims to have been a master."[72]

3

Wool Trade and Printing

$\mathcal{T}$he exact nature of the disputes between printers, stationers, and booksellers on one side and wool producers on the other remains mysterious, unless these disputes are filled with details and put into context. This chapter will therefore examine some preliminary yet fundamental conditions of printing in Renaissance Florence. Most of the protagonists of this new art shared a cultural background, which one does not necessarily have to think of as "social" or "civic" humanism in order to detect common cultural interests. In a very open way these men—and sometimes women—were interested in ancient literature, often known through translations in *volgare*, medieval and contemporary religious or chivalric texts, and, exceptionally, even the works of contemporary humanism.

As has often been observed, the production of manuscripts was not interrupted or substituted by the printing press, especially in a book center like Florence. For instance, the wealthy innkeeper Zanobi di Zanobi del Cica, who had probably played a role in the printing of the Cennini Servius in 1471-1472, bought (around 1478) a manuscript of Virgil ("uno Vergilio"), for the relatively high sum of six gold florins,

written by the scribe ser Francesco di ser Niccolò Berti (Gentiluzzi) da
San Gimignano and commissioned by the stationer Zanobi di Mariano
di Giovanni.[1] Virgil's writings—in this case, probably all of his three
major works—were available in many non-Florentine printed editions
from 1469 onward, and Zanobi's preference for an expensive manuscript
must therefore have been a deliberate choice for either aesthetical or
philological reasons. Two years later, another stationer, Iacopo di Bartolomeo *cartolaio,* sued Zanobi del Cica over the lesser price of two lire
and ten soldi for what was presumably a printed book.[2]

Other examples come from the printer Giovanni di Piero da Magonza's circle. The wool dealer Francesco di Goccio di Bartolomeo (called
"Rosso"), who in 1473 had sued the two partners Giorgio di Niccolò
Baldesi and Giovanni di Piero da Magonza, was the administrator of the
wool company owned by Piero di Giovanni Capponi and Giovanni di
messer Sallustio Buonguglielmi da Perugia; the latter, son of a famous
lawyer and brother-in-law of Antonio di Tuccio Manetti, left a considerable library of manuscripts after his death in early 1470.[3] The stationer
Giorgio Baldesi in 1489 bought for more than six gold florins cloth from
the wool dealer Leonardo di Francesco Tornabuoni, leaving as collateral
a handwritten breviary which was later valued at the lesser sum of five
florins.[4] Baldesi's son Niccolò copied as late as 1509 a manuscript of the
chivalric romance known as *Ugone d'Alvernia.*[5]

In order to understand the business relation between wool merchants and printers or stationers one must first consider the status and
value of the woolen cloth known as *panni di garbo* in fifteenth-century
Florence. The historian Hidetoshi Hoshino has shown how this not particularly fine type of wool was produced in large quantities for the export to foreign markets, especially those of central and southern Italy
and the eastern Mediterranean.[6] Thanks to its omnipresence, in Rome
it was used in payments as a substitute for money. It comes as no surprise that one of the most important economic transactions of the late
1480s involved Lorenzo de' Medici settling Pope Innocent VIII's debt of
one hundred thousand florins who on his part accepted Florentine
woolen cloth as partial payment.[7] In Florence "fine" *garbo* wool could also
be used to pay the rent for a house, as an example from 1472 shows.[8] The
status of wool as an alternative medium of exchange was not restricted
to Florence or Rome: in Ferrara in the 1470s Duke Ercole d'Este tried to

overrule the local wool corporation in an attempt to ban woolen cloth as a substitute for cash; the long-standing privilege of the corporation's payments in textiles was, however, defended by two famous lawyers.[9]

In Renaissance Florence, which is known for its "industrial fluidity," the underlying economic mechanism which became fundamental for the printing industry was quite simple.[10] At its basis was the assumption that credits given for material were to be cashed in only after the final products had been sold or "finished," to use the terminology of the age. Benedetto Cotrugli, the merchant and writer from Ragusa (Dubrovnik), dedicated one of the longest chapters in his trade handbook on the subject of selling merchandise on forward commitments (*a termine*).[11] In another instance, he used an example from shoemakers' activities to illustrate a point which lay not only at the heart of the Florentine wool business but also that of printing.[12]

Contracts for the sale of *garbo* clothes were usually concluded on the understanding that full payment was postponed to a later time, often one year, allowing the resellers on the local markets to cash in their credits. These contracts were called *a mercato* or *a termine*, and their conclusion lay in the hands of the professional brokers, the *sensali*.[13] A law from 1446 ruled that these agreements had to be written out, signed, and copied in special registers; in another law from December 1467 the clerks' role was further defined. *Sensali* were officially elected by the guilds and had to be approved in the court of the Mercanzia.[14] In the Mercanzia registers, unfortunately, their names were rarely and incompletely registered—as, for example, in February 1472 and February 1474.[15] With regard to the wool guild, a law from January 1477 limited the brokers' number to twenty who had to be experienced and of good reputation ("persone pratiche et intendenti et di buona fama"). Direct sales of wool of *lanaiuoli* and retailers were, of course, allowed, but only in their shops. The same was true for dyers and other professionals working in the wool trade ("tintori, gualcherai, purgatori, cimatori, tiratoiai"), but in contrast with the retailers their trade was limited to their own, intact products ("panni interi per loro manifacture").[16]

The time span between the delivery of the wool on one side and its clearance on the other allowed the printers to face both running costs and earlier debts—for example, for setting up the workshop, the purchase of paper and other material and, finally, the stipends of the workmen.

Once the final products, the printed books, arrived on the market, the newly generated gains would, it was hoped, suffice to pay off the debts with the *lanaiuoli:* the circle closed in. As payment in kind was the rule in all printing shops of the period, printers themselves were at times recompensed with wool, as an example regarding Ugo Ruggeri—who worked in Bologna, Reggio Emilia, San Cesario sul Panario and Pisa—shows.[17] The same also happened in Milan, where in 1499 the printer Alessandro Minuziano, backed by two Milanese citizens, bought wool for the considerable sum of 264 lire. The understanding was that the printer provided for the sum one year later. Minuziano presumably exchanged this wool to finance his four-volume edition of Cicero's works and move the printer's shop to his new home.[18] And even north of the Alps this mechanism was known—as, for example, by Michel Wenssler in Basel, who has been mentioned before in the introduction. Before 1487 he received cloth for no less than two hundred gulden from the largest trading company in Basel; this cloth could easily have been exchanged with paper.[19]

Although the sources for the Florentiner printer Giovanni di Piero da Magonza do not specify this, it seems that the stationer Giorgio di Niccolò Baldesi guaranteed around 1472 for exactly this sort of loan with the two *lanaiuoli.* In the second part of his career, the independent printer Niccolò di Lorenzo della Magna and his different partners often made use of similar wool loans, as Part III will show.

A second reason for the close cooperation between early printers and wool merchants was the fact that the latter were directly involved in the commercialization of the products.[20] Three short examples from the well-known Ripoli press will illustrate this point. On 2 April 1479 the press presented to Bartolomeo Fonzio, Giovanbattista di Roberto Boninsegni, and Giraldo di Francesco Giraldi 650 copies of the so-called *Vite de' pontefici e imperatori,* astutely but wrongly ascribed to Francesco Petrarca in the colophon.[21] Although the three men had in various ways promoted the printing of this work, the copies remained for the time being in the hands of the Ripoli press, until the promised sums of money had been fully paid.[22] According to the account book of two wool merchants, Bernardo di Giovanni Rustichi and Antonio di Francesco Giraldi (Giraldo's brother), in December 1479 they finally received not only two hundred copies of the pseudo-Petrarch for 192 lire—considerably less than the official selling price fixed on 2 April—but also "166 *Salusti Giugurtini et Chat[e]llinari* gittati a chomune" for the lower sum of one hundred lire. The term "gittati a chomune" in this case refers not so much to the content of the 1478 Ripoli edition of Sallust's works (which followed one of the many earlier, non-Florentine editions and was not even recorded in the so-called diary), as to its shared sponsorship between various merchants, maybe the stationer Bartolo di Domenico di Guido and certainly the Giraldi brothers themselves.[23] In the following years, the *lanaiuolo* Antonio Giraldi bought other books from Bartolo di Domenico—for example, "un Burchiello legato" for 18 soldi, presumably Francesco di Dino's edition from 24 November 1481.[24] Some of these books were then handed over to Giraldi's sales agent, a certain ser Giovanni d'Agostino di ser Niccolaio da San Gimignano.[25]

Another Florentine merchant who sold the Ripoli products was Cipriano di Iacopo Antonio Rucellai, about whom very little is known.[26] In 1480, at the age of twenty-eight and with a wife and four children, he declared to the Catasto officials that he was still living with his elder brother and was without any profession ("nonn à esercizio nesuno").[27] His professional situation must have changed soon later. Before 1483 one of his business partners seems to have been a certain Niccolò di Simone di Lapeggia Bardi.[28] In 1484 Cipriano moved into a house in the parish of Santa Lucia d'Ognissanti and later was unable to pay the rent.[29] From a list of his confiscated books on behalf of the wool merchant Giovanni di ser Piero Braccini in April 1486 one learns that Cipriano then still possessed no less than 190 "Donadelli"—that is, the common Latin grammar for beginners (see Appendix B, no. 9). This was presumably a Ripoli print from 1476 of which no copy has survived. Alternatively, however, it could also have been another unknown edition sponsored by Rucellai himself. And as it seems, Cipriano was almost certainly involved in publishing: already on 22 March 1480 the apothecary Tommaso di Luca di Betto Bernardi had charged him for the considerable debt of seventy-seven lire "for paper sold and given to him" ("per fogli a llui dati et venduti").[30]

The books confiscated from Cipriano in 1486, most of them undoubtedly Ripoli prints, were then estimated at twenty gold florins, as was confirmed in a second valuation in the fall which arrived at the sum of hundred lire. The *lanaiuolo* Giovanni Braccini could possibly have sponsored these books with his wool, although Cipriano Rucellai retained the main responsibility for the printing.[31] Soon later his trading company entered into its final crisis; in March 1487 the silk merchant Francesco di Berlinghieri Berlinghieri confiscated a second group of books worth 105 lire from a certain Giovanni di ser Antonio. This man had previously "received and bought" them from Cipriano, who was by now considered an "insolvent and fugitive" merchant ("cessante et fuggitivo").[32] Unfortunately, too little is known about Cipriano's book dealings to know whether his bankruptcy originated only from them or from other commercial activities.

Wool traders were thus frequently collaborating with the Ripoli press. When on 26 May 1479 an arbiter for the case with the stationer Bartolo di Domenico had to be elected, the two Dominican friars who directed the press chose, for example, the merchant Tommaso di Iacopo Tani (see Appendix B, no. 2). Decades earlier this man had been a Latin scribe and secretary for Giannozzo Manetti.[33] In the late 1450s Tommaso Tani had acted as a partner and agent in Naples for his son, the *lanaiuolo* Bernardo di Giannozzo Manetti.[34] And at least once there he had also been involved in the book trade, when in 1456 he sold a richly illuminated manuscript of Ptolemy's *Geography* to the royal court.[35]

Part II

Niccolò di Lorenzo della Magna's
First Years of Activity

4

In the Service of the Mercanzia, 1464–1475

*T*oday the Florentine printer Niccolò di Lorenzo della Magna is appreciated for his central role in the first editions of the works of Florentine humanists and for the introduction of engravings in his books—notably, Dante Alighieri's *Divine Comedy* from 1481 with the commentary of Cristoforo Landino. In the colophons of his works he variously signed himself as "Nicolaus," "magister Nicolaus Laurentii alamanus," "Nicolò di Lorenzo della Magna," or "Nicholaus diocesis vratislavriensis."[1] Not surprisingly, confusion dominated in the earliest accounts of his life: Orlandi's bibliography from 1722 counted five editions of "Niccolò di Lorenzo alemano" and, quite distinctively, two others by another "Niccolò di Brestavv."[2] Only later these names were recognized as belonging to just one individual.[3] An early biographical study from 1921 numbered eighteen signed editions from the years 1477–1486, many of which were, once again, without any dates; another group of twenty-five editions had then been attributed to his press on the grounds of the character types used.[4] In the sixth volume of the *Catalogue of Books Printed in the XVth Century Now in the British Museum* (*BMC*), Victor Scholderer described twenty certain and two dubious editions of Niccolò di Lorenzo.[5] Dennis

Rhodes, in his definitive synthesis in 1988 of early Florentine printing, critically followed by the modern *Incunabula Short Title Catalogue at the British Library* (ISTC), counted altogether forty-seven editions of Niccolò. The ongoing Berlin-based *Gesamtkatalog der Wiegendrucke* (GW) assigned to Niccolò di Lorenzo another two, taking the total to almost fifty.[6] This amounts to only about 5 percent of the recorded book production in Florence from the fifteenth century (for which the *ISTC* counts 891 titles). If this seems little, on the other hand, the printer's biography can be written in more detail than those of his Florentine colleagues.

As the aforementioned colophon indicates, he originally came from the diocese of Vratislava (i.e., Wrocław or Breslau in Silesia), a highly important, cosmopolitan urban center and crossroads of international trade, where the Florentines had many interests.[7] Both his cultural and linguistic background—apart from his ability to write and read—and the date of his arrival in Florence are unknown. Surprisingly, however, his working experience lay not at all in printing or other professionally relevant activities. Instead, for roughly a decade, from 1464 until January 1475, he was employed as a *donzello* (Latin, *domicellus*) in the Florentine court of the Mercanzia.[8]

With its majestic building in the Piazza della Signorìa, this institution represented from the fourteenth century onward the supreme (albeit not the only) tribunal for commercial conflicts among Florentine citizens and foreigners alike. It was formally headed by a non-Florentine lawyer, the so-called official, who sat in office for six months and was responsible for signing the final sentences. Six Florentine counselors, the so-called Sei della Mercanzia, who were extracted from the five major and the fourteen minor guilds, controlled him and expressed their opinion in any more complicated matters. In most cases, the controversies brought to the court were resolved rather quickly after the first charge (*richiesta*), often in the form of a private compromise, to avoid the relatively high costs of a trial.

Similar to the Sei della Mercanzia, the college of the *donzelli* was made up of six members. Officially dressed in red-and-green tunics, they often served, thanks to their modest but regular stipend of twelve lire per month, in tenured employment for long periods of time.[9] They also received small contributions from the subjects seeking justice in the court, as one of many obligatory taxes. From 1418 on they were obliged to demonstrate their writing and reading abilities.[10] Their activity consisted primarily, as far as is known, in public appearances representing the tribunal itself; three times, in 1469, 1471 and 1472, Niccolò di Lorenzo was also the official representative of the court (*sindaco*) to invite and accompany the newly elected officials from abroad to Florence.[11]

Reading their personal tax returns to the Catasto officials and the lists of debtors and creditors contained in these sometimes very detailed declarations, one discovers that the *donzelli*—many of whom were Germans—often had a wide range of commercial interests and relations. This is also true for Niccolò di Lorenzo, who was, unfortunately for us, never called to deliver any such tax declarations.[12] In his years of public service he occasionally claimed to be a creditor of minor sums of money, normally without explaining their nature or origin. A first example comes from 1467, when he exonerated a servant of the confraternity of Orsanmichele, a certain Guasparre di Giovanni, from paying a small debt.[13] In 1467 he was living in the central parish of San Bartolomeo del Corso and by early 1472 had moved to that of Sant'Ambrogio, possibly by consequence of his matrimony.[14] Before that he could have shared his premises with a cloth worker from whom in November 1472 he asked four lire for "rent."[15] His wife's name is known from only a single document: on 10 February 1476 Niccolò affirmed that his household belongings were no part of her dowry (i.e., that of "domina Domitilla uxor dicti magistri Nicolai").[16]

This home, which at the latest from 1480/1481 also housed his workshop with the presses, was situated in the east of Florence, close to the city walls. It lay at the far end of Via Ghibellina, between the famous Benedictine female monastery known as Le Murate and another house owned by Donato di Giovanni d'Amerigho Benci.[17] From a legal act, the temporary confiscation of this building in August 1485, it is further known that Niccolò shared it with a cobbler, Francesco d'Andrea (see Appendix B, no. 7). In 1467 it had been bought by Francesco's father, the cobbler Andrea di Giovanni di Nicola from Poppi. The house seems to have been a relatively spacious building, with a courtyard, a garden, a well, and other structures.[18] The date and method of its division between the two families are not known; in his Catasto returns of 1470 and 1480 Andrea claimed his residence there without even mentioning Niccolò di Lorenzo's family.[19] On the other hand, the legitimate property of Donato Benci's neighboring house seems to have been a matter of dispute with the monastery: in Benci's Catasto returns he refrained from naming it, and in his testament from 1489 he donated it to the Murate, mentioning the fact that in the adjacent building was still living the (unnamed) cobbler and, possibly, even the printer.[20]

Between 1471 and 1474 Niccolò di Lorenzo presented himself in several Mercanzia cases as the legal representative of a certain Giovanni di Filippo Benizi, acting against other debtors ("cessionario," "procuratore delle ragioni").[21] Giovanni di Filippo Benizi came from an ancient Florentine family from the Oltrarno region which had been exiled for twenty-five years in 1458, and he was the cousin of Giovanni di Matteo Benizi.[22]

This man has already been named as the runner of a mill in Poggibonsi. For a certain compensation, Niccolò di Lorenzo was also working as his collector in the early 1470s ("cessionario delle ragioni").[23] Giovanni di Matteo Benizi was a multifaceted and interesting man who had also been banned for political reasons in 1458; he was authorized to return to the Florentine dominion a year later and formally reallowed into Florence in 1466.[24] In that year he became one of the conductors of the communal galleys to the Eastern Mediterranean and then invested in various commercial enterprises.[25] Their failure caused him serious economic troubles. Around 1472 Benedetto Dei included the Benizi among the families notable for having lost its ancient riches.[26] At least twice Benizi was imprisoned for debts, and by 1478 had been declared an "insolvent and fugitive merchant" ("cessante et fuggitivo").[27] In June of the same year he signed a setting with his wife's family that temporarily resolved some of his legal problems.[28] He then went to Lucca, where he traded an important supply of iron bars for a Florentine blacksmith ("libbre 1207 ferri in virgis," July 1478).[29] In the 1480 Catasto he declared he was indebted for more than three thousand florins, and in November 1481 he was accused of helping some prisoners escape the same prison where he had been held three years earlier; the exact circumstances of this episode remain mysterious.[30] A year later he acted as one of the arbiters in a mercantile dispute in the silk merchants' corporation, the Arte di Por Santa Maria.[31]

Politically he always remained distant from the Medici regime and never held any public office. Only after the fall of the Medici in late 1494 did he regain a certain visibility.[32] In April 1496, however, he was condemned to perpetual jail when it was discovered that he had plotted against the new popular government.[33] The humanist scribe and modestly successful politician Lorenzo Guidetti gave a detailed account of this intrigue, but unfortunately no closer personal portrait of "il Benizo."[34] Presumably Benizi had some literary interests, too, and this may have guided him in appointing in the 1480s the humanist Piero Domizi as chaplain of his family chapel at the church of Santa Felicita.[35] And undoubtedly he also had some interest in printing: in the spring of 1477 he collaborated with both the printer Giovanni di Piero da Magonza and the Ripoli press, to which he lent a set of matrices ("cinquanta tre madri di lettera anticha") that could have come from the typographer.[36]

Did the business relation between Niccolò di Lorenzo and the Benizi in the early 1470s have its origin in book printing as well? A positive answer to this question might strengthen the recent hypothesis that Niccolò was responsible for the aforementioned edition of Boccaccio's *Decamerone* known as *Deo gratias* and that he was thus identical with the anonymous "Printer of Terentius, Pr. 6748" (see Chapter 2).

This supposition, however, is more than doubtful. One has to wonder whether Niccolò's work as a *donzello* of the Mercanzia between 1464 and 1475 would have allowed him to learn and exercise the printer's profession, which was both time-consuming and tiring.[37] And the answer cannot be but negative: the court of the Mercanzia would and could not have possibly permitted him to hold a double position, in negligence of his public duties. Although one may still argue that the mysterious "Printer of Terentius, Pr. 6748" was working in Florence, it cannot have been Niccolò di Lorenzo himself.

As a parallel, one might consider the case of the printer Lienhart Holl from Ulm in Southern Germany.[38] Between August 1467 and 4 December 1471, Holl worked in a very similar position as that of Niccolò di Lorenzo, as a *donzello* of the Florentine wool corporation, the Arte della lana. He then abandoned his post with the intention to move, as he claimed, to Venice.[39] Since Venetian incunabula arrived in Florence at a very early stage, it is quite possible that Holl was already thinking about a professional career in printing. No Venetian sources seem to record his sojourn there, but he must have acquired his skills either in Venice or in

Germany, presumably with Johannes Zainer. Temporary stays in Florence were again recorded on 11 March 1475 and between December 1476 and February 1477, before he settled in Ulm in 1478. There he soon published at least six important books, among them Ptolemy's illustrated *Geography*, which was based on a manuscript he had acquired in Florence from the well-known priest and geographer or "astrologist" Don Niccolò tedesco, also known as Niccolò Bleymint. Although a family member of Lienhart Holl continued to live in Florence, it is not clear whether he ever returned after that.

5

The Collaboration with Giovanni di Piero da Magonza, and Marsilio Ficino's *De Christiana religione*, ca. 1474–1476

*B*ibliographers use the descriptions of character types not only to identify printers' names but also to date their works. Throughout Niccolò di Lorenzo's career as a printer he used seven different types (all but one Roman), starting with a 113R ("Type 4*").[1] Regarding this, Victor Schold-erer actually distinguished two different types that developed out of each other, an earlier 114R (for the Ficino) and a 113R (from 1477 onward).[2] The very first book attributed to Niccolò di Lorenzo's press with this type was the rendering in *volgare* of Marsilio Ficino's *De Christiana religione*, of which more than fifty copies have been preserved in public collections, often in imperfect condition.[3] Not only Roberto Ridolfi but also Dennis Rhodes, Piero Scapecchi and, most recently, Guido Bartolucci have as-signed this work to Niccolò di Lorenzo.[4] The colophon recited rather anonymously, ":FINIS DEO GRATIAS AMEN. / /:AMEN."

A general indication of its printing date derives from the owner's note in a copy preserved in the National Central Library of Florence, in which a certain Francesco di Bartolomeo Nelli recorded that he had bought it "immediately" after its printing in 1474 ("inmediate fu chomposto ne l'anno 1474"); according to the Florentine calendar *ab incarnatione,* this could refer to any date between 25 March 1474 and 24 March 1475.[5] Francesco Nelli was the brother of the professor of canon law messer (Giovan) Battista Nelli and of Antonio Nelli, who in these years worked for a trading company of the Martelli family which had very strong interests in the book trade, especially with Venice.[6]

Marsilio Ficino had originally planned to publish both this and the Latin edition of *De Christiana religione* simultaneously. In the preface to the *volgare* edition, he stressed that he would—in the very near future—be dedicating the Latin version to Lorenzo de' Medici, whereas the first, "Tuscan" version ("el libro toscano") was now dedicated to the politician Bernardo del Nero, an ardent lover of his fatherland ("ardente amator della patria nostra").[7] As it turned out, in any case, the following Latin edition contained several additions.

In his highly ambitious treatise Ficino presented an "all-comprehensive," philosophical justification of the Christian religion in the light of an union between ancient and modern religion, wisdom and science. In its second part, following the precepts of the Franciscan pope Sixtus IV, Ficino gave his arguments a strong anti-Jewish polemical twist, drawing on at least three medieval controversialists. He may have known their writings through his nephew, the priest Sebastiano Salvini; only one of these texts had previously been printed.[8] At the same time, *De Christiana religione* showed a sincere interest in ancient and medieval Hebrew literature—Ficino actually distinguished between Hebrew and Jewish, (i.e., before and after the Christian "law")—in order to demonstrate arcane continuities in the theological reflections of both religions. It has been shown how much he depended in this on the Greek church father Eusebius of Caesarea, whose *De praeperatione evangelica* he must have known from its Latin translation in the Venetian *editio princeps* by the hand of Nicolas Jenson (1470). This much is evident from Ficino's notion of the "Jewish Aristotles," which actually derived from a misprint in Jenson's edition.[9] Marsilio Ficino's scribe Luca Fabiani intervened by hand on the printed text of *De Christiana religione* in a few volumes—as, for example, in the copy today preserved in the Bodleian Library—and a nonsystematic way. Some of these corrections were motivated by the author's fears regarding the theological orthodoxy of his own formulations.[10] Although it is not known who financed the printing of the Italian *De Christiane religione,* Ficino's personal interest in the publication was obvious: with this text he strived to assume the "public role of guide and master of spiritual life" in Florence.[11]

Doubts about the role of Niccolò di Lorenzo in printing this work are, as has been shown herein, more than justified. Already Scholderer observed in part six of the *Catalogue of Books Printed in the XVth Century Now in the British Museum* that in Florence

> the only craftsman known to us at this date [i.e., 1474/1475], however, is Petri [i.e., Giovanni di Piero da Magonza], who supplied the Ripoli press with a part, if not the whole, of its original outfit and more particularly with the very fount of roman nearest akin to that of the Ficino books ... so that it can scarcely be doubted that he had a hand in the latter. This, of course, is not to exclude Laurentii from a share in their production, and they are in any case intimately connected with his earliest work, but we know too little about Florentine printing in the years immediately prior to 1477 to make a more definite statement.[12]

It has therefore been suggested that not only Niccolò di Lorenzo's type 114R but also "its several mutations: 113R, 115Ra, 115Rb, and perhaps 111Ra" all originated with Giovanni di Piero, who "owned the punches and sold different sets of matrices to different printers."[13] The few historical sources at our disposal do not resolve the problem. It could be argued, however, that even Florentine goldsmiths like Banco di Filippo and Domenico di Bernardo Cennini, were in such relations with the German printers as to produce and sell them typographical material. It is with a certain dose of skepticism that one should meet Scholderer's suggestion—which has become "classic"—that Giovanni di Piero da Magonza was identical with the "Giovanni tedescho," who in the summer of 1477, and with the mediation of a certain "Cassino," briefly collaborated with the Ripoli press and was in contact with Niccolò di Lorenzo's workshop, as this Giovanni could also have been an itinerant printer.[14]

On the other hand, one has to uphold Konrad Haebler's and Victor Scholderer's hypotheses about Giovanni di Piero da Magonza acting as a mentor for Niccolò di Lorenzo in learning the printing trade.[15] The latter's new qualification as typographer following his work at the Mercanzia was probably due to the collaboration with the temporarily unemployed printer Giovanni di Piero da Magonza. Some "matches" in their biographies seem to be more than mere coincidence. Both of them lived with their families in the parish of Sant'Ambrogio, in the quarter of Santa Croce. There were no overlapping periods of time in which both of them independently signed colophons of their own printed books. Giovanni officially reassumed his activity only after Niccolò di Lorenzo's bankruptcy in 1486/1487. It is therefore quite possible that the two cooperated closely, presumably in the very same workshop and in alternate roles, throughout the 1470s and 1480s.

The following Latin version of Marsilio Ficino's *De Christiana religione* in quarto is again undated but seems to have been printed at the end of 1476, when Ficino dedicated it to some of his friends.[16] This work also evidenced several imperfections and became (in)famous for its erratic setting and orthographic variations, which were corrected only in successive print runs. Ficino himself, instead of meticulously correcting his proofs, reacted very harshly against the "oppressors" of his book ("oppressores librorum").[17] In his bibliographical analysis Curt Bühler has furthermore suggested that Niccolò di Lorenzo printed this book on "at least two presses," possibly three.[18] No names of editors or proofreaders of *De Christiana religione* have been reported from the time of its printing.[19] The Florentine copy which Ficino dedicated to the eminent humanist Giorgio Antonio Vespucci was also sent in the name of the rich merchant Giovanni di Niccolò Cavalcanti, who was a friend of Ficino and could have been one of the publishers of the edition.[20]

6

Cappone Capponi and His Circle, 1475–1480

According to archival documents, Niccolò di Lorenzo triumphantly reappeared as a "master printer" on 10 February 1476, roughly one year after resigning his post at the Mercanzia ("magister Nicholaus Laurentii Nicholai alamannus"). After his apprenticeship—presumably with Giovanni di Piero da Magonza—he now signed a formal and very detailed contract with the Florentine citizen Cappone di Bartolomeo Capponi; on 22 October 1475 both parties specified the terms of their collaboration in detail. The text of this agreement is unfortunately preserved only in its first lines. Two conditions were mentioned on later occasions: first, the printer's obligation to deliver one copy of each finished book to Capponi and, second, Niccolò's debt of 163 lire, or more than thirty gold florins (probably the sum spent for setting up his workshop); this was, by the way, a very similar sum to that contended between Francesco Berlinghieri and Giorgio Baldesi in 1471/1472.[1] On 10 February 1476 Niccolò promised to return this money in one year. With all probability, his company with Capponi was to last for five years; in fact, on 11 November 1480 the printer was "free" to consider a new contract with the convent of San Iacopo di Ripoli and the stationer Bartolo di Domenico di Guido (see Chapter 10).

Cappone di Bartolomeo Capponi came, just like Giorgio Baldesi and Giovanni Benizi, from the quarter of Santo Spirito. His long and well-documented life was, just like Benizi's, characterized by manifestations of true, multifaceted entrepreneurial spirit and political hardship. Already in 1444, at the age of eight, he had joined the silk merchants' corporation, thanks to his father's membership.[2] After having committed a murder and being absolved (1459), he married Mona Francesca, the daughter of the Florentine knight Giannozzo Pitti, with an outstandingly high dowry.[3] From Capponi's testament from 1508 it is clear that by then she was still active in the administration of her property.[4]

Two years after the so-called conspiracy of Luca Pitti, Capponi was banished from the Florentine republic for the "preservation of the peaceful state" (1468). He now invested in various commercial activities, both in Florence and in the Lower Valdarno, Volterra and the Maremma.[5] As it seems, only in spring 1471 did he return to Florence, when his father Bartolomeo thanked Lorenzo de' Medici for helping to liberate Capponi from the banishment.[6] The following October, Capponi established a trading society together with the humanist Alamanno Rinuccini, his brother-in-law.[7] Six years later, in Lucca, he set up a company for book printing together with the sculptor Matteo Civitali, which was ended by May 1478 and from which no products have survived.[8] Lucca was clearly a town with which Capponi had close links. In early 1479 he returned there escaping the Black Death, and then invested in the silk trade together with a merchant from Villa Basilica, not far from Lucca (1480).[9]

With rather typical understatement, in the Catasto records of 1480 Capponi defined himself as being of forty-four years of age and "without any occupation" ("sanza exercitio").[10] His relationship with the Medici was characterized by deference: in the summer 1472 he humbly wrote to Lorenzo de' Medici at his villa at Cafaggiolo that as one of the electors of the Florentine Podestà he would clearly adhere to the Magnifico's will.[11] Occasionally he was in direct business relations with him.[12] More often he acted as a legal representative of his ecclesiastical family members, and sometimes these activities resulted in bitter conflicts with other citizens. In 1497, for instance, in defending the rights of one of his kinsmen, Capponi tried to impede the passing of the old Vallombrosan monastery of Santa Trinita under the obedience of the abbot of Vallombrosa, Dom Biagio Milanesi. In his records, Milanesi noted with satisfaction that in this case an important politician, Luca d'Antonio degli Albizzi, openly defended him and threatened to throw Capponi out of the windows of Palazzo Vecchio in order "to teach him and give an example to others."[13]

Unfortunately, Capponi's diary of *ricordanze* seems to have survived only in later extracts which do not mention his supporting early Florentine printing.[14] The same source also names the godfathers (*compari*) chosen for his children who came from all social classes. In 1467 one of these godfathers was the spice dealer or apothecary Antonio di Mariano *speziale*. This man is known to have commissioned a painted tabernacle by the artist Neri di Bicci two years earlier.[15] As a consequence of his insolvency in early 1472, Mariano's family home was—maybe only briefly—confiscated.[16] In 1476 he was named as a witness in two notarial acts regarding Niccolò di Lorenzo, and in February 1478 was again described as a "former" apothecary and an "insolvent and fugitive" debtor when his belongings were confiscated for a debt dating back to May 1477.[17] He now likely chose a profession that had already been among his former activities—that of itinerant bookseller. In this occupation he was recorded in Bologna in 1485.[18]

Among the godfathers of Capponi's children were the humanist Piero Domizi, whom Capponi described in 1477 as "teacher at the clerics' school at Santa Reparata" and who later became the chaplain of Giovanni Benizi's chapel. Others were the merchant Iacopo di Borgianni di Mino (1481), the medical doctor Matteo di maestro Girolamo Broccardi (1481), the painter "maestro Antonio" from Lucca (1485),[19] and the philosopher and priest Marsilio Ficino (1493). Capponi was also in direct relations with a cleric called "ser Meo" who could be the same man identified as a worker at the Ripoli press between 1478 and 1480.[20] He was finally on friendly terms with other humanists, not only with his brother-in-law Alamanno Rinuccini but also with the sons of Giannozzo Manetti (Capponi was one of the arbiters regarding their father's inheritance), and with Cristoforo Landino.[21]

Printing for the Convent of Santo Spirito, ca. 1476–1477

$\mathscr{I}$n his publishing company with Niccolò di Lorenzo ("in arte et exercitio imprimendi et formando libros et volumina"), Cappone di Bartolomeo Capponi was the legal and, above all, commercial head of the enterprise. Niccolò was only responsible for the book production. This distribution of tasks was, of course, very much as in the earliest "division(s) of responsibility between craftsmanship and business operation"—for example, in the company of Johannes Gutenberg and Johannes Fust.[1] The obligation of bookkeeping lay presumably in the hands of both men, each for his own part; from a later court case we know that Niccolò di Lorenzo's account book was begun in 1476.

In an attempt to shield himself from further financial obligations, on 30 July 1476 Capponi appointed two notaries to legalize the first contract both partners had signed on 22 October 1475, and similarly on 23 October 1476.[2] This step was presumably due to the charges brought to the court of the Podestà on 7 September 1476 by the learned prior of the Augustinian convent of Santo Spirito, Fra Andrea d'Alessandro de' Trotti d'Alessandria.[3] As he claimed, Niccolò di Lorenzo had received from him the enormous sum of about one hundred gold florins for printing a volume titled *Egidio sopra el secondo* (i.e., the commentary of Aegidius Columna on the second book of the *Sentences* of Peter the Lombard), which however never saw the light of day.[4]

This theological textbook was commonly used in all Augustinian *studia*, and a short digression is needed here. One of Trotti's predecessors as prior of Santo Spirito, then general of the order and bishop of Fiesole, Guglielmo Becchi, had for many years lectured on the text of the *Sentences*, leaving after his death several manuscripts and commentaries on it.[5] Although the crucially important commentary of Aegidius Columna itself is not mentioned among his books, it must be assumed that Becchi owned such a manuscript which could have served as a printer's copy; in 1482 the text finally went to press in Venice.[6]

The friendly relations between the convent of Santo Spirito and the printer did not suffer from the legal conflict of 1476. Already the few lines known from the *volgare* contract of 22 October 1475 refer to the central role played by certain "venerabili et religiosi etc."—obviously the members of a religious order. And even later the printer's name turned up in the convent's accounts for a rather generic commission of printing books.[7] Nothing is known about the location of Niccolò's first workshop, but if it was different from his family home, it cannot be excluded that it was in one of the buildings of Santo Spirito.[8]

In any case, on 26 July 1477, Niccolò finished an important volume for the convent. It was the only text ever set by him in a Gothic script, the *Quaestiones super libris De anima Aristotelis* by the Augustinian theologian Alphonsus de Vargas.[9] This author had himself written a commentary on Peter the Lombard's *Sentences* and had died as Bishop of Sevilla in 1366; his lectures on Aristotle's books on the human soul were used almost exclusively by students of his own order and were published at least five times by 1609.[10] Although there is no documentary evidence for it, the first edition of the *Quaestiones* by the hand of Niccolò di Lorenzo was almost certainly commissioned by the aforementioned Fra Andrea de' Trotti, who was interested—if not directly involved—in the teaching of Aristotle at Santo Spirito.[11] Probably copies of the *Quaestiones* were also sent to other Augustinian *studia*.

In the case of the *Quaestiones,* Gothic types were probably employed on specific request of the friars, who in their academic context preferred this "traditional" script.[12] On the Florentine book market, however, there was little use for them. Soon later these types were therefore sold to another printer, Bonus Gallus de Béthun, who after some time in Padua had settled in Colle Valdelsa, a center of paper production, where he printed two scientific texts with these types (1478–1479).[13]

Institutional and Private Commissions, ca. 1476–1480

$\mathcal{L}$ooking at the approximately twenty titles attributed to Niccolò di Lorenzo's press from the years of his collaboration with Cappone di Bartolomeo Capponi (and excluding from this list the text falsely attributed to Leon Battista Alberti, *Ippolito Buondelmonti e Dianora de' Bardi*),[1] some preliminary observations can be made. The titles may be divided into approximately three phases. The first phase comprises seven religious or philosophical titles up to the year 1477, mostly printed with Niccolò's type 113R, as in the case of Marsilio Ficino's *De Christiana religione*.[2] The numbers of extant copies from this group vary a great deal, from more than twenty to very few or single exemplars (for example, the very short *Confessione* of Paulus Florentinus, preserved only in Siena). As always, no conclusions can be drawn from these numbers regarding the original press runs.

In the second phase, after 1477, the printer also used smaller types ("Type 3: 92R" and "Type 2: 106/107R"), and opened up to a large variety of texts: theological, philosophical, humanistic, political, and even *volgare* literature (e.g., Luca Pulci's *Driadeo*). Again the number of extant copies differs immensely from case to case. More than seventy copies have, for example, survived of the Cornelius Celsus, and more than thirty of the Petrus de Crescentiis, both from 1478. On the other side stand the single or extremely rare exemplars of the *Esortazione ai Veneziani*, or those of the three pamphlets against Pope Sixtus IV in defense of Lorenzo de' Medici after the so-called Pazzi conspiracy.

A new type was introduced by Niccolò di Lorenzo in the very last year of his partnership with Capponi.[3] He still signed himself as "Nicolaus Laurentii Alamanus" as in the colophon of the Latin *Ethics* of Aristotle (before 25 March 1480), and continued to direct the workshop in 1480. He probably also played a role in the choice of the last titles—for example, the neither original nor voluminous editions of the *Epistolae et Evangelia* in Italian and Petrarch's *Trionfi*. The first of these two was printed in Niccolò's "Type 4: 114R," the other in his smaller "Type 3: 92r" from 1477/1478. Both titles were cheap, and easy sellers—there had been at least five earlier editions of the *Epistolae et Evangelia*, among which was one of the already known "Printer of Terentius, Pr. 6748"—and the Petrarch was very similar if not directly modeled on Giovanni di Piero da Magonza's earlier edition from 1472.[4]

Despite these fluctuations, the initial activity of Niccolò di Lorenzo and Capponi regarded mostly religious and devotional texts. This could either depend on Capponi's personal preferences—if indeed he ever played an active role in the choice of the titles—or the influence of Santo Spirito, but was more likely due to the single commissions the two partners accepted from their publishers.

Whereas his edition of *De Christiana religione* still demonstrated the limits of Niccolò di Lorenzo's printing expertise, the following publication of Antonio Bettini's *Monte sancto di Dio* (10 September 1477) introduced a revolutionary novelty in Italian illustrated books: the use of copper engravings. This new technique dates from more or less the time of the first printed books. The first dated Italian engraving is inscribed 1461.[5] Although the earlier tradition of illustrating printed books with woodcuts remained popular all over Europe, copper engravings soon also found their way into them. In Italy they were employed from around 1477—as, for example, in the single maps in Domenico Lapi's Bologna edition of Ptolemy's *Geography* from that year.[6] Following a more complex procedure, however, the three engravings for Bettini's three pious tracts *Monte sancto di Dio*, *Della gloria del paradiso*, and *Delle pene delli dan-*

nati had to be printed directly on the pages, necessarily in successive print runs and after that of the text.

The most famous of these engravings is certainly the allegory of "God's mountain." In the center of the image one sees a humble friar climbing the ladder of the virtues up to heaven, where Christ is waiting for him, whereas in the left foreground an elegantly dressed but blindfolded youth is being captured by the devil. The other two pictures present the savior in glory and, just before the last tract on the punishments of the damned, hell with Satan. These illustrations must have been produced especially for this edition and by somebody familiar with all three texts. Traditionally they have been attributed, not without a large margin of doubt, to the Florentine goldsmith and engraver Baccio Baldini, about whom very little is known. The most recent attribution to an as yet unknown "Dante workshop" seems therefore equally justified.[7]

Just as in the case of *De Christiana religione,* Niccolò di Lorenzo's *Monte sancto* reveals several imperfections. In the copy preserved today at the National Central Library of Florence, a contemporary hand added some missing phrases from a more complete manuscript source and corrected the text where passages had been printed twice (employing the note "vacat").[8] No direct sources on the names of the financial backers of the edition have survived. Recently, the name of the religious poet and writer Feo Belcari as the possible financial backer has been suggested. In Belcari's biography of the founder of the Jesuate order, Blessed Giovanni Colombini da Siena (1304–1367), the merchant's religious conversion was attributed to the irresistible attraction of a devotional book that belonged to his wife, so different from the daily accounting and mercantile correspondence he was used to.[9] Studying "the right texts" was clearly one of the main aims of the order, which actively promoted religious reading.[10] Regarding the illustrations of Niccolò di Lorenzo's *Monte sancto,* Belcari was certainly "well placed to provide an iconographic programme" for them.[11]

However, some curiosity has also been aroused by the testament of the author of the *Monte sancto,* the Jesuate Antonio Bettini da Siena, Bishop of Foligno (1396–1487). Among the possessions cited in his will, there were actually several printed books—for example, three copies of his *Monte sancto,* together with other editions that seemingly stem from

Niccolò di Lorenzo from the same years: four copies of Domenico Cavalca's *Pungilingua* and six legends of Giovanni Colombini ("sei leggende del B. Gio[van]ni").[12]

If these titles circulated among the Jesuates, who, despite their membership in a religious congregation were mostly laymen, it is also possible that they had commissioned them and were responsible for their distribution.[13] If thus both the printing of the *Monte sancto* and of Belcari's life of Giovanni Colombini, and possibly even that of the *Pungilingua*, originated with the Jesuates, a closer look at their Florentine convent is obligatory. For roughly a century after 1434, the date of the first concession of Pope Eugene IV, they inhabited an elder thirteenth-century foundation called San Giusto outside the city walls at Porta Pinti.[14] Soon the convent became famous for its production of stained glass windows. The Jesuates also copied and translated numerous religious texts in *volgare*, some of which are still conserved in the Florentine libraries.[15] The importance of their Florentine house for the whole congregation can be seen from the fact that general chapter meetings were held at San Giusto in 1450 and in 1467. A profound reform of the order had to wait until 1485, again at a chapter meeting in Florence.[16]

Despite the precepts of a perpetual circulation of the Jesuate friars between different convents in order to prevent the formation of regional clusters, in the 1470s the Florentine element predominated at San Giusto. In these years the convent was headed by a certain Fra Antonio di Leonardo Strozzi, from a minor branch of this important Florentine family. We first hear of him in 1468 as "one of the friars," when he was responsible for the relations with local artists like Neri di Bicci.[17] In 1471 he was sent as the convent's delegate to attend the general chapter meeting in Siena and by August 1472 was elected prior himself.[18] With the very same humble title already employed by Antonio Bettini, in 1474 he signed himself "fr. Antonio degli Ingesuati povero di virtù" when he pleaded with Lorenzo de' Medici to pay for a certain quantity of ultramarine color he had acquired, apparently with his brother's help.[19] Lorenzo himself was on good terms with the Jesuates. He reputedly donated a saint's relic to the church of San Giusto and wrote on their behalf to the government of Lucca.[20]

Fra Antonio seems to have served as the convent's prior until late 1477, when he was replaced.[21] The Jesuates' general chapter at San Giusto in May 1477, for which the Florentine commune, awaiting between seventy and eighty participants from all over Italy, financially contributed with a sum of two hundred lire, paid directly to the prior on 21 April, falls into his period.[22] It was also the last chapter meeting which bishop Antonio Bettini personally attended. The printing of the *Monte sancto* that so strongly interested his religion could thus be related to this solemn occasion and his last visit in Florence. Considering Fra Antonio Strozzi's artistic relations, we should take seriously the possibility that in the chapter's aftermath he also arranged for the printing of both Belcari's and Bettini's texts.[23] The images in the 1477 edition of the *Monte sancto* were therefore intended to illustrate both the Jesuates' spirituality and the excellence of Florentine craftsmanship. Thanks to a series of private donations, in the following years the convent of San Giusto was able to expand and beautify its church with important works of art, like the high altar painting from the hand of Domenico Ghirlandaio and the frescoes and panels by Pietro Perugino; in 1529, alas, all the buildings were destroyed in fear of the imperial troops of Charles V.[24] Some of the remaining books from San Giusto were, at the beginning of the eighteenth century, in the private library of the Doni family and then passed on to the Biblioteca Riccardiana.[25]

Similar in aim to Niccolò di Lorenzo's works for the Jesuates were two other publications of 16 October 1477 with a new, very small type ("Type 3: 92R"), the *Regola della vita spirituale* and the *Regola della vita matrimoniale*, by a certain Fra Cherubino from the Franciscan order. Modern scholarship has established that this was the popular Franciscan Observant preacher Cherubino da Spoleto (1414-1484), whose two "rules" had begun to circulate in manuscript copies already in the 1460s.[26] During Lent in 1466 Fra Cherubino preached in the Florentine convent of Santa Croce and a decade later convinced the communal government of Prato to inaugurate one of the first Tuscan charitable pawnshops known as Monte de' poveri della pietà di Prato.[27] He was obviously well connected to various members of Florentine society. When he was preaching in Bologna during Lent in 1472, for instance, the exiled Giandonato Barbadori thanked both him and Lorenzo de' Medici for putting in a good word for a possible future return to Florence.[28] Another of Fra Cherubino's followers was Pandolfo di Giovanni Rucellai, later Fra Santi of the San Marco convent.[29]

In the first printed edition of 1477, Fra Cherubino's two treatises on spiritual and matrimonial life were dedicated to a Florentine whom he addressed as "my blessed son Iacobus de Bongannis" (or "Iacobus de Borgannis"). This man has been identified with Iacopo di Borgianni di Mino di Borgianni, the son of a dyer from the quarter of Santa Croce. In his youth he had composed religious rhymes and copied the poetry of popular Florentine authors—for example, Burchiello.[30] In the early 1470s he stayed on as a merchant in Bologna, in close epistolary contact with Lorenzo de' Medici, who confidentially called him "il Borgiannino," possibly alluding to his physical stature.[31] Thereafter he became a partner in an important banking firm, first with Iacopo Venturi and Giovanni di Paolo Rucellai, and then only as Rucellai's administrator (1476–1477).[32] His brother Matteo was a merchant in Avignon in Southern France, but Iacopo's own economic activities after these years are still little known.[33] Today he is mostly remembered for his generous patronage of the Observant Clarissan convent of Santa Chiara Novella, where three of his sisters became nuns.[34] It was thanks to his patronage that the convent church was rebuilt in the 1490s, and in his testament he requested to be buried there in Franciscan habit (1506).[35] On spiritual grounds, a direct contact between Iacopo di Borgianni and Fra Cherubino would not be surprising, even without the latter's dedication to "his blessed son." Despite his apparent interest in the subject of marriage, Iacopo remained a bachelor.

But was he also behind the publication of Fra Cherubino's writings in 1477? In the accounts and records of Lorenzo Guidetti one finds a note that he had bought a book described as a "bound Cherubino from those belonging to Iacopo di Borgianni," as if this copy had been left by Iacopo in the stationer's shop.[36] And although this copy could have been any of the printed editions of either Niccolò di Lorenzo (1477, 1482, 1483), San Iacopo di Ripoli (1483), or even of a non-Florentine press, it can be demonstrated that Iacopo was indeed the publisher of the *editio princeps*.

As it turned out, on 18 February 1478, the merchant Iacopo di Borgianni di Mino presented himself in the court of the Mercanzia, claiming that Niccolò di Lorenzo had been obliged to print a book titled *The Spiritual Life*, written for him by Fra Cherubino, by the end of July 1477. For this work the typographer had received the sum of forty-four gold florins without ever finishing the volume; even if some parts—or, as one may guess, some number of copies—had been printed, this was not what he had promised to his partner in their contract. Therefore Iacopo protested against Niccolò and claimed the refunding of the anticipated sum (see Appendix B, no. 1).

Evidently their quarrel was not settled in the following months. As a consequence, on 20 August 1478 the initial protest became a formal charge. Instead of calling him a printer, Iacopo now claimed from the "former servant of the Mercanzia" the lesser sum of forty gold florins, six soldi and four danari. This was for the cash received and all "the other things they had had to do with each other, as appears in Iacopo's account book on page 90." Again Niccolò was either unable or unwilling to pay this sum.[37] In order to give more weight to his charge and make it "executive," Iacopo deposited on 25 August five lire and seven soldi as the requested tax (the so-called *diritto*) from the Mercanzia. As Niccolò did not present himself, the final sentence in Iacopo's favor over the whole sum was pronounced on 7 October 1478.[38]

At the present stage it can only be speculated on what went wrong with this edition. The colophons of the more than eleven copies preserved in public collections do not actually indicate Niccolò di Lorenzo as printer but read "PERFECTODIEXVI.OCTVBRIS.M//CCCC. LXXVII.//DEOGRATIAS" (as in the copy in the National Central Library of Florence), or, with a spelling variant, "PERFECTODIEXVI. OCTOBRIS.M//CCCC.LXXVII.//DEOGRATIAS" (as in the copy in the Biblioteca Casanatense in Rome). As mentioned, the type used was Niccolò di Lorenzo's small new "Type 3: 92R," which was used only one later time, in his Cornelius Celsus, *De medicina*, of 1478. If therefore the Cherubino had really been finished with a few months' delay in October 1477, albeit not in the form and number of copies as promised, one should think that Iacopo di Borgianni would have refrained from a court case. On the other hand, the colophon might be a deliberate attempt to confuse the reader about the date of the edition, which was really printed a year later, in October 1478, and thus only after the final Mercanzia sentence. In this case, the use of a smaller type could have been due to paper shortage or an attempt to limit the printing costs. A final, more radical hypothesis could be that the book was not at all produced by Niccolò di Lorenzo but by somebody else using this type.

Although the printer had already been cited before a judge once before—in 1476 by the prior of Santo Spirito—this is the first time a legal dispute on the printing of a single book is documented in the Florentine archive sources for the Mercanzia. As much as one might desire that the notaries of the Mercanzia had also transcribed the terms of the contract, such a relative "completeness" of the documents would be very exceptional. Whatever the solution to the bibliographical riddle, the 1477 sentence probably bore no immediate fruits: Iacopo di Borgianni could not force the printer into paying his debt and presumably did not intend to deprive him of his liberty and workforce, denying him the possibility of a future clearance of his debt. It must finally not be forgotten that Niccolò was still in a partnership with Capponi, who could have mediated in this case; as has been noted, four years later Iacopo di Borgianni even became the godfather of one of his children.

The traumatic events following the Pazzi conspiracy in April 1478 left a deep mark on Florence. For the printer Niccolò di Lorenzo, the violent clash between Pope Sixtus IV and Lorenzo de' Medici created an occasion for producing, presumably in late summer 1478, three short and undated pamphlets in a "comprehensive scheme to counter the propaganda issuing from the papal printing press,"[39] In precedence, as Sixtus IV gloried himself, the two printed papal bulls of 1 and 22 June containing the Medici's and the civic government's excommunication had been "sent to the whole world." It was therefore one of the first propaganda wars that was fought in both the Florentine and Roman printing shops. The three authors who responded to the papal claims all belonged to the "inner Medici circle." Although no documentary evidence has survived on this, it would only be natural to assume a direct role of Lorenzo de' Medici in the publication and then also the public distribution of their writings: Gentile Becchi's *Florentina Synodus*, Angelo Poliziano's *Pactianae coniurationis commentarium*, and finally Bartolomeo Scala's *Excusatio Florentinorum*.[40] Whereas the first and the last survive in just one printed exemplar, Poliziano's classic account of the Pazzi conspiracy has been preserved in four copies. Again in this case one finds two different print states, with three copies containing corrections added by hand and a single one, that of the Biblioteca Corsiniana in Rome, presenting a more correct printed text. Rather curiously, in two copies the printing date in the colophon was changed by hand from 1478 to 1479 before being readapted to the original 1478. This procedure has be explained as an attempt to "update" these copies in the presumed year of their sale—that is, 1479.[41]

Several other books were printed by Niccolò di Lorenzo in the years of his association with Capponi, which ended in November 1480. The most important of these were undoubtedly the Petrus de Crescentiis, *Ruralia commoda* in *volgare* (15 July 1478), the first edition of Cornelius Celsus's classic medical handbook *De medicina* (1478), Luca Pulci's short *volgare* poem *Driadeo d'amore* (3 April 1479), Sebastiano Salvini's translation of Rabbi Samuel of Morocco's *Epistola* against the Jews (after 25 November 1479), and Aristotle's *Ethica ad Nicomachum* in Latin (before 25 March 1480). Nothing certain is known about the financial backing or direct commission of any of these works. It nevertheless seems that now the printer reached out toward new readerships, less interested in religious or pious works than with *volgare* and humanistic literature. The success of these works almost certainly fueled in him further ambitions for the second part of his professional career after 1480/1481.

The *volgare* translation of the first and most systematic agronomical work of the Middle Ages, Piero Crescenzi's *Libri commodorum ruralium*, was still printed in the weeks of acute political crisis (15 July 1478). In March 1481 the book dealer and editor Piero Pacini sold an unbound copy of this work for the considerable sum of forty-five soldi, or two lire and five soldi.[42] The edition was a powerful demonstration that "business as usual" continued among those Florentine patricians who allowed no distraction from their economic interests and cultural inclinations. Crescenzi's popular work had already been printed several times in Latin (Augsburg, 1471; Louvain, 1474, 1475, 1478). In Tuscany it continued, however, to be read mostly in its fourteenth-century translation, which is known from many manuscripts (*Il libro della agricultura*).[43] After the fortunate *editio princeps* by the hand of Niccolò di Lorenzo, a second reception of the text was triggered north of the Alps, where numerous translations in other European languages made the text available to new readers.

Through his work the printer presumably entered into relations with the humanist Bartolomeo Della Fonte, or Bartolomeo Fonzio. As an editor he was responsible, sometime between 24 March 1478 and 25 March 1479, for another *princeps,* that of Cornelius Celsus's medical handbook *De medicina,* in eight volumes.[44] This work, a wide-ranging encyclopedia on dietetic, pharmaceutical, and surgical treatments of disease; plastic operations; and many other subjects, had been rediscovered in the fifteenth century and won immediate applause.[45] The philological form of the text, however, posed serious problems: Lorenzo Guidetti, for example, as an intermediary in early 1470, arranged for the copying of a *De medicina* manuscript for the Neapolitan book market and two years later turned to the Medici library in search of a better manuscript."[46] When Bartolomeo Fonzio decided to prepare a new "critical" edition, the humanist had already printed, with the press of San Iacopo di Ripoli, his interpretation of the Latin satires of Persius (1477).[47]

In a short presentation letter to the Florentine banker Francesco di Tommaso Sassetti which was probably added in a second moment (as it is present only in some copies), Fonzio passed from a short history of the invention of letters in Egypt and their introduction in Italy to the merits of contemporary printers who secured eternity to ancient and modern writers and therefore deserved the praise of all readers.[48] After Marsilio Ficino's rather unfair attacks on the *oppressores librorum,* this could be read as a full restoration of Niccolò di Lorenzo's reputation. As Fonzio knew well, the typographer's work had to be completed by that of the proofreaders and correctors. Despite this, even his *De medicina* is known in at least two different print states.[49]

As the humanist furthermore explained in his preface, his edition retrieved Cornelius Celsus's text from "squalor and deformation" to a "renovated and restituted" form through the help of some "very old manuscripts" acquired by Francesco Sassetti in France ("vetustis exemplaribus tua opera e Gallia conquisitis"). This Florentine banker was not only the owner of an important library and business partner of Lorenzo de' Medici but also, with all probability, the financial backer of the 1478 publication.[50] Some time before, Fonzio had dedicated him a lavishly decorated manuscript of *De medicina,* which in 1489 was destined to be sent to the king of Hungary, Matthias Corvinus. After his death, however, it remained in Florence and is now the Codex Laurentianus Pluteo LXXIII.4 (also known as "F").[51] Albinia de la Mare noted the curious coincidence that in the same year of the printing of *De medicina* two other medical works entered Sassetti's library, both dedication copies and "concerned with means of combating the plague, and [*which*] were presumably composed during the plague which broke out in 1478."[52] Evidently Sassetti had a personal interest in the subject. For his part, Fonzio may have drawn inspiration from the humanistic exercise of Francesco Filelfo, who some decades earlier had translated ancient medical texts for a prince who was constantly preoccupied with health matters.[53]

As has been demonstrated, one of Bartolomeo Fonzio's direct sources for his edition could have been the Codex Laurentianus Pluteo LXXIII.1 (also known as "L") from the tenth century, which, however, did not belong to Sassetti; it originally came from the church of Sant'Ambrogio in Milan, was in Bologna around the time of Fonzio's edition, and then found its way into the Laurentian Library only after 1490. The mystery remains as to how Fonzio got hold of the text of this manuscript. In the highly competitive context of Florentine humanism, some scholars from Angelo Poliziano's circle downplayed Fonzio's philological efforts some years later.[54] A relatively high number of printed copies of his book have survived—at least seventy in public collections. It was also mentioned in several Florentine libraries of the fifteenth century.[55]

With the first edition of Luca Pulci's mythical pastoral in *volgare* octaves known as *Il Driadeo (d'amore)* from 1479, Niccolò di Lorenzo served for the first time a much more "popular" readership. The literary style of the poem has been described as a combination of "high" and "comic" language, very similar to that of Luca's more famous brother Luigi.[56] As it was published anonymously, some Florentines actually attributed it to Luigi Pulci himself.[57] Several manuscripts of this text are known from before its publication in print and only five copies of the Florentine *princeps* are preserved today in public libraries.[58] Approximately seven reprints of the work by other Florentine presses before the year 1500 demonstrate its huge success among local readers—among them even Leonardo da Vinci.[59] The 1479 edition contained at its beginning Luca Pulci's dedication letter to Lorenzo de' Medici from around 1465, although the author had already died in 1470: one may thus wonder who was responsible for printing his work.[60] It cannot be excluded that his two remaining brothers, Luigi and Bernardo Pulci, organized the publication of this easy "best seller," which certainly could have helped to improve their sagging fortunes; about two years earlier, and together with a business partner, Luigi Pulci had organized—with an as yet unidentified typographer—the printing of the lost *princeps* of his chivalric poem *Morgante*.

The edition of John Argyropoulos's Latin translation of Aristotle's *Ethics* in its last, third redaction was another publishing success of Niccolò di Lorenzo before 25 March 1480.[61] As has been mentioned, it was printed with a new type, and at least twenty-seven copies of this book have survived in public collections.[62] Single unbound copies sold for two lire and six soldi—as, for example, in October 1481 to the convent of Santissima Annunziata.[63] The initiative of printing this text obviously came from someone in contact with Argyropoulos, while he was teaching philosophy in the Florentine university, the Studium Generale, for the second time (1477-1481).[64] However, one may wonder to what degree the Greek was actually involved in commissioning the edition. If that was the case, he would presumably have added a second presentation letter or substituted altogether the original dedication of the *Ethics* to Cosimo de' Medici, *pater patriae* and Lorenzo de' Medici's grandfather.

The publication of the *Ethics* was also connected to the earlier folio edition of Donato Acciaiuoli's *Expositio Ethicorum Aristotelis*, which had probably been printed by the Ripoli press in 1477 and not in "1478" as its colophon stated.[65] In this work Acciaiuoli twice refers to the "new translation" of Aristotle's *Ethics* brought to Florence by Argyropoulos, but it is rather uncertain whether he was referring to its printed form. More than Acciaiuoli's *Expositio*, the new translation of the *Ethics* in quarto became also a commercial success. It was even found in princely libraries—such as, for example, in that of Federico da Montefeltro.[66]

Despite the doubts about his active role in the printing of Aristotle's *Ethics*, John Argyropoulos was clearly on good terms with the Florentine circle of Capponi. With a notarial act dated 23 February 1480 in which he identified himself as the procurator of his son Isaac, papal organist and holder of a priory at Pisa, Argyropoulos nominated in fact Capponi's cousin, the rather infamous master of the hospital of Altopascio, Guglielmo di Niccolò Capponi, as his general representative.[67] In this case, Capponi could have acted as an intermediary for both Argyropoulos and his relative.

In the same months, Niccolò di Lorenzo also printed the priest Sebastiano Salvini's Italian translation of Rabbi Samuel of Morocco's *Epistola*. As in this text the date 25 November 1479 is mentioned, the edition must clearly be dated after. The new translation belonged to the wider context of Ficino's anti-Jewish polemic, as contained in his *De Christiana religione* (see Chapter 5). Salvini was the humanist's nephew, scribe, and pupil, and in a fundamental study on him, Paul Oskar Kristeller noted that he seemed "to have studied with the Augustinian Hermits of Santo Spirito."[68] As the theological school of the Augustinians until 1469 had resisted the mounting anti-Semitic tension raised by the Observant mendicant preachers, at first glance this publication may surprise.[69] Salvini, however, approved the actions taken against the Jews by the newly elected bishop of Volterra (1478), Francesco Soderini.[70] When on 1 January 1481 Salvini was promoted to master of theology at the convent of Santo Spirito, this occurred after a "tremendous and rigorous" exam by the convent's vicar, who was also Francesco Soderini's legal procurator, by two Augustinian masters, among them Fra Andrea de' Trotti d'Alessandria, and by the "most learned man" (*eruditissimus vir*) Marsilio Ficino himself.[71] So far it is not clear in which way Salvini's publication of Rabbi Samuel's *Epistola* and his other religious works was related to his theological promotion, and whether and how far his promoters were involved in the publication, but they could have certainly directed him toward the printer Niccolò di Lorenzo.

The End of the Company, 1480–1482

*A*fter five years, the partnership between Niccolò di Lorenzo and Cappone di Bartolomeo Capponi came to an end in November 1480. A final balance sheet had to be drawn up to regulate the outstanding debts and credits with other business partners. From a notarial act of January 1482 it appears that the two partners arrived at a formal agreement ("compositio et concordia") only after the printer's short imprisonment ("captura") in the jail of the Podestà a year earlier.[1] Unfortunately, no archive sources regarding this court case seem to have survived. Also, by that time Niccolò di Lorenzo was already busy on another important project, Cristoforo Landino's edition and his commentary on Dante Alighieri's *Divine Comedy*. According to the final settlement with the typographer, in any case, Capponi was to pay all the company's debts, whereas Niccolò promised to compensate him with thirty gold florins, presumably the overall costs for setting up the printing shop.

As was customary after the end of a business venture, some of the unsatisfied creditors claimed their due in the court of the Mercanzia. The first to present himself was the goldsmith Domenico di Bernardo, the son of the goldsmith and printer Bernardo Cennini. In his deposition of 1 December 1480 he correctly described Niccolò as an ex-typographer whose partnership had ended ("per l'adrieto inpressori di libri").[2] As was argued, in the printer's account book begun in 1476 ("libro di forma"), Cennini was recorded as his creditor of thirty lire, the remainder of what had been a higher sum. The printer did not reply to this charge, and two weeks later, on 15 December, the debt was confirmed by a formal sentence (see Appendix B, no. 3). So far a collaboration be-tween Domenico Cennini and Niccolò di Lorenzo has never been taken into consideration. If Cennini's work for the printer consisted in the very same products he had presumably fabricated for the Servius in 1471-1472 (i.e., the design and cutting of the printing types), the question arises as to which of the several type sets used by Niccolò are being referred to. From the Ripoli diary it is known that in 1478 the rather obscure gold-smith Benvenuto di Chimenti sold the Ripoli press three different alpha-bets ("abbici, cioè dua antichie e una moderna") for the nearly fourfold higher sum of 110 lire; these were presumably the punches.[3] The simi-larity of the Ripoli types 85R and 105R with Niccolò di Lorenzo's small 92R (used for the Cherubino da Spoleto and the Cornelius Celsus, 1478) and 106R, has convinced Riccardo Olocco that Benvenuto di Chimenti also made the latter types.[4] If this was indeed the case, Domenico Cen-nini must have been the cutter or founder of earlier types, such as the Ficino "Type 4*: 113R" or the Gothic "Type 1: 102G" used by Niccolò di Lorenzo for the Alphonsus de Vargas (1477).

The second creditor to state his case in the Mercanzia was a medical doctor, Ludovico di maestro Piero dal Pozzo Toscanelli, a nephew of the great scientist Paolo di Domenico dal Pozzo Toscanelli, on 19 January 1481 (see Appendix B, no. 5).[5] According to his petition, the "writer" Niccolò di Lorenzo from the parish of Sant'Ambrogio owed him fourteen gold florins which in an unspecified date he had advanced on Niccolò's behalf with some apothecaries, Baldino di Bartolomeo di Cambio, Niccolò di Bartolomeo del Troscia, and their partners; many times he had urged the "writer" to honor this debt, but to no avail. As proof, Ludovico showed the apothecaries' account book to the notaries of the Mercanzia.[6] Despite his medical profession, Ludovico seems to have worked predominantly as a merchant of raw metals like copper, es-pecially after the marriage of his daughter Maddalena to the most important merchant in this market, Tommaso di ser Bonifazio Marinai

(1481).[7] The still extant registers of the two aforementioned apothecaries "in the Old Market, under the sign of the column," do not resolve the mystery of the origin of this debt.[8] It is therefore impossible to forward any hypothesis on what the printer had acquired from their well-established shop—for example, paper, the ingredients for ink, or similar materials needed in typography.[9] In any case, given Niccolò di Lorenzo's unwillingness or impossibility to respond to the court, the Mercanzia official ordered him on 17 February to pay exactly this sum.

The very last charge in the Mercanzia acts on 5 February 1481 regarded the modest sum of ten lire which three heirs who claimed to be creditors of the carpenters Giovanni and Bartolomeo d'Ulivante di Bartolomeo requested from Niccolò di Lorenzo; the printer seems to have been the debtor of the two, whom he had actually known for a long time. This case never arrived at a formal sentence, probably because the debt was paid immediately.[10] Possibly it originated in "the carpenter's service in assembling the printing press," as has recently been suggested for another, similar dispute between a woodworker and the printer Michel Wenssler in Basel.[11]

The five-year-long partnership with Capponi offered Niccolò di Lorenzo the opportunity to grow professionally and collaborate with important members of Florentine society from different cultural backgrounds. As both new requests and professional experience guided him to a new challenge in printing, the use of book illustrations, his flourishing contacts with emerging humanists laid the grounds for the second phase of his career, which will stand at the center of Part III.

Part III

At the Peak of Niccolò di Lorenzo's Career

10

A Work Proposal for the Ripoli Press,
11 November 1480

*I*n 1480 the conditions for printing in Florence had changed considerably from what they had been in the early 1470s. Certainly peace had returned after the conclusion of the uneasy truce between King Ferrante of Naples and Pope Sixtus IV on one side and Florence and Milan on the other (13 March 1480). Not all the lost territories returned immediately under the town's control, however, nor could all the destruction wrought by the war be repaired. War damage presumably affected also the paper production at Colle Valdelsa.[1] It comes therefore as no surprise that in 1483, when the Florentine merchant Battista d'Agnolo Vernacci decided to print a breviary for the Camaldolese order, his son was first sent as far away as Parma and then even to Brescia to acquire the necessary four bales of paper.[2]

With regard to the book trade, the late 1470s had witnessed the growing influence of the Venetian printing industry. When Nicolas Jenson, with at least ninety-one editions before 1480, and the associated company of Johannes Manthen and John of Cologne, merged their activities into one large syndicate (29 May 1480), they soon inundated the Florentine market with their exports.[3] Their books were universally admired not only for their care for correct scholarly texts but also for their high standards regarding the paper, the layout, and the beauty of their Roman (or Gothic, when required) characters. These merits immediately caught the attention of Florentine merchants.[4] The "big company" of Nicolas Jenson, John of Cologne, and partners counted numerous local stationers among its customers, and in a list of the shop's clients from 1482 one finds leading Florentine citizens—for example, Braccio di Domenico Martelli, with the large debt of eighteen gold florins and the humanist Cristoforo Landino, with a debt of eight gold florins.[5] Landino was evidently an eager reader of Venetian incunabula and an attentive critic. In his commentary on Dante Alighieri's *Divina Commedia* from 1481 he criticized, for example, the reductive use some printers had made of Mattia Palmieri's *De temporibus*.[6] From what is known, the Florentine book sales to the North seem to have been rather modest: the Ripoli press occasionally sent its products to a Florentine stationer in Venice, Sano di Battista di Domenico, but without any lasting success.[7]

From the early fifteenth century onward, most Florentine bookshops were grouped in the area of the Badia Fiorentina, between Via del Garbo and Via del Proconsolo.[8] In direct response to the Venetian book syndicate, the miniaturist and commercial head of the Ripoli press, Bartolo di Domenico di Guido, also rented a shop there (ca. 1480–1481).[9] In September 1480 he thus signed a new contract with the stationer Miniato di Tingo, who was hired as Bartolo di Domenico's salesman for the new shop.[10] According to their agreement, Miniato was authorized to sell his books up to the sum of twenty-five lire when he saw a profit, without Bartolo's formal permission. This partnership was to last until 1 January 1483; if neither of the two companions declared it officially finished in and by the guild of doctors and apothecaries (here called *ars aromatariorum*) and at least six months before its expiration, it was to continue for another five years.[11]

Bartolo di Domenico built his commercial hopes on a renewed editorial program of the Ripoli press. Shortly afterward, on 11 November 1480, he thus concluded an accord for a new typographical enterprise together with the governor of the Ripoli convent, Fra Domenico da Pistoia, and the humanist Bartolomeo Fonzio.[12] The latter seems to have been acting in the name of the printer Niccolò di Lorenzo, or pretended to be. Just like the shop lease with Miniato di Tingo, this company was to last until 1 January 1483 and was clearly understood as the "productive basis" of their commercial activities. If both agreements are considered together, this was presumably the most comprehensive and ambitious project the Florentine book market had seen so far. According to the contract, all profits had to be distributed equally between the three partners. The general control of the printing shop was under the twofold responsibility of Fra Domenico da Pistoia and Niccolò di Lorenzo. These two were to run their presses independently and had to guarantee that at least one of them was always working; as a consequence, the two presses could also be used for different books at the same time. If, as was written, Niccolò di Lorenzo refused these conditions, the contract still remained valid for the other two partners. In this case another typographer had to be found.[13]

Bartolo di Domenico's role was that of executive head of the company. He thus bore the responsibility for supplying the printer's copies and the necessary paper and for paying the two workmen needed at each press: the compositor (or typesetter) and the pressman.[14] The contract also gave him the power to hire and dismiss these workmen. At the end of each year a balance had to be drawn up in order to distribute the possible gains and losses between the different partners. Metals or work instruments like matrices and punches, the type metal, and any other instruments, on the other hand, had to be acquired by the printers themselves once the relative costs had been approved by Bartolo di Domenico.[15] If any of the printed books went missing, either the printer himself or Fra Domenico were held responsible for his workmen and made to reimburse double the value of the stolen books; none of the partners could trade or give them away on his own initiative, especially as payments in kind to their workmen. The monthly income for both Fra Domenico da Pistoia and the printer was set up to a sum of fifteen lire—approximately three gold florins.

On the dissolution of the company on 1 January 1483, all the unsold books were to be sold to the partner who offered the best price for them. One of the last conditions regarded print commissions from other, private customers. These had to be executed in the best of all possible ways and exactly as arranged, with respect to both the printers' copies and corrected proofs ("secundum degustationes et monstras que prebuntur pro campione et exemplari").[16] In these cases, the responsibility for eventual imperfections in or "damage" to the books fell back on the printers and not on the whole company, especially if a workman of either the printer (Niccolò di Lorenzo) or Fra Domenico had caused them.

The stationer Bartolo di Domenico is known from various sources to have traded in printed books. For instance, on 16 October 1481 he sold an unbound copy of Aristotle's *Ethics*—that is, Niccolò di Lorenzo's work— to the convent of Santissima Annunziata; his agent in this case was an otherwise unknown typesetter, presumably a priest, ser Lorenzo di Iacopo d'Agnolo *formatore*.[17] In the following years his activities also reached other Tuscan towns. In Pistoia his salesman was a certain Iacopo di Benedetto Bellucci, who before November 1483 was condemned by the Florentine guild of doctors and apothecaries to pay Bartolo more than thirty-nine lire.[18] A new compromise was signed in December 1486 by the hand of Piero Pacini.[19] As Bellucci explained in a letter shortly afterward, this was to put an end to the dispute in which the guild, after more than three years, had declared him in default (*contumace*), inhibiting him to trade books from Florence. On the advice of his brother, the notary Lorenzo Bellucci, he had been forced to accept this arbitration without realizing that Bartolo di Domenico and Pacini were business partners, and the latter therefore not impartial.[20]

Another case from late 1486 saw Bartolo in conflict with a wool merchant, Antonio di Giovanni del Caccia. The stationer requested of him the sum of 148 lire and four soldi for "books and merchandise" which Antonio del Caccia had promised to market. Unfortunately, the Mercanzia acts do not tell us where. Del Caccia responded that as previously agreed he had sold these volumes in one year's time and was therefore obliged to pay only the sum that had been fixed in their original contract. Bartolo rebutted on his part that the wool merchant had sold them without his consent—that is, below their price and thus against his will.[21] The outcome of the case is unknown.

In order to conclude the contract with the Ripoli press of 11 November 1480, Niccolò di Lorenzo was legally represented by the humanist Bartolomeo Fonzio. Fonzio's interest was to continue the collaboration initiated with the printing of Cornelius Celsus's *De medicina* two years earlier. As it seems, however, this contract did not offer Niccolò ideal conditions. It not only compelled him to work on the convent's premises on Via della Scala but left him very little autonomy and, with only one printing press, also lower profits. In the very same weeks, in fact, a better offer was maturing. For this reason, the cooperation with San Iacopo di Ripoli soon lost its appeal.

11

Cristoforo Landino's Commented Edition
of Dante's *Divine Comedy* (1481)

*J*n 1480 Cristoforo di Bartolomeo Landino, a famous professor of poetry and rhetoric at the Florentine university, the Studium Generale, intended to publish Dante Alighieri's *Divine Comedy* with a new, exhaustive commentary on the basis of his own lectures on the subject.[1] His intention was to render all the other, "medieval," commentaries obsolete and present Dante in a more "modern," platonic light. His was furthermore a patriotic effort to "bring back home" the *Divine Comedy*. The question had become a matter of civic pride after the publication of several non-Florentine editions of the text. These prints had appeared in Foligno (1472), Mantua (1472), Venice (1472), Verona (1472), Venice (1477), Naples (1477, 1478), and, above all, Milan, where the *Comedy* had been edited and commented by the humanist Martino Paolo Nidobeatino (1478).[2] Cristoforo Landino was therefore keen to explain in his long introduction that he intended to liberate Dante from all barbarian, non-Florentine linguistic influences. After presenting an ornate "apology" of Dante and the city of Florence, his foreword turned into a eulogy of all those Florentines who excelled in their professions and disciplines before arriving at a discussion of the role of poetry, its divine origins, and the concept of "divine fury." A Latin presentation letter by Marsilio Ficino and a short treatise on the site of Dante's *Inferno* concluded the introductory parts of Landino's commentary.

Cristoforo Landino was not only a university professor, public lecturer on Dante, and a writer, editor, commentator, and translator of ancient texts but was also a secretary of the Parte Guelfa, a functionary of the communal chancery in Palazzo Vecchio, and a businessman who published his works with more than only one typographer. From his *volgare* translation of Pliny's *Natural History* onward (1474–1475, printed by Nicolas Jenson in Venice in 1476), most of his publications betrayed the extreme haste with which they had been composed.[3] Rightly or wrongly, the humanist hoped that his commentary on Dante and the donation of a richly illuminated dedication copy of the printed text to the Signorìa would help him with his academic projects, securing him a safe income for the rest of his days.[4]

Although the definitive text of the commentary was still in the course of being written, a detailed agreement for its publication was signed on 24 December 1480 by Landino, the merchant Bernardo d'Antonio di Ricciardo degli Alberti, and the printer Niccolò di Lorenzo (see Appendix B, no. 4).[5] To him this contract must have appeared more attractive than Bartolo di Domenico's and Bartolomeo Fonzio's proposal regarding the press of San Iacopo di Ripoli. No monthly income was mentioned in it, but it was presumably not lower than the fifteen lire guaranteed in precedence. What was more, the three partners promised to share the profits regarding the sale of no less than 1,125 copies of the *Comento* to be printed in large folio volumes, of the estimated value of no less than three gold florins each.[6] The major financial burden—that is, the purchase of paper, ink, the cost of the illustrations ("storie") and the daily payments to the workmen ("garzoni")—initially all lay on the shoulders of Bernardo degli Alberti, the nephew and heir of the great Leon Battista Alberti, who had died eight years earlier.[7] Whereas Landino contributed to the partnership with his commentary, master Niccolò had to supervise the printing process. This was particularly complex because three different presses had to operate separately and contemporaneously on all "three comedies," as the *Inferno*, the *Purgatorio*, and the *Paradiso* were still generally known. The printer even possessed a fourth press which, according to the contract, could only be used for the same work. This demonstrates that by now the printer had (re)gained full control over the instruments and tools of his first workshop; one may recall that already some years before he had used two or possibly three presses for Ficino's *De Christiana religione*. In an attempt to avoid possible confiscations in the court of the Mercanzia, by the middle of the 1480s some of these instruments had become the property of the priest Lorenzo Tinghi (see Chapter 13), but before 1493 Niccolò di Lorenzo must again have owned at least two of his printing presses (see Epilogue and Appendix B, no. 12). In 1480/1481 many new workmen had to be hired for his workshop, from type founders to compositors, pressmen, inkers, and assistants. Most of these presumably came from the—unfortunately for us, anonymous—"stock" of traveling journeymen who after each employment looked for alternative jobs elsewhere. In conclusion, it is quite difficult to imagine how Niccolò di Lorenzo could have resolved his financial difficulties after the company with Cappone di Bartolomeo Capponi and begin his new typographical adventure without Bernardo degli Alberti's or Cristoforo Landino's direct help.

Where was this new workshop? From the fact that the very first copy of Landino's printed *Comento* was promised as a gift to the renowned Benedictine monastery Le Murate on Via Ghibellina, one might suspect that the spacious premises of this nunnery were in some way used for storing, printing, or drying the printed sheets, and that the presses therefore stood either there or in Niccolò's neighboring home. From a court case in the Mercanzia in April 1482 one also learns that the printer—presumably in the weeks of the printing contract—had leased a house for his workmen ("garzoni") from a certain grocer named Giovanni di Bartolomeo di Rutino (Rontino). This house was situated on Via Pietrapiana, close to the church of Sant'Ambrogio, just a short walking distance away from Niccolò's printing shop.[8] For this the typographer had promised a yearly rent of twenty-four lire—of which, however, only six lire had been paid.[9] Exactly eight days after the first petition Niccolò was therefore condemned to make up for the rest (see Appendix B, no. 6). From the conditions laid down in the printing contract for the *Comento*, one might guess that it was again Bernardo degli Alberti who paid not only Niccolò's workmen but also cleared this debt.

The priest who had drafted the agreement on Christmas Day 1480 was a certain ser Piero di Francesco Pieraccini from Pratovecchio in the

Casentino. He was probably the son of a crossbow archer who in the 1460s had served in the citadel of Arezzo.[10] Even Landino's own family originated from Pratovecchio and in his role of chancellor of the Parte Guelfa, he was in daily contact with these soldiers whose supervision lay in the hands of the Parte. Ser Piero seems to have grown up in Florence and in the early 1470s studied in the religious company of the Purification, "Florence's premier confraternity specifically catering for adolescent boys."[11] By early 1476 he had first become the chaplain and then the administrator of the central church of Santa Maria in Campidoglio.[12] Interestingly, in many of the documents relating to his administration he was given the surname "De Landinis," as if he had been living with Cristoforo Landino or had formally been accepted into his family.[13] At least once he stood as a formal witness together with one of his collaborators, the humanist priest Carlo di Simone Altoviti (1477).[14] From around 1480 onward, he served as a chaplain in the church of Orsanmichele and even in this office was known as "ser Petrus Francisci Landini" (1483).[15] In May 1489 he took up his residence at San Miniato al Monte, outside the city walls, when he became the monastery's "perpetual chaplain."[16]

In which way could ser Piero have belonged to Landino's family? Some years earlier the latter had actually adopted a son, Taddeo, but in his tax return from 1480 he did not mention either Piero or Taddeo.[17] Similar cases of "borrowing" new surnames were, however, quite frequent among Florentine humanists, as Marsilio Ficino's example shows. In his case, the notary who copied his landlord's manuscripts and edited them for printing, Luca Fabiani, temporarily assumed the name Ficini or was known in this way, before becoming independent and assuming another last name.[18] Whenever these surnames indicated only an individual's temporary residence, they were usually dropped with the move to a new home.[19] It seems therefore quite possible that in exchange for Landino's hospitality Piero da Pratovecchio took up comparable tasks to those of Luca Fabiani, and that apart from drafting the contract for the printing of Landino's *Comento* he also had a role in the preparation of the printer's copy and in the typographical process itself.

Like Ficino, Cristoforo Landino was running a *scriptorium*, or scribes' workshop, whose single members have not yet been identified. Their handwriting, however, can be clearly distinguished in the dedication copies of his *volgare* translation of Pliny's *Historia naturale* (1475) to King Ferrante of Naples. Three of these were those of the translator himself (i.e., Cristoforo Landino), of the Florentine scribe Niccolò Riccio, and of the Neapolitan humanist Giovanni Brancati. However, another hand which corrected the manuscript at an early stage has remained nameless. As his corrections often coincided with the text as it finally went to press in Venice in early 1476, this nameless person must have been a very close collaborator of Landino.[20] In the shortly later case of Landino's *Comento*, such hand-in-hand cooperation was needed even more, and it is certainly not wrong to assume that the priest Piero di Francesco da Pratovecchio was one of these collaborators.

As Neil Harris showed, the presses used by Niccolò di Lorenzo for the Dante were still the so-called one-pull presses on which, according to the contract, "one sheet" ("una carta") or four pages, had to be produced every day. For all the three presses this actually accounted for twelve pages.[21] The proofs of this huge amount of text had then to be corrected overnight as the contract prescribed that every night the fresh proofs had to be brought to Cristoforo Landino and Bernardo degli Alberti for correction. Even for this labor, a valuable assistant like Piero da Pratovecchio could evidently be a great help.

The *Comento* was finished by "Nicholò di Lorenzo della Magna," if its colophon is to be believed, after approximately eight months on 30 August 1481. It was printed with two Roman typefaces differing in size. According to Victor Scholderer, the first was a 115RA/115RB used for the text of the *Commedia* which derived from Niccolò's earlier "type 4*: 113R."[22] For Landino's commentary, which was printed on the very same page as Dante's text, a much smaller 91R was used which again derived from Niccolò's earlier "type 3: 92R."[23] In their new forms, these characters had not been used before.

As no printer's copy or manuscript of the *Comento* has ever come to light, the elaboration of a critical edition was necessarily based on the printed copies. The variant states in the more than 150 copies present in libraries and collections all over the world are, however, a serious challenge. In his critical edition of the *Comento* Paolo Procaccioli carried out the arduous task of collating an important sample of copies and discovered a total of 103 variants, in nine cases involving the resetting of a full page. In most cases the variants involving the same setting were minor, though in some settings multiple states were discovered—as many as four in one instance (i.e., at folio 6v: "intellccto/intellceto/intelleeto/intellecto").[24] Simultaneous printing and revision of the three "comedies" on all three presses, and partial revisions, caused this rather intriguing state of things; Procaccioli even contemplated the possibility of a third corrector, and here one might again think of Piero di Francesco da Pratovecchio.[25] Nonetheless, supplementary corrections were still added even after 1481.[26]

From the beginning, even before the contract was signed on Christmas Day 1480, all three partners had decided to embellish the *Comento* with illustrations (*storie*). These were supposed to add up to exactly one hundred, one for each canto of Dante's poem.[27] As is widely known, however, just a few of these engravings were executed, presumably between 1481 and 1487.[28] In the individual copies of the *Comento* they amount to somewhere between two and nineteen.[29] Only the first two were directly impressed on the pages in a successive print run, exactly as with the three engravings in Antonio Bettini's *Monte sancto* from 1477. The remaining later engravings, however, were cut and pasted into the empty spaces left on the pages. The exact chronology, the causes of the delays, the authorship of the engravings—attributed either to the rather unknown Baccio Baldini or an equally mysterious "Dante workshop"—and their obvious inspiration by Sandro Botticelli's drawings have often been discussed, with different conclusions.[30]

The 1481 edition of the *Comento* contained a series of imperfections for which Niccolò di Lorenzo could only partially be held responsible. One of the consequences of this was, however, that the high-minded artistic and commercial expectations of the three partners could not be met. Already in 1482 in the Mercanzia, Cristoforo Landino started to quarrel with Bernardo degli Alberti about the organization of the volumes' sales. The arrival of cheaper northern copies of the same text two years later had serious repercussions on the Florentine market. In June 1484, Ottaviano Scoto's pirated folio edition of Landino's *Comento* was sold in Venice for just one ducat, approximately the equivalent of one gold florin.[31] At the end of August 1484 a commented Dante sold in Florence for a slightly higher sum, seven lire.[32] The relative inadequacies of the city's printing industry became evident to everyone when in 1487 a banned Florentine merchant, Miniato di Neri del Sera, financed in

Brescia a fully illustrated edition of the *Divina Commedia*, including also Landino's commentary.[33] Shortly afterward the bulk sale price of Niccolò di Lorenzo's *princeps* dropped to only one-third its 1483 value: one gold florin.[34]

One year after Landino's first complaints in the Mercanzia, the dispute with his partner Bernardo degli Alberti had a sequel in the court of the Podestà (June 1483). This time, however, the charges came from other creditors. On closer examination, there were at least two wool merchants who in the summer of 1483 were pressing for their credits. The first was Francesco di Roberto Martelli and his partners, who on 9 July claimed more than thirty-six florins *di suggello* for woolen cloth from both Cristoforo Landino and "Nicholò di Lorenzo impressore." According to his claim, the two—presumably more than a year before—had underwritten this debt in Martelli's account book ("dove sono soscripti di sua mano").[35] On 4 August 1483, the Mercanzia commanded both the humanist and the printer to honor this debt.[36] Martelli then continued his action between September and December 1483 when he arrived at a legally valid, formal confiscation of Landino's home and real estate.[37] In order to avoid any scandal, however, he did not pursue the actualization of these verdicts, which thus remained without any practical consequences. Nevertheless, between March and June 1484 Martelli seized other, unspecified goods of Landino for the same amount of money.[38] And this was not yet the end of their business relation: in a semipublic meeting on 9 June 1486 in the palace of the Florentine government, Palazzo Vecchio, Landino confessed that he still owed Martelli another fifty-four florins "as part of a bigger sum." Payment was promised in three tranches (i.e., every year a sum of eighteen florins).[39]

Two other wool merchants took legal action against Landino in the summer of 1483. They were Antonio di Giovanni del Caccia and Francesco di Giovanni del maestro Libero and partners; Del Caccia has already been mentioned as a salesman for the stationer Bartolo di Domenico. On 20 August the Florentine Podestà condemned Landino to pay them fifty gold florins, again presumably for woolen cloth.[40]

The humanist's interest in wool can easily be explained with the well-known economic mechanism used in financing print publications in Florence and elsewhere. Wool purchases from these merchants almost certainly covered part of Landino's printing costs around 1481 / 1482.

From the summer of 1482 on, he also bought expensive cloth on behalf of the noble cleric Carlo di Simone Altoviti, a doctor of ecclesiastical law and prior of the church of Ciggiano in the Valdichiana, but without a fitting income.[41] Just as in the case of Piero di Francesco da Pratovecchio, who probably helped with Landino's *Comento,* one may presume that either Altoviti had a role in his other publications or that he was a direct business partner in the printing enterprise.[42]

12

From Cristoforo Landino's *Disputationes camaldulenses* (1480?) to Francesco Berlinghieri's *Geographia* (1481–1482)

*I*n these years, Niccolò di Lorenzo was also responsible for printing Cristoforo Landino's *Disputationum camaldulensium libri IV.* After having studied Marsilio Ficino's masterwork, the *Theologia Platonica*, in early 1474, the humanist had composed this Latin dialogue in four books, in which he discussed the concepts of the active and passive life, its final goals and the allegorical interpretation of the first six books of Virgil's *Aeneis*.[1] In both its original manuscript form and its undated printed *editio princeps* the text was dedicated to the Duke of Urbino, Federico da Montefeltro, who died in September 1482. Around fifty copies or fragments of this edition in quarto survive in public libraries. It was printed with the same characters as Aristotle's *Ethics* and Landino's *Comento* on Dante Alighieri's *Divine Comedy* (see Chapter 11), leaving free spaces for the Greek words.[2] However, no colophon indicated the printer's name or the date of printing. Opinions on the date have thus been discordant; the Oxford University copy at Corpus Christi College was bought by the English humanist John Shirwood in Rome on 12 September 1481.[3] Niccolò di Lorenzo had thus probably finished it before the *Comento*, as it appears difficult to imagine that for all the combined efforts in printing this huge work, the *Disputationes* could have run in a parallel way; an earlier printing date seems more likely. In conclusion, the *Disputationes* must have signaled the official beginning of Niccolò di Lorenzo's long collaboration with Cristoforo Landino. Incidentally, the year 1480 also seems to mark the beginning of most of the humanist's commercial transactions. However, the reason of a contract signed between Landino and the two young brothers Lorenzo and Felice di Francesco di Filippo Lapaccini from the quarter of Santa Maria Novella on 4 March 1480, confirmed three days later in the Parte Guelfa (of which Landino was the chancellor), remains for now mysterious.[4]

The two wool purchases which ended up in court in 1483 were presumably linked to the publication of the *Comento*. But other, similar transactions in Landino's name arouse our curiosity as well. To detect whether these were related to his publications, one needs to take a closer look. If one sets aside for the moment Landino's short public orations, of which at least two were actually printed by Niccolò di Lorenzo (one for the presentation of the Dante copy to the Signorìa and the other for the funeral of the military captain Giordano Orsini), two major works stand out which certainly needed additional funding: Landino's commented edition of Horace, printed in folio on 8 August 1482 by Antonio Miscomini, and his edition of Virgil, again with his commentary, from 18 March 1488, by an anonymous printer and likewise in folio.[5]

According to a document from the Medici archives, the cloth dyer Francesco di Iacopo Doni on 30 July 1485 lent Landino the sum of fifteen hundred florins *di suggello*. Although details are not specified, this loan almost certainly consisted of woolen cloth; the date of clearance in this case was set for eighteen months later, on 29 January 1487, and guaranteed by Lorenzo di Pierfrancesco de' Medici's commercial agent, Sandro di Piero Pagagnotti.[6]

The date of 30 July 1485 roughly coincides with the printing of Leon Battista Alberti's *De re aedificatoria*. In a famous letter Lorenzo de' Medici's secretary Niccolò Michelozzi wrote on 11 September 1485 that his nephew Lorenzo di Pierfrancesco de' Medici was among the first citizens to receive the print proofs, even before his uncle.[7] It is therefore plausible that Lorenzo di Pierfrancesco was one of the main supporters of this important edition. A similar case to be considered here is that of Landino's commented edition of Virgil, by an unknown

printer (18 March 1488).[8] As Lorenzo di Pierfrancesco's business relation with Landino continued in 1487 and 1489, again through Sandro
Pagagnotti he might have sponsored this edition either directly or indi-
rectly.[9] The Virgil itself, however, was not so much dedicated to Lorenzo
di Pierfrancesco as to his direct cousin, Piero di Lorenzo de' Medici.

Landino's *Comento* to Dante's *Divine Comedy* was the typographically
most challenging book Niccolò di Lorenzo produced in these years, after
the end of his partnership with Cappone di Bartolomeo Capponi. Although he now was a formally "independent" typographer, in court cases
he was most often represented by Landino, with whom he shared more
than just a working partnership. In 1485 the printer was among the official witnesses at the payment of the rest of the dowry of Landino's
daughter Mona Aura to her husband Piero di Manno Temperani.[10] Naturally, Niccolò continued to also print other humanists' works—for example, Bartolomeo Scala's oration for the military captain Costanzo
Sforza (after 4 October 1481), and maybe Angelo Poliziano's short poem
Ambra (after 4 November 1485).[11] However, the three best-known works
from this second period are, apart from the *Comento* and the *Disputationes
camaldulenses*, Francesco Berlinghieri's *Geographia* (1481–1482), Leon Battista Alberti's *De re aedificatoria* (29 December 1485), and the large folio
volumes of Saint Gregory's *Morali in Job* (15 June 1486).

Francesco di Niccolò Berlinghieri has already been mentioned
because of his early investment in printing (1470–1472, see Chapter 2).
The famous folio edition of his *Geographia*, a liberal and extended *volgare*
version of Ptolemy's *Geography* in terzina rhyme, has recently been celebrated as the "single most-labor-intensive, complicated, and we can specu-
late, expensive illustrated edition undertaken in Renaissance Florence."[12]
Berlinghieri belonged to the humanistic circle of Ficino and Landino
and wrote his text approximately between 1465 and 1478/1479.[13] One
must, however, wonder whether already in their earlier printing company Berlinghieri and Piero del Massaio had in mind the publication of
the *Geographia*. Its thirty-one double-paged engravings of maps, including
a world map, actually derived from Massaio's and other contemporary
Florentine maps.[14]

According to a now lost letter from 1476, Berlinghieri publicly dis-
puted with Landino on Ptolemaic problems and was then planning to
contact a German printer in Rome, Konrad Sweynheym, to print his

work.[15] In 1477 he got married and received a rich dowry.[16] Nothing came as yet of his publication plans, but he remained close to the Florentine book world: in May 1482 Berlinghieri acted, for example, as a witness in a lawsuit in the archbishop's court in which the heir of a stationer was condemned to pay no less than 474 lire to the apothecaries Tommaso and Antonio di Luca di Betto Bernardi, presumably for paper.[17] In September 1483 he was himself faced with a charge from one of their colleagues, Folco di ser Amerigo da Pratovecchio *spetiale*, over twenty-five lire.[18] In the following year he was mentioned as being among the publishers, together with Filippo di Bartolomeo Valori, of Ficino's famous Latin translation of Plato's works.[19] This important work was to come out with the Ripoli press but was actually finished by the printer Lorenzo d'Alopa; it is, however, not clear whether and how much Berlinghieri contributed to it.[20] When in 1485 the Florentine convent of Santissima Annunziata ordered from him a copy of his *Geographia*, he personally oversaw its binding and the illumination of the engraved maps, for the enormous cost of more than twenty-eight gold florins.[21] Still, in late 1492 Berlinghieri had a dispute with the stationer Domenico di Giovanni Parigi in the Mercanzia which was resolved by an arbitration.[22]

Two richly illuminated dedication manuscripts of Berlinghieri's *Geographia* have survived, and more than a hundred copies of the finished volume, "printed by Nicolò Todescho and corrected with the outmost diligence by the author," as the colophon claimed. The sponsorship almost certainly lay in Berlinghieri's own hands and that of his family. In a similar way to Landino's publication of the *Comento*, Marsilio Ficino contributed with a short letter of presentation (*apologus*) to the Duke of Urbino, Federico da Montefeltro.

On the basis of Scholderer's indications, in 1982 Paolo Veneziani studied this edition in more detail.[23] Like Niccolò's other books it was scattered with typographical errors which were only occasionally corrected. Sometimes several different character typefaces were used on the very same pages.[24] Veneziani concluded that the many shortcomings of this edition were not so much due to the excessive speed of the printing process as to its frequent interruptions. Apparently the work started with the fourth, fifth, sixth, and seventh books before turning to the earlier volumes. This could have happened either because the printer's copy was not yet ready, or for other unknown reasons. In any case, printing seems to have run for some time parallel to that of Landino's *Comento,* possibly on Niccolò's fourth press, and was finished in 1482.[25] Sean Roberts has explained in detail how the lack of practical knowledge resulted in a rather poor quality of the engraved copperplate maps. Many copies remained unsold. In the sixteenth century the Florentine publishers and booksellers Giunti added a red title page and a colophon to them naming both the author and the printer; this demonstrated that after more than three decades they were still remembered favorably.[26]

13

From Niccolò Perotti's *Rudimenta grammatices* (1483) to Saint Gregory's *Morali* (1483–1486)

*F*or many years, Niccolò di Lorenzo remained formally an independent printer. This is clear from a Mercanzia sentence from 7 April 1483 with which "Niccolò the German who prints the books" was condemned to pay a debt of eight lire for certain "merchandise" to an otherwise unknown blacksmith, Piero di Filippo *fabbro*.[1] It is not difficult to imagine that this man had in one way or another contributed to the running of the workshop.

Niccolò continued to produce both Italian and Latin editions—for example, a long-term best seller like Niccolò Perotti's *Rudimenta grammatices,* finished, according to the colophon, on 16 April 1483 ("Per Prudentem Virum // Nicolaum Laurentii. Impressa Sunt Florentiae.").[2] One may quietly assume that the blacksmith was paid in kind—that is, with copies of exactly this edition. But the "prudent" printer also produced ephemeral devotional instant books like that of Lorenzo di Giacomo Olbizi (Oppizzi), *Miracoli della vergine Maria delle carceri di Prato* (after 6 July 1484).[3] Shortly after this came his Latin edition of the sermons of Gilbert of Hoyland, abbot of the English Cistercian abbey of Swineshead (died around 1172), on the biblical Song of Songs (16 April 1485). This edition in folio was presumably commissioned by a clergyman, survives in dozens of copies, and again presents various typographical errors and variants; no printer's copy has been preserved.[4] Another Latin grammar book of these years was the undated *Regulae grammaticales* of the priest Gaspare di Giovanni di Roberto da Massa (c. 1485), a Latin teacher who taught at the convent of Santa Maria del Carmine and was also a friend of Sebastiano Salvini.[5] As Victor Scholderer justly noted, however, this was the only one of Niccolò's books which contained printed capitals and "was perhaps not printed by Laurentii himself."[6]

The two most important editions which occupied Niccolò di Lorenzo in the last years of his activity were Leon Battista Albertis's *De re aedificatoria* and the thirty-five books of *Moralia* (*Morali*) of Saint Gregory on the book of Job in *volgare*. Although begun three years earlier (i.e., in 1483), this last work was finished, as the colophon claimed, only after Alberti's masterwork on 15 June 1486.

The Florentine poet Zanobi da Strada had begun translating Saint Gregory's *Morali* in the middle of the fourteenth century in Naples. After his death the work was terminated, from book 19, chapter 19, by the Camaldolese monk Giovanni da San Miniato in the Florentine convent of Santa Maria degli Angeli (1415).[7] The *Morali* was both a comprehensive and an immensely popular reference book for theological teaching and preaching, and its *volgare* translation began to circulate immediately in Florentine convents and monasteries.[8] Vespasiano da Bisticci reports that even Cosimo de' Medici—who knew very little Latin—claimed to have read all of the "thirty-seven" books in six months.[9] Not unexpectedly, the first printed editions of the Latin text were already a success. When the book arrived, for example, in a Pisan shop, a hermit living close to Lorenzo de' Medici's villa at Agnano humbly asked to buy him a copy.[10] In Florence the idea to publish the *volgare* version of the *Morali* may have matured quite early. Although no printer's copy of Niccolò di Lorenzo's edition has survived, the form of the printed text has been related to some manuscripts in the monastery of Santa Brigida del Paradiso outside the city walls, not far from Bagni a Ripoli.[11]

On 5 July 1483 Niccolò finished with printing a book of hours which has recently been described in more detail.[12] Approximately one month after, on 8 August 1483, "Nicholò di Lorenzo tedescho, del popolo di Sancto Ambruogio di Firenze, inpressore di libri overo stanpatore di forma" signed a new contract with the apothecary Antonio di Luca di Betto (Bernardi) regarding the publication of Saint Gregory's *Morali*.[13] Two versions of this contract have survived, of which one bore the signatures of both partners. To judge from the handwriting, it was drafted by the notary ser Francesco di Piero di Neri (Molletti), who from the early 1470s had been drawing up many documents for the Betti Bernardi brothers.[14] Incidentally, Niccolò di Lorenzo's signature under this contract presents his only autograph to survive today. In the presence of the chancellor of the Mercanzia and the father-in-law of Antonio di Luca's brother Tommaso, Bencivenni di Bencivenni di Bencivenni, the agreement was then also registered in a special Mercanzia register.[15] Bencivenni was himself an important member of the guild of doctors and apothecaries (he had been its consul in 1479), but this corporation was not directly involved in the partnership.[16] On the other hand, it somehow guaranteed the fundamental condition that the society remained both legally and financially limited; this type of partnership was known as *accomandita*, different from a *compagnia*.[17]

Already the historian Roberto Ridolfi wondered about the "lion's courage" of the printer. For the relatively modest sum of 150 gold florins, Niccolò di Lorenzo obliged himself to deliver no less than 1,025 copies of this massive work in only seven months, by 12 March 1484. As an editor he was fully responsible for the print's beauty and the text's accuracy; the formulation in the contract "di buona lettera e corretti d'ogni e qualunque cosa a somma perfectione" actually records that of Giorgio Baldesi's printing shop of 1470 (see Chapter 2). It was furthermore specified that whereas the running costs of the publication should be advanced by Antonio di Luca, the printer had to acquire the mass of the paper in his own name ("fogli che decto Nicholò à a tôrre sopra sè proprio"), using his partner's guarantee only up to the promised sum of 150 gold florins. In no way was Antonio intended to spend a larger amount of money. At the end, all the printed copies of the *Morali* were to be handed over to him. Until his expenses had been fully paid back, Antonio was the only one entitled to sell the *Morali*; thereafter the gains had to be divided at a rate of two-thirds for Antonio and only one-third for Niccolò di Lorenzo.

Still today the contract provokes bewilderment, as there was no realistic provision for how Niccolò would finish his work once the initial investment of 150 florins had been spent. His motivation to accept these absurd conditions might in fact be related to some of his financial troubles at the time, especially the charges of two wool merchants against him and Cristoforo Landino in the summer of 1483 (see Chapter 12). The sums advanced by Antonio di Luca for publishing the *Morali* could actually have been used to cover part of the debts deriving from his previous publications.

But who were Antonio and Tommaso di Luca di Betto Bernardi? We have already met the brothers as the vendors of paper to Cipriano Rucellai and Francesco Berlinghieri. Unlike most other stationers, Tommaso (age forty-seven in 1483, with a large family) and Antonio (age forty-three in 1483, and presumably still a bachelor) came from a well-established family. Born as the grandsons of a rich butcher from the quarter of Santa Maria Novella, in their profession as apothecaries they followed the footsteps of their father and maternal grandfather.[18] They resided with their families in a house that belonged to the church of Sant'Appollinare and had rented the adjacent shop on the corner of Via del Proconsolo, which contained a warehouse and other buildings.[19] When their father had died in 1465, only the middle brother Tommaso had accepted his part of the inheritance, whereas the other two had refused theirs.[20] Five years later, Benedetto Dei listed their shop under the name of the eldest brother, Piero di Luca di Betto Bernardi.[21] After his death, around 1472, his brothers Tommaso and Antonio continued his business, aptly downplaying its importance in the 1480 Catasto.[22]

The trade of paper was one of the main activities of the two apothecaries through the 1470s and 1480s.[23] Presumably even their cooperation with Niccolò di Lorenzo had started long before the printing of the *Morali*. On 25 January 1482 Antonio was actually a witness in the court of the Podestà when the printer paid thirty gold florins to Cappone di Bartolomeo Capponi in order to put an end to his first company.[24] In 1485 his brother Tommaso was recorded as the creditor of the large sum of five hundred lire of a bankrupt merchant, Matteo di Dino Dazzi, who incidentally also owed Landino 140 gold florins, possibly for copies of the *Comento*.[25] A close business partner of the brothers was Galeotto di Francesco Cei, who lived not far away in Borgo de' Greci.[26] He was a very important member of the guild of doctors and apothecaries and served as their consul in 1464, 1469, 1472, 1477, 1480, and 1490.[27] It cannot be excluded that he was the "mastermind" or one of the secret sponsors behind the printing of the *Morali*.[28]

Despite the ambiguous contract, the partnership between Antonio di Luca and Niccolò di Lorenzo came as no surprise. As no other sources hint at any intellectual or religious interests of the two apothecaries, theirs was foremost a commercial enterprise. Printing started soon on large folio pages in two columns in Niccolò's "Type 6: 111R." This character type had already been used in his second edition of the Cherubino da Spoleto (22 October 1482) and the book of hours (5 July 1483). As Victor Scholderer noted and Roberto Ridolfi confirmed, two different states of this type can be distinguished: a 111Ra, which in the *Morali* was used from the beginning to quire "gg" (i.e., after the completion of little more than one-third of the whole work) in the fourteenth book. Thereafter a different typeface was used.[29] Victor Scholderer's logical conclusion was that "the printing of this book was perhaps interrupted for some time after the completion of quire gg."[30]

Circumstantial evidence confirms that at an unknown date in 1484 the presses stood still. After Niccolò di Lorenzo had given up on the possibility of finishing the *Morali* on his own, on 5 November 1484 in the church of Santa Croce a new contract was drawn up. This time a priest, a certain ser Lorenzo di Girolamo di Domenico Tinghi, promised to finish the interrupted work.[31] Whereas the printer had to serve his financial obligations for the acquisition of paper, Tinghi declared himself willing to set the types and correct the text for all of the remaining parts of the *Morali*. As in the case of Landino's *Comento*, at the end of a day's work, the printed sheets had to be shown to Antonio di Luca in order to be checked. For four quires every month until the end, Tinghi was to receive the considerable sum of seventy lire, or approximately fourteen gold florins. Discussions on eventual shortcomings of his work had to be judged by two stationers, Bartolomeo di Angelo Tucci and Antonio di Filippo (di Ventura).[32]

Ser Lorenzo was one of four sons of a small merchant (*merciarius*), who after some time in Avignon and Rome had settled in Via della Scala in the quarter of Santa Maria Novella. In the early 1470s the father's debts overwhelmed the family. In 1472 they had to sell both their home in Via della Scala and a farm at Malmantile; thereafter the numerous family moved into a rented house in Via degli Angioli (today Via degli

Alfani). In the 1480 Catasto the twenty-two-year-old priest ser Lorenzo Tinghi confirmed that he had no stable occupation but sometimes substituted as a chaplain in the church of San Biagio.[33] A year later he organized the dowry payment for his sister Caterina with a deposit on an account of the hospital Santa Maria Nuova.[34] By 1482 he had been appointed a chaplain in the church of Orsanmichele, just like the aforementioned ser Piero di Francesco "Landini" from Pratovecchio (see Chapter 11).[35]

This coincidence calls for a short digression. From around 1479 onward, yet another and later very prolific printer served among the Orsanmichele chaplains: ser Bartolomeo di Francesco di Bartolomeo, better known as Bartolomeo dei Libri.[36] It actually seems as if these priests formed a sort of literary elite in the broader ranks of the town's clerical hierarchy. On the occasion of a public document drawn up on 27 December 1485, for instance, among the chaplains named as witnesses were not only Piero "Landini" and Bartolomeo de' Libri, but also Giovanni Dominico d'Antonio dell'Azzurro, who worked as grammar teacher.[37] Unfortunately, no lists or records of the chaplains' names have survived.

Traditionally the church's governing body, the "company" of Orsanmichele employed nine chaplains who theoretically were to receive a monthly stipend of seven lire for "officiating the oratory."[38] It can, however, not be excluded that their interest in alternative occupations like printing was related to their unstable economic situation following a public law from early 1481. In order to safeguard God's honor, it was then ruled that from now on the "temple" of Orsanmichele could not be used any longer as a mere workshop for constructions used during the annual procession and celebrations of the civic patron San Giovanni Battista—for example, the famous "clouds" (*peginata seu nubes*) and the firework charts, the *girandole*. No liberal or mechanical arts could be exercised in Orsanmichele; neither could school classes be taught there unless in religion.[39] Printing could therefore have presented a welcome and new source of income for some of the chaplains.

In 1484 / 1485 the printer Lorenzo Tinghi and the two apothecaries needed new funds to finish Saint Gregory's *Morali*. Not surprisingly, Niccolò di Lorenzo's solution was the traditional practice followed in Florence: obtaining new credit with local wool merchants. In order to legally pursue this, he assumed a new business partner, Tommaso di Scolaio Ciachi (or Ciacchi), who descended from an ancient family of leather workers (*vaiai*) from the quarter of Santa Croce and had become an orphan in 1480 at the age of twenty-two.[40] The following year he had married Mona Margherita di Tommaso Antinori.[41] No other economic activities are known from these years except his partnership with Niccolò di Lorenzo.[42] The precise terms of Ciachi's investment are unknown, but he could have been paid with copies of the *Morali* themselves; from the projected print run of 1,025 the two apothecaries Tommaso and Antonio di Luca di Betto Bernardi later possessed only 825 copies, so the remaining two hundred may have been Ciachi's.[43] Presumably, his interest in this operation was again more commercial than intellectual. On 28 January 1485 Ciachi and Niccolò di Lorenzo together contracted a debt of thirty-eight gold florins with the company of the wool merchant Roberto di Pagnozzo Ridolfi; his *garbo* wool had to be repaid after one year.[44]

In the midst of this new fervor, however, the printer was imprisoned on behalf of Tommaso di Luca, who claimed a sum of forty gold florins (July 1485).[45] Not surprisingly, it was again ser Lorenzo Tinghi who defended Niccolò "for the love of God and the sake of piety and misery." On behalf of the printer the priest promised to pay this debt in the following two years from the profits deriving from the sale of the *Morali;* otherwise Tommaso would receive a printing press and two hundred pounds of type with which the book had been printed.[46] A year later, on 1 August 1486, Tinghi confessed to owe the landlord of Tommaso and Antonio's workshop a sum of three gold florins, possibly part of the apothecaries' rent, which he had previously accepted to pay.[47] With a rather unusual choice for a cleric, on 17 October 1485 Tinghi even contracted a wool purchase on his own for the sum of thirteen florins and fourteen soldi, to be paid back at a rate of one florin per month.[48] Tinghi's clerical status in this case actually was of crucial importance, as his creditors could not sue him in any other than an ecclesiastical court.

If this and Roberto di Pagnozzo Ridolfi's wool loan to Ciachi and Niccolò di Lorenzo on 24 January 1485 were exceptionally recorded by a public notary, other similar loans are known only from judicial acts. In October 1485 Ciachi had to face yet another court case initiated by the two wool merchants Niccolò and Luca di Giorgio Ugolini for over fifteen gold florins.[49] In 1486 other *lanaiuoli* from the San Martino convent—namely, Battista di Giovanni Serristori, Angelo di Sinibaldo Dei, and partners—had Tommaso Ciachi and "Nicolaus Laurentii teutonichus et magister stampe librorum" commanded to pay an even higher sum of 108 gold florins for "Perpignan woolen cloth," not counting the procedural costs. Serristori's charge arrived first in the court of the Mercanzia in April and then, as it bore no direct fruit, moved to that of the Podestà.[50] The printer was certainly found in fault there in 1486, although it is not clear on whose behalf.[51] As nothing could be gained from the two partners, Serristori was forced to seize some livestock, harvest, and belongings in the countryside from one of Tommaso Ciachi's land workers (July–September 1486).[52] Further funding of nineteen gold florins for unspecified "merchandise" had been provided for him and Niccolò di Lorenzo by the merchant Rosso di Gentile da Sommaia, who asked for compensation after a year on 22 December 1486.[53] It is unfortunately impossible to know whether these businessmen were all aware that they were financing the printing of Saint Gregory's *Morali*. More likely, they had signed their contracts with the mediation of the agents, the *sensali*, in a rather anonymous way. If, in conclusion, this cannot yet be called "crowdfunding," there was certainly a large number of individuals who knowingly or unknowingly sustained this book's production.

Thanks to these investments and Lorenzo Tinghi's daily labor in the printing shop, the *Morali* was officially terminated after nearly three years on 15 June 1486. As the colophon generously stated, it had been produced "in the most dignified city of Florence by Niccolò di Lorenzo della Magna." This, however, was not yet the end of the story. Both Tommaso and Antonio di Luca di Betto Bernardi had still to face an exhaustingly long court case with the merchants from Fabriano who had provided the paper stock for the book (see the Epilogue). The *Morali*, usually bound in two or three big volumes, sold only slowly. For this reason, early in the beginning of the sixteenth century a number of unsold volumes were embellished with a one-page woodcut depicting Saint Gregory on a throne, generally considered of Venetian origin. This woodcut could actually be used for more than only one saint, as both Saint Gregory's head and the church in his hands could be substituted by a different head and other identifying attributes.[54]

14

Baptista Siculus and Leon Battista Alberti's
De re aedificatoria (1485)

*A*n even more prominent book from this time was the *princeps* of Leon Battista Alberti's *De re aedificatoria,* dated 29 December 1485.[1] This posthumous edition of a work on which Alberti had worked for nearly two decades, presented by then the most systematic and intriguing Renaissance treatise on classical architecture.[2] It was widely read, and some humanists, like Giorgio Antonio Vespucci, even possessed more than one copy.[3] The care of the publication lay in the hands of a hitherto unidentified Sicilian named Battista (Baptista Siculus), the publisher Bernardo di Antonio degli Alberti, and Agnolo Poliziano, who proudly presented the "most accurate" print in a Latin dedication letter to Lorenzo de' Medici.[4]

Bibliographers have detected various print states and pointed to variants even in the work's colophon. In some copies, interestingly, in one of the middle gatherings ("l") and the very last gathering, Niccolò's type "111Rb" was exchanged with another type, the "Nerlius 110R" (according to Victor Scholderer) or, other terminology, that of the "Printer of Vergilius, C 6061" (according to Roberto Ridolfi and Adolfo Tura), before returning to the previously used types.[5] The paper quality in the various quires was surprisingly different.[6] A letter published in 1965 shows that some weeks before September 1485 the book had arrived at the quire "n," more than halfway through the whole work. In these months Lorenzo de' Medici was receiving the single pages from his cousin Lorenzo di Pierfrancesco who—if he was indeed entitled to see the first proofs—must have been involved in the financing of the project.[7] This said, the "patron" addressed in Poliziano's dedication letter must have been the Magnifico himself. A careful analysis of the printer's copy used for Niccolò di Lorenzo's edition, today the manuscript Laurenziano Pluteo 89 sup. 113 in the Laurentian Library, has allowed Silvia Fiaschi to conclude that the printer was now using a two-pull press. This new device had been introduced in Florence in the 1480s and thus only after the completion of Cristoforo Landino's *Comento* on Dante Alighieri's *Divine Comedy*.[8] From the distinct marks left by one or more compositors on the margins of this manuscript, Fiaschi concluded that not only printing was interrupted more than once but also that more than one press was employed. The same copy finally betrays the signs of a textual revision for the press. This was possible, as has become clear, by the use of a second, now lost, manuscript.

To explain these vicissitudes and the possible involvement of more than one typographer in the printing of *De re aedificatoria,* one must remember that the summer of 1485 marked a very critical moment in Niccolò di Lorenzo's career. In these months he was—however shortly—imprisoned (July 1485, see Chapter 13), and—possibly—even out of his home in Via Ghibellina (6 August; see Appendix B, no. 7).[9] These difficulties originated from two separate court cases. On one side Niccolò was facing the charges of the apothecary Tommaso di Luca di Betto Bernardi regarding the paper costs for Saint Gregory's *Morali.* On the other he had to deal with the claims of the woodworker Francesco di Giovanni di Matteo Cappelli against Niccolò's landlord, the cobbler Francesco d'Andrea. Cappelli's charge was actually directed against the religious confraternity of Sant'Alberto in the church of Santa Maria del Carmine, for which he and his brother had constructed wooden furniture.[10] In his role as a prominent member of this confraternity Francesco d'Andrea was condemned to pay Cappelli eighteen lire; Niccolò di Lorenzo's role in this case seems to have been quite marginal.[11]

Whereas some aspects regarding the making of the *princeps* of *De re aedificatoria* have been studied quite thoroughly, others have only been touched upon. One of these is the role of the mysterious Battista from Sicily, who in a colophon at the end of the book addressed the reader in the form of a classicizing poem (*carmen*) in Latin hexameter. As he claimed, even Archimedes and Daedalus would have drawn advantage from Alberti's masterpiece. The interested reader only had to conquer his stinginess and pay the stationer with cash money ("aere sonanti") to hold in hand what "our work" ("nostros labores"), in collaboration with the printer's expert hand, had produced ("callidus arte impressor doctae perstrinxit robore dextrae").[12]

It has been speculated that either the Sicilian humanist Giovanni Aurispa or even Leon Battista Alberti himself hid under the name *Baptista Siculus*.[13] But nothing could be further from the truth, as he really was the book's typesetter ("componitore di lettere"). On 20 August 1485 messer Battista di Antonio da Sicilia presented himself in the court of the Mercanzia to tell his story. On request of the agent ("factore") of the printer Niccolò di Lorenzo, he had arrived from Siena in March of that year. This agent, a certain Domenico Doni, had promised him a monthly income of five gold florins for a four-month job. Thereafter Battista had worked in the printing shop over the summer, but without receiving the guaranteed salary. When he finally asked permission to leave, both the printer and Doni urged him to complete his work but remained vague about his outstanding payments. In the court of the Mercanzia Battista therefore protested the broken promise and demanded from them no less than ten gold florins (see Appendix B, no. 9). Regarding the history of the *princeps* of *De re aedificatoria,* Battista's request is an important document. Not only does it indicate its compositor's name but it allows us also to attribute to him some of the signs in the manuscript Laurenziano Pluteo 89 sup. 113.

Battista di Antonio da Sicilia was probably a learned cleric but, despite his title ("messer"), no doctor. As early as 1475 he had been working as a compositor for the edition of Pietro da Monte's *Repertorium iuris* in Bologna; Albano Sorbelli presumed that his family name was "Caffari."[14] Many Sicilians studied in these years at the University of Bologna, and the printing industry presented a professional opportunity after their academic studies.[15] In the late 1470s Battista could have earned his living elsewhere and in 1482 briefly returned to Bologna.[16] It cannot be excluded that already in 1484 he worked in Florence, where a certain "ser

Battista compositore" was employed by Antonio di Bartolomeo Misco-mini for printing the *Breviarium Camaldulense;* in this case the composi-tor's monthly income was set at four florins a month.[17] Messer Battista was, in conclusion, a very experienced professional who on his own would have been perfectly able to edit the first edition of Leon Battista Alberti's *De re aedificatoria.*

His counterpart, Domenico di Benedetto di Matteo Doni, was ap-parently not so much involved with printing itself as with bookselling. He came from the parish of Santa Felicita in the quarter of Santo Spirito and bore his first name in tribute to his grandfather, Domenico Dei. Doni was therefore related to the Dei, a well-known family of gold-smiths.[18] In a letter from 1467 his cousin Benedetto Dei mentioned a dispute with some of Doni's family members.[19] From 1464 Doni was married to the daughter of a small merchant (*merciaio*), Mona Tommasa di Francesco di Romolo di Giovanni, with whom he had two children.[20] From the early 1470s on he must have been in close contact with Ber-nardo di Antonio degli Alberti, whom he nominated as his arbiter in a dispute regarding a farm with his brother Matteo and an apothecary from the parish of Santa Trinita.[21] By 1474 this farm had to be sold, as both Doni brothers declared to the Catasto officials in 1480, adding that they had gone bankrupt that year and moved with their families to An-cona on the Adriatic Sea.[22]

The date of Domenico Doni's return to Florence is unknown, but it seems that in these years he gained his living as a peddler or trav-eling salesman, almost certainly also with printed books. He also was in direct relations with the Ripoli press, but cannot be identified with its worker mentioned in 1484 ("Domenico nostro lavorante").[23] A year later he was one of the two legal witnesses of Niccolò di Lorenzo's wool purchase from Roberto di Pagnozzo Ridolfi, and in summer 1485 became the agent of Martino di Angelo di Lumia, a paper merchant from Fabriano.[24] In 1487 he was recorded as the debtor of Priore di Francesco Strinati, a brother of Strinato Strinati, who presumably in 1483 has acquired a very substantial number of copies of Landino's *Comento.*[25] In these years he was again living in the Florentine parish of San Giorgio in the quarter of Santo Spirito and was frequently mentioned for his debts with other Florentines in the acts of the Mercanzia.[26]

Thereafter nothing more is heard of Niccolò di Lorenzo's printing partners in the acts of the Mercanzia. After the two important editions of Alberti's *De re aedificatoria* and Saint Gregory's *Morali* in 1486, he did not sign any more colophons. This does not necessarily imply, however, that he lost his work, left the town of Florence, or died. As will be argued in the Epilogue, the question was instead directly related to his professional status after the disaster of the publication of the *Morali*.

Epilogue

$\mathscr{T}$wo opposing views on Niccolò di Lorenzo's last years have been offered thus far. In a recent biographical study it was argued that the lack of historical documents regarding his life and work after 1486 was due to his death, presumably in Florence.[1] A differing hypothesis was presented by Giuseppe Ottino in 1871, who claimed to have seen a book printed by Niccolò di Lorenzo together with Lorenzo Morgiani in 1491. He therefore concluded that his activity must have continued for at least five years after 1486.[2] However, as the mysterious volume mentioned by Ottino has remained a bibliographical ghost, the first claim bears more weight.

In the years from around 1490 to 1497, Niccolò's alleged partner, the priest Lorenzo di Matteo Morgiani, was actually a business partner of Giovanni di Piero da Magonza. In January 1495 the latter confessed himself to be Morgiani's debtor of 135 lire before starting with him a new company for three years.[3] Together they printed a series of important, often illustrated, editions of religious texts in *volgare*.[4] Given the earlier cooperation between Niccolò di Lorenzo and Giovanni di Piero, a similar collaboration between the former and Morgiani in 1491 could actually not be excluded. And as the following pages will show, Niccolò di Lorenzo was indeed not yet out of business, although he did not sign any more books.

Already in late 1486 Giovanni di Piero da Magonza had reassumed his printing activity under his own name. Before 28 August of that year, he may already have been responsible for the edition of Niccolò Perotti's *Rudimenta grammatices*,[5] produced for the book dealer Giampiero di Cristofano Buonuomini from Cremona, and on 23 December signed the *Libro da compagnia, ovvero Fraternita dei Battuti* in quarto.[6] In the month of February of a unknown year, but possibly in 1488, and certainly before joining the company with Morgiani, he hired the Florentine priest Iacopo di Carlo as his typesetter (see Appendix B, no. 10).[7] Iacopo di Carlo actually signed a series of colophons either under his own name or together with a certain Piero di Nofri Buonaccorsi—that is, the brother of the printer Francesco di Nofri Buonaccorsi—but, curiously, never together with Giovanni di Piero da Magonza.[8] Once again, historical documents, even where they exist, sometimes complicate the attribution problems regarding Florentine incunabula *cum notis* or *sine notis*.

The growing number of churchmen among Florentine printers and the frequent collaborations between typographers and priests was due to their exemption from common law and communal jurisdiction.[9] Although clerics could prosecute their own debtors in lay courts, especially that of the Podestà or the Mercanzia, they could not be sued in these tribunals.[10] Whereas in Rome the clerical status was considered the first step to gaining an ecclesiastical benefice—the aspiration of many printers—in quarrelsome Florence obtaining a legal shield seems to have been equally if not more appealing. The first printer to use this stratagem was presumably Bartolomeo de' Libri, professionally active from ca. 1479, who, despite his clerical status, was the father of another printer, Michelangelo.[11] Another stationer who might have taken minor orders to avoid the confiscation of his worldly goods was ser Francesco di Benedetto di Giovanni (Vannuccio) di Geri, who after his father's death explained more than once to his surprised creditors that he was not subject to the Mercanzia court but only to that of the archbishop (1483-1484).[12] On the other hand, his clerical status did not prevent him from bringing action in this court against his father's creditors for their unpaid book purchases.[13] Eventually, however, even Francesco was forced to pay some of his father's debts, especially those for paper to a certain Battista di Piero (Peterlini) da Fabriano. This paper had been sold some years before, thanks to the mediation of the two apothecaries, Tommaso and Antonio di Luca di Betto Bernardi. Necessarily, this case was brought to trial in May 1484 in the archbishop's court.[14]

This study has so far avoided the most important economic question in early printing, that of the paper supply. Only rarely is this argument touched upon in extant account books from the period, and even less so in the court cases in the Mercanzia. However, the year 1490 witnessed the legal showdown between Tommaso and Antonio di Luca di Betto Bernardi on one side, and on the other their paper dealers from Fabriano. These were Rinaldo di Piero di Bartolomeo Peterlini (or Petrelini), the aforementioned brother Battista, and their uncle Gabriele di Bartolomeo Peterlini. The family had been selling their paper on the Florentine market from the 1460s onward; when Lorenzo de' Medici in a letter from 1466 jokingly mentioned "all that paper from Fabriano," he presumably referred to their company.[15] Five years later, on 19 July 1471, Piero and Gabriele di Bartolomeo Peterlini, "paper dealers from Fabriano," presented their (first?) cause in the Florentine Mercanzia against their many debtors among the local stationers.[16]

Nearly two decades later the new dispute arose on the printing of Saint Gregory's *Morali*. Rinaldo Peterlini's first charge was brought to the court of the Mercanzia on 29 March 1490. Directly referring to the account books of the two apothecaries, he asked them for the considerable sum of two hundred lire for paper that had been delivered at an unspecified date, but possibly over a longer period.[17] The brothers refused not only to acknowledge this debt but also the consultation of their account books, without further ado (15 April).[18] Instantly Peterlini insisted that they present at least copies of their accounts ("sumpto delle partite," 17 April), and then showed his own books.[19] On 16 June the tribunal nominated two accountants, Piero di Taddeo Gaddi and Gualberto di Giovanni Morelli, to examine the documents of both parties.[20] After their verdict—which had to be finished in fifteen days but is unfortunately lost—on 13 August, Tommaso and Antonio di Luca were officially declared to owe Peterlini two hundred lire for paper sold between 1480 and 1485.[21]

Roughly a month after his first accusation, Rinaldo Peterlini submitted a second, this time much more detailed, petition (30 April). For the first time he now directly cited Niccolò di Lorenzo and partners ("Nicholò di Lorenzo tedescho impressore et compagni impressori"). According to this accusation, Tommaso and Antonio di Luca had been the typographer's main and thus fully liable partners in the printing of Saint Gregory's *Morali*. As a consequence they together now owed him the enormous sum of 4,174 lire for the paper that Battista Peterlini had sold them to print 1,050—and not 1,025, as was recorded in the 1483 contract (see Chapter 13)—copies of this book. Although Niccolò di Lorenzo had obligated himself and his heirs for this sum, now all the remaining copies of the book were in the hands of the two apothecaries.[22] Rinaldo was offering to demonstrate this at the court's request. His claim regarded in fact only these volumes, which he formally asked to be handed over as a deposit, until his full financial satisfaction. According to the Mercanzia rules, the judge therefore sent his messenger ("messo") to the houses of the printer and of Tommaso and Antonio to notify them of the petition; this was duly executed (30 April).[23] The following judicial steps are not all perfectly clear, in particular regarding the role of Niccolò di Lorenzo himself. Evidently he never presented himself in the Mercanzia court, despite several convocations. He may actually have benefited from some higher level of protection, so that the court official accepted his position as so marginal as to exclude him from the case.

Tommaso and Antonio di Luca di Betto Bernardi presented themselves on 11 May and sternly denied the claim that they had ever been the official, and thus liable, partners of Niccolò di Lorenzo. On whether they had convinced Battista Peterlini to sell Niccolò the paper, the two brothers seemed to be in disaccord: whereas Tommaso categorically denied this, his younger brother Antonio—who was, as we know from the original contract, directly involved in the publication of the *Morali*—didn't wish to incriminate himself.[24] Thus, four days later Rinaldo Peterlini returned to the court, insisting on the fact of a full partnership between the printer and the two apothecaries. According to Peterlini, the delivery of forty bales of Bolognese paper ("balle quarante di carta bolognese etc., sicome appare per scripta privata fatta tra loro") was totally imputable to their intercession. Previously his brother Battista had not even known the printer. All Florentines, especially those living in the parishes of Sant'Apollinare and San Firenze, knew this. To prove his allegations, Rinaldo presented several witnesses whose names were unfortunately omitted in the Mercanzia register.[25] On 27 and 29 May Tommaso and Antonio refuted this once again, this time adding the rather clumsy argument that even if they possessed some copies of the *Morali* printed by Niccolò di Lorenzo, these could have been produced on somebody else's paper.[26]

As has been mentioned, Peterlini claimed to have brought to Florence only forty bales of "Bolognese"—that is royal—paper (the *Morali* were printed in folio). Although the bale's unitary price was not stated in the Mercanzia acts, the overall sum of 4,174 lire seemed to refer to this quantity. One thus arrives at an approximate unitary price of more than a hundred lire or twenty gold florins per bale. If this were correct, the cost would be considerably higher, more than the double, than the 731 ducats forwarded by the Agostini in Venice for no less than eighty-six bales of royal paper in 1476 (eight and a half ducats per bale).[27] It must be assumed that the requested sum was therefore either hiding other charges or that the quantity of paper had been considerably higher than forty bales.

Presumably due to the dilatory tactics of the two apothecaries and the difficulties of the two accountants, Piero Gaddi and Gualberto Morelli, the dispute could not be settled in the summer of 1490. As Peterlini knew, Florentine jurisdiction prescribed that any major Mercanzia dispute that could not be terminated in four months, had to be handled by a special commission of the court ("The Ten of the *Ricorso*").[28] The repeated nomination between July and September of Peterlini's legal guarantor ("mallevadore"), the stationer Francesco d'Angelo Tucci, was already related to this new procedure.[29] Promptly on 1 September Peterlini represented his case and on 10 September Antonio and Tommaso refuted the charges, as before.[30] On this occasion, however, the apothecaries showed for the first time some of their own account books. Ten Florentine merchants from the most important families were called to examine these accounts.[31] Likewise, on 23 September Rinaldo Peterlini deposed all relative documents in his possession, among which was also the original contract between Niccolò di Lorenzo and Antonio di Luca. His notarial documents and letters demonstrated furthermore the long business connection between the two apothecaries and his brother Battista Peterlini, certainly from 1475.[32]

After having spoken to the printer ("udito etiam decto Nicholò impressore"), on the following day, 24 September 1490, the tribunal of the Mercanzia decided that Peterlini's claims were largely justified: he was judged to be Niccolò di Lorenzo's creditor of 3,583 lire for the paper needed for the *Morali,* and Antonio and Tommaso di Luca were condemned to consign to Peterlini all of their 825 copies. Overruling the terms of Antonio's limited partnership (*accomandita*), the court therefore concluded implicitly that their conduct had been "fraudulent and deceptive."[33] All the volumes of the *Morali* were now "obligated" to Rinaldo Peterlini. The two apothecaries were asked to consign them in fifteen days to as yet unnamed stationers, where they had to remain for six months; Peterlini had the right to nominate them.[34] After this the volumes were to be offered for sale under the condition that Peterlini inform the two apothecaries on the selling price and who had a prepurchase option on this basis.[35] There was still discussion on around twenty-five copies of the *Morali* that had been sent to Perugia in Peterlini's name; Peterlini, for his part, denied this commission.[36] Other previous consignments were not recorded. After six months a balance had to be drawn.[37]

After one week Tommaso and Antonio di Luca di Betto Bernardi returned to the court, protesting yet another time against the assumption that they were the liable partners of Niccolò di Lorenzo and denouncing the fact that Rinaldo Peterlini had not yet nominated the stationers to receive their 825 copies of the *Morali.* In order to avoid negative consequences for themselves, they declared to deposit them with "Bartolomeo di Domenico cartolaio sotto la Badia di Firenze," a capable bookseller ("buono et idoneo").[38] This was, of course, the well-known stationer Bartolo di Domenico di Guido who long before had been the commercial head of the Ripoli press (see Chapter 10).[39] On this matter Rinaldo thought differently, and on 11 October named the three stationers Domenico di Bartolo, Michele di Biagio Caccini, and Filippo di Giunta (the local head of the Giunti dynasty) as the three booksellers among whom the volumes should be distributed.[40] The paper dealer also pressed Tommaso and Antonio to finally inform him about all those debtors for whom they had ever acted as intermediaries for acquisitions of his paper. Since these sums really pertained to himself, the two apothecaries were obliged to hand over their credits, as they had always promised. On the following day the brothers offered to deliver their volumes to the three chosen stationers; Tommaso di Luca added that in his brother's name he already had given Peterlini a power of attorney to cash in his paper credits (13 October).[41]

This notarial deed from the very same day named, in fact, Battista and Rinaldo as entitled to receiving different sums of money from fifteen Florentine citizens and stationers. The highest sum of 591 lire and sixteen soldi fell on Niccolò di Lorenzo, but the document did not actually state to whom these sums legally pertained. As it turned soon out, the list was furthermore incomplete.[42]

Two days later, therefore, Rinaldo reaffirmed that the 825 copies of the *Morali* be consigned to the three chosen stationers in no more than fifteen days. Regarding the notarial deed, he insisted on a public document drawn up by one of the official Mercanzia notaries (15 October).[43] After two weeks he returned to the court with the claim that so far he had only received a partial list of debtors; for his part, he had himself added four more stationers with their relative (paper) debts.[44] Rinaldo therefore challenged the two apothecaries to finally consign to him the definitive list of these credits. On 30 October Tommaso and Antonio contradicted him, stating that they had already done so, including in the list "Nicolò di Lorenzo tedescho impressore di libri" with his debt of 591 lire.[45]

This specific claim, however, was refuted by Rinaldo Peterlini on 3 November, unfortunately without giving a specific motive. It thus remains dubious whether Peterlini had understood the printer's marginal role and wanted to exclude his name altogether or whether he believed that his debt was actually even higher, as seemed to appear "in another part or on the other hand" of the definitive debtors' list of 5 November.[46]

On 5 November 1490, Tommaso and Antonio di Luca di Betto Bernardi had the Mercanzia notary ser Niccolò di Guido del Trincia copy Peterlini's definitive authorization to cash in his paper credits (see Appendix B, no. 11). This second list began with the names of six stationers who had never been recorded before—maybe those uncovered by Peterlini himself. It then indicated the debts of other citizens like Francesco

Berlinghieri, Cappone di Bartolomeo Capponi, and Guido Mannelli. For the highest sums stand out the names of Niccolò di Lorenzo (again with more than 591 lire), and, surprisingly, also that of Cristoforo Landino, with more than 469 lire. The inclusion of the humanist's name is indeed startling. It must be assumed that in one way or another he was involved in the printing of the *Morali* and that he continued to support Niccolò di Lorenzo even after their direct collaboration. Maybe his role resembled that of a "secret partner" or "friend" (*amico*), as these sponsors were known in Florentine accounting. The deeper reasons of why Tommaso and Antonio had not mentioned his name before were presumably dictated by their own hidden interests. At the end of the notarial document, "in another part or on the other hand," the two apothecaries finally appointed Peterlini as their representative to cash in the whole and highly hypothetical sum that had been calculated in the sentence of 24 September—3,583 lire—as if all the other minor sums were no part of this.

After Rinaldo Peterlini's deposition of 3 November 1490, the registers of the Mercanzia remained silent for several months, probably thanks to the delivery of the *Morali* copies to the various stationers indicated. However, on 28 April 1491 the paper merchant from Fabriano returned to the court, claiming that the two brothers still owed him a sum of more than six hundred lire.[47] In the next few weeks Peterlini formally seized not only the farm of Tommaso and Antonio but also those of their legal guarantors (29 April–18 May 1491).[48] After the passing of several deadlines, on 31 May the Mercanzia official decreed to have the brothers publicly called out as "insolvent and fugitive merchants" ("cessanti et fuggitivi").[49] On the following day, Tommaso and Antonio successfully contested both these confiscations and the public declaration on the basis that Peterlini was no Florentine, a "stranger" (1 June).[50] Therefore, Rinaldo now concentrated on confiscations from the belongings of one of the two legal guarantors of the brothers, Bartolomeo d'Antonio di Bartolomeo del Rosso Pieri.[51] He furthermore seized in Tommaso and Antonio's workshop several domestic objects and cloth worth 150 lire (21 July 1491).[52] In October 1492 Peterlini even jailed Antonio in the Mercanzia prison, forcing his elder brother Tommaso to guarantee for the requested sum.[53]

The question of the *Morali* must have agitated the two apothecaries and Rinaldo Peterlini and their heirs for many years to come. As Peterlini knew—because he had stated so in his deposition of 23 September 1490—Antonio di Luca di Betto Bernardi sold single copies of this book for twelve lire.[54] In other words, to arrive at the expected sum of the 3,583 lire, nearly three hundred copies of the bulky work had to be sold. This could have only been possible over a longer period of time and in various markets. In any case, Antonio di Luca died on 24 March 1494.[55] His brother Tommaso presented his tax declaration four years later on his own.[56] The printing of the *Morali* had not brought them any fortune.

Niccolò di Lorenzo's professional activities after 1486 remain for now unknown. Some of his types could soon have circulated, as the enigmatic edition of the *Rivelazione* of Antonio da Rieti shows (1485?, see Appendix A, no. 39). Similarly, the exact relation of Niccolò with the mysterious "Printer of Vergilius, C 6061," to whom no less than seventeen books printed between around 1487 and 1492 have been attributed, still needs to be established.[57] Following the discovery that this anonymous printer used some of Niccolò's characters, one might consider different types of collaboration in two workshops, or possibly just one. Given the insistence of his creditors, however, one easily understands why Niccolò could not sign any more colophons after 1486. However, he did not altogether abandon his profession.

This is confirmed by a document from 13 August 1493 which states that at an unspecified date—but presumably shortly before—he had sold two printing presses and other typographical material to his colleague, the priest Francesco Buonaccorsi, and that some of this material had revealed itself to be unusable. The resolution of the ensuing dispute was placed into the hands of two other printers, Giovanni di Piero da Magonza for Niccolò, and Antonio Miscomini for ser Francesco Buonaccorsi (see Appendix B, no. 12).[58]

In conclusion, Niccolò di Lorenzo's long professional career appears in many aspects exceptional. Over more than a decade he was repeatedly confronted with serious difficulties, both technical and economic. He tried to resolve them by adopting various strategies, but too little is known about the general circumstances and his direct competitors to interpret them in an adequate way. Although Niccolò's often pioneering work may sometimes have been met with indifference or hostility, it was both copied and refined abroad. Important Florentine humanists like Bartolomeo Fonzio or Cristoforo Landino recognized his merits and protected him from the more critical consequences of bankruptcy, exile, or a long jail term; his business was clearly judged as too important to fail. This, however, was not so much "capitalistic" or "protocapitalistic" thinking, as, in a debt economy, common sense.

ABBREVIATIONS

ASF   Archivio di Stato, Florence.

BMC   *Catalogue of Books Printed in the XVth Century Now in the British Museum. Part VI, Italy: Foligno Ferrara Florence Milan Bologna Naples Perugia and Treviso*. London: British Museum, 1930.

BNCF   Biblioteca Nazionale Centrale, Florence.

DBI   *Dizionario biografico degli Italiani*. Rome: Istituto della Enciclopedia Italiana, 1960-. Also available online at www.treccani.it.

GW   *Gesamtkatalog der Wiegendrucke*. Available online at www.gesamtkatalogderwiegendrucke.de.

ISTC   *Incunable Short Title Catalogue*. Available online at www.data.cerl.org.

BOOKS PRINTED BY NICCOLÒ DI LORENZO DELLA MAGNA OR ATTRIBUTED TO HIS PRESS

1. Marsilius Ficinus, *De Christiana religione* (in Latin, between 10 November and 10 December 1476).[1]

2. Domenico Cavalca, *Pungi lingua* (about 1476–1477).[2]

3. Alphonsus de Vargas, *Quaestiones super libris De anima Aristotelis* (26 July 1477).[3]

4. Antonio Bettini da Siena, *Monte Santo di Dio* (10 September 1477).[4]

5. Cherubino da Spoleto, *Regola della vita spirituale*. Add: *Regola della vita matrimoniale* (16 October 1477).[5]

6. Feo Belcari, *Vita del B. Giovanni Colombini* (about 1477).[6]

7. Paulus Florentinus, *Confessione* (about 1477).[7]

8. *Esortazione ai Veneziani: "Al nome sia di Dio"* (about 1477).[8]

9. Petrus de Crescentiis, *Il libro della agricultura* (15 July 1478).[9]

10. Bartholomaeus Scala, *Excusatio Florentinorum ob poenas de sociis Pactianae in Medices coniurationis* (after 11 August 1478).[10]

11. Gentile Becchi, *Florentina Synodus ad veritatis testimonium et Sixtianae caliginis dissipationem* (after 19 August 1478).[11]

12. Angelus Politianus, *Pactianae coniurationis commentarium* (1478).[12]

13. A. Cornelius Celsus, *De medicina* (1478).[13]

14. Luca Pulci, *Il Driadeo* (3 April 1479).[14]

15. Rabbi Samuel, *Epistola contra Judaeorum errores* (in Italian, after 25 November 1479).[15]

16. Aristotle, *Ethica ad Nicomachum* (in Latin, before 25 March 1480).[16]

17. Robertus Caracciolus, *Sermones quadragesimales* (1 April 1480).[17]

18. Francesco Petrarca, *Trionfi* (18 November 1480).[18]

19. *Epistolae et Evangelia* (in Italian, about 1480).[19]

20. *Uffici della città di Firenze* (about 1480).[20]

21. Sixtus IV, *Sommario della bolla contro i Turchi del 4 dicembre 1480* (after 4 December 1480).[21]

22. Cristoforo Landino, *Disputationum Camaldulensium libri IV* (presumably before 24 December 1480, see Chapter 12).[22]

23. Sixtus IV, *Indulgentia* (between 4 December 1480 and 31 March 1481).[23]

24. Sixtus IV, *Indulgentia* (about 1481).[24]

25. Angelus Carletti de Clavasio, *Declaratio seu interpretatio bullarum super bullis Sixti IV* (about 1481).[25]

26. Bartholomaeus Scala, *Oratio pro imperatoriis signis Constantio Sforzae dandis* (not before 4 October 1481).[26]

27. Francesco Berlinghieri, *Le septe giornate della geographia* (about 1481–1482).[27]

28. Cherubino da Spoleto, *Regola della vita sprirituale* (22 October 1482).[28]

29. Cristoforo Landino, *Orazione alla Signoria Fiorentina quando presentò il suo Comento di Dante* (about 1482–1483).[29]

30. Cristoforo Landino, *Oratio in funere Iordani Ursini* (after 13 March 1483).[30]

31. Nicolaus Perottus, *Rudimenta grammatices* (16 April 1483).[31]

32. *Horae Beatae Mariae Virginis ad usum Ecclesiae Romanae* (5 July 1483).[32]

33. Cherubino da Spoleto, *Regola della vita spirituale* (31 July 1483).[33]

34. Lorenzo Oppizzi, *Miracoli della Vergine delle Carceri di Prato* (after 6 July 1484).[34]

35. Gilbertus de Hoilanda, *Sermones super Cantica canticorum* (16 April 1485).[35]

36. Pius II, *De duabus amantibus* (in Alessandro Braccesi's Italian translation, about 1485).[36]

37. Gaspar Massanus, *Regulae grammaticales* (about 1485).[37]

38. Antonio Pucci, *Storia di Apollonio di Tiro* (about 1485).[38]

39. Antonio da Rieti, *Rivelazione che ebbe frate Antonio di Rieti* (dubious, around 1485).[39]

40. Leon Battista Alberti, *De re aedificatoria* (29 December 1485).[40]

41. Angelus Politianus, *Silva cui titulus Ambra* (not before 4 November 1485).[41]

42. Bartholomaeus Scala, *Oratio ad Innocentium VIII* (1485–1486).[42]

43. Gregorius I, *Moralia sive Expositio in Iob* (15 June 1486).[43]

APPENDIX B

DOCUMENTS

All the dates, except in the sources themselves, have been modernized. The following documents are unknown and unedited, except no. 4, the printing contract for Cristoforo Landino's commentary of Dante Alighieri's *Divina Commedia*, which has been edited in Böninger (2016), pp. 111–113.

1. ASF, Mercanzia, 4482 (Cause straordinarie, 7 January–
    25 February 1478), no pagination, n. 174.

Die 18 februarii 1477.[1]

Iacopo di Borgianni di Mino cittadino et mercatante fiorentino che infino a dì VIIII di giugno 1477 o in altro più vero tempo, come appare per la infrascripta scripta, allogò a Niccolò di Lorenzo di Niccolò della Magna a fare uno libro di vita spirituale compostogli frate Cherubino da Spoleti, et di che et come nella infrascripta scripta privata si fa mentione, et quello doveva dare fornito per tutto luglio allora proximo futuro et hora lungamente passato,[2] come tutte le predecte cose apparischono et contengonsi per una scripta et cautione privata, ad che decto Iacopo in quella solamente parte et parti feceno per lui et non più né altrimenti si riferì et la produsse, usò et allegò dinanzi al decto messer uficiale et sua corte et diposela apresso a ser Giorgio di ser Sancti notaio in decta corte ad farne tanto quanto si richiede, et fu et è certa cosa che dipoi decto Niccolò à 'uto et ricevuto dal decto Iacopo fiorini quarantaquattro d'oro larghi, di che li à servito per potere lavorare et fare el bisogno come chiaramente appare, et fu et è certa cosa che esso Niccolò non à facto decta opera né libro né observato cosa promettese di fare, et se alcuna particella n'avesse facta, quella non sarebbe secondo e pacti et conventioni avute insieme, el perché decto Iacopo richiese et richiede instantissimamente decto Niccolò che infra tre dì proximi futuri dia, renda et restituisscha a esso Iacopo detti fiorini quarantaquattro larghi et le spese et dampni suoi, altrimenti come esso Iacopo li protestò et protesta d'ogni suoi dampni, spese et interesse, et che passato decto termine lo converrà et farà contra a esso Niccolò quello et quanto li fia permesso et contro di lui userà le suoi ragioni et questo acciò che delle predecte cose esso Niccolò mai/per alcuno tempo possa né vaglia pretendere et allegare alcuna ingnorantia, et tutte le suprascripte cose disse et dice, protestò et protesta et fa insiememente, congiuntamente, divisamente et per ordine, subcessione et per ogni migliore modo etc. Et produsse li statuti etc.

El quale messer uficiale sedente pro tribunali al suo et di decta corte usato banco delle ragioni, ad petitione di decto Iacopo, veduto le infrascripte cose et ciò ch'è stato da vedere, commisse, impuose et comandò a Pasignano messo di decta corte et a qualunque altro messo di decta corte et a qualunque di loro et in tutto che vada et da parte, commissione et mandato di decti uficiale et corte richiegga decto Niccolò ad vedere la infrascripta comparigione, protesto, notificagione, productione et depisitione de decta scripta di ragione et tutte le infrascripte cose, et qualunque d'esse trarne copia, dire et opporre contra etc., alias etc., et più li protesta richiedi et notifichi in tutto et per tutto come et quanto di sopra si contiene et è scripto etc.

El quale Pasigniano messo rapportò al decto m. uficiale et sua corte et a me notario infrascripto se da parte, commissione et mandato di detti uficiale et corte essere ito et avere richiesto decto Niccolò per questo di et hora ad vedere la infrascripta comparigione, protesto, notificatione, requisitione, productione et depositione di decta scripta privata di ragione et ciò che in essa si contiene, torne copia, dire contra etc., alias etc., et in tutto et per tutto rapportò decto messo avere protestato, notificato et richiestolo secondo et come di sopra si contiene et ebbe in commissione et mandato, et tutto rapportò decto messo avere facto decto dì et dopo detta factali commissione cum cedola et alla presentia d'esso Niccolò.

> 2. ASF, Notarile antecosimiano, 16783 (ser Piero di Andrea di Michele da Campi, 1477–1481), fol. 271r.

Item postea dictis anno [1479], indictione predicta, die vero XXVI mensis maii, actum in civitate Florentie in populo Sancte Marie Novelle, presentibus testibus etc. presbitero Marcho Dominici Pauli barbitonsoris rectore ecclesie S. Iusti de Champi et Francesco Benedicti Pacini pictore populi S. Laurentii de Florentia,

Frater Dominichus olim Daniellis de Pistorio et

Frater Pierus olim Salvatoris de Pisis, } fratres S. Dominici ordinis predicatorum, habitatores ad monasterium Ripolis de Florentia et quilibet eorum in simul in solidum, coniunctim et de per se et omni modo etc., eorum et cuiuslibet eorum propriis et privatis nominibus, et pro omni eorum et cuiuslibet eorum interesse ac etiam ut et tamquam sindici et procuratores quilibet eorum in solidum monialium monasterii, capituli et conventus Sancti Iacopi de Ripolis de Florentia et quilibet eorum quolibet dictorum modorum et nominum in solidum et de per se et omni meliori modo etc., fecerunt etc., constituerunt et substituerunt suos dictis modis et nominibus procuratores etc., Thomasium

Iacobi Tani civem florentinum licet absentem etc.,[3] spetialiter et nominatim ad transigendum et componendum etc., cum Bartholo Dominici Guidonis[4] cartolario et sociis de et super quocumque traffico et societate facta inter ipsos super formando et formari faciendo libros et litteras scultas in libris etc., et prout vulgariter dicitur "sopra gittare libri in forma" etc., et quamcumque compositionem et transactionem faciendum etc., eo modo et forma de quibus et prout et sicut dicto procuratori videbitur et placebit et propterea etc., saldandum et in saldo et [com]puto ponendum quascumque scripturas et alias quascumque etc.,[5] item ad commictendum et compromictendum etc., cum dicto Bartholo de et super predictis etc.,[6] et laudis interessendum et ipsis seu ipsos ratificandum et seu ab eis appellandum et notificari et bapnum faciendum, et generaliter etc., dans etc., promictens[7] sub ypoteca etc.

3. ASF, Mercanzia, 7263 (Sentenze, 1 December 1480–17 February 1481), no foliation, under the day.

Die XV decembris.[8]

Ad petitione del detto Domenico di Bernardo orafo, Passigniano messo della detta corte rapportò al detto messer ufficiale et corte et a me notario infrascripto se di licentia di detto messer ufficiale et cortte avere richiesto detto Nicholo di Lorenzo tedescho habitante in Firenze et compagni per l'adrieto inpressori di libri et qualunque di loro per questo dì et hora et prehemptorie ad vedere et udire la infrascripta sententia, confermatione di comandamento di libro, condepnagione et tassatione di spese et ciò che in essa si contiene, dire contra et opporre alias, et decta richiesta rapportò detto messo haver fatta a dì XII di dicembre 1480 alla casa della usata habitatione d'esso Nicholò con cedola et in detto luogo [di] detti suoi per adrieto compagni.

Al nome di Dio amen. Noi Vandino de' Vandini da Faenza iudice et officiale prefato sedente pro tribunali ut supra, insieme di volere, consiglio et deliberatione de' nobili et prudenti huomini

Antonio di Lorenzo Buondelmonti
Averardo d'Antonio Serristori
Francesco di Zanobi Lapaccini
Gino di Francesco Ginori
Simone d'Amerigho Zati, et
ser Nicholò di Michele Fedini,} gli Signori Sei consiglieri collegialmente ragunati et sedenti pro tribunali ne' luogo della nostra usatta residentia,

veduta una petitione et domanda data et fatta in ditta corte per detto Domenicho a dì primo del mese di dicembre 1480 o altro più vero tempo, per la quale domandò che fusse comandato al detto Nicholò et compagni che infra otto dì allora proximo futuro producesse in iudicio dinanzi al detto messer ufficiale et corte[9] il suo et di detti suoi compagni libro di forma per lui et compagni tenuto in Firenze da l'anno 1476 dove, c. 10, essi Nicolò et compagni ànno scripto per loro creditore detto Domenico et infra detto tempo desseno et pagasseno al detto Domenicho lire trenta p[iccioli] per parte di maggior somma, et oltre acciò domandò che si dichiarasse detto Nicholò et compagni essere stati et essere veri debitori di detto Domenicho di dette lire XXX p[iccioli] per parte di maggior somma, et così si condepnassino detti Nicholò et compagni et ciascuno in tutto, et veduto ciò che in detta domanda si contiene et veduto il diretto pagato et finalmente veduto la suprascripta richiesta, la forma della ragioni, statuti et ordini et ciò che fu da vedere, il nome di Dio invocato, sedente pro tribunali ut supra, prima fatto, messo et celebrato tra detti consiglieri solepne et segreto squittino a fave nere et bianche et obtenuto el partito tra lloro secondo gl'ordini,

Pronumptiamo, sententiamo et dichiariamo il detto comandamento di libro essersi dovuto et potuto fare et fatto valere et tenere et doversi et potersi confermare, et così quello in tutto et per tutto confermiamo et approviamo, et oltre acciò dichiariamo i detti Nicholò et compagni predetti et qualunque di loro in tutto uno pagamento bastando essere stati et essere veri debitori di detto Domenicho di detta quantità di lire XXX p[iccioli], et così dichiariamo essi Nicholò et compagni predetti et ciascuno in tutto uno pagamento bastando per questa nostra presente sententia condepniamo a dare et pagare al detto Domenicho ditte lire XXX p[iccioli] per parte et per sorte, et de più lire[10] ... per le spese della corte, le quali così et tanto tassiamo et dichiariamo.

Lata,[11] data, letta et in questi scripti sententialmente pronunptiata et promulgata cum la decta sententia, condepnagione et tassatione di spese, et tucte le dicte chose facte furono per decti m. ufficiale et Sei sedenti pro tribunali ut supra dell'anno del Signore 1480, indictione XIIII et a dì 15 di dicembre, presenti Francesco di Giovanni et Iacopo di Paolo donzelli di decta chasa.

4.   ASF, Podestà, 5193 (Cause civili, quartieri S. Spirito e S. Croce, 2–24 June 1483), fols. 891r–893r.

Al nome di Dio a dì XXIIII di dicembre MCCCCLXXX in Firenze.

Sia noto et manifesto a qualunche persona vedrà la presente scripta chome questo dì decto di sopra chome lo egregio doctore in iure civili messer Cristofano di Bartholomeo Landini et lo expectabile huomo Bernardo d'Antonio di Ricciardo degli Alberti et maestro Nicolò di Lorenzo della Magna impressore del popolo di Sancto Ambrogio di Firenze si sono convenuti et hanno facto compagnia ha imprimere le tre Comedie di Dante chol chomento nuovamente composto dal soprascripto messer Cristofano, chon queste conditioni et pacti, cioè che el decto messer Cristofano sia tenuto et debba dare di mano in mano la sopradecta opera al sopradecto maestro Nicolò, et similmente correggere tucte le monstre in forma che el decto maestro Nicolò possa imprimere ogni dì quanto di socto si dirà, cioè una carta per dì per istrectoio per insino alla somma di tre strectoi che fieno ogni dì tre charte, et non observando perda il quarto del guadagnio che gnen'avessi[12] a toccare, et oltra questo non possa decto messer Cristofano dare copia della decta opera né di parte di quella ad alchuno altro, né prestarla insino a tanto che ' libri che s'imprimeranno non sieno finiti di vendere, et non observando perda tucto el guadagnio. Et maestro Nicolò sia tenuto et debba curare sì et in tal modo che e sopradecti quinterni o fogli, così dello originale come degli impressi, con ogni diligentia guardargli et fargli guardare a ffine che per suo mancamento o da altri per lui non ne dieno parte alcuna in altre mani che di messer Cristofano et di Bernardo sopradecti, accioché per altri non se ne possa havere né di tucti né di parte copia alchuna fino a tanto che decti volumi che a ffar s'ànno, chome in questa si dirà, / non sieno venduti, et contrafaccendo a quanto di ciò è decto, el sopradecto maestro Nicolo s'intenda havere perduto ogni et qualunche ghuadagno segli appartenessi, e piu debba el sopradecto maestro Nicolò seguire di lavorare et lavorare fare nella somma et quantità di somma di libri mille cento venticinque, e quali mille cento venticinque più giorni fa s'impongono a uno strectoio, et per tutto dì quindici di gennaio proximo che de' venire debba seguire con due altri strectoi, a ffine che tucti a tre debbano imprimere ogni dì raghuagliato carte tre di tucta la somma, cioè carte tremila trecento septantacinque per dì, cioè ragionando e dì che si lavora, e tucti e sopradecti quinterni debba come finiti saranno mandargli tre a messer Cristofano et tre a Bernardo et chosì di mano in mano fino a opera finita, et che nelle mani del decto maestro Nicolò non debba rimanere né dello originale né dello impresso, né parte né tucto libro alcuno, et contrafaccendo a quanto è decto perda ogni guadagno che gliene toccassi.

Et più s'obliga el sopradecto Bernardo di prestare fiorini trecento sexanta larghi, de' quali danari se ne debba pagare fiorini cento larghi per l'arra et parte de' fogli, e 'l resto che sono fiorini dugento sexanta larghi s'abbino a pagare dì per dì per le spese et storie et salari de' garzoni ha imprimere decti volumi et ogni spesa occorrente, come dirà el sopradecto maestro Nicolò, di che decto maestro Nicolò ne debba tenere diligente conto di quanto per decta opera si spenderà, che al fine che saranno impressi decti volumi debba darne buono conto.

E 'l decto Bernardo, se per caso alcuno non facessi buoni dì per dì quello che è di bisogno per insino alla somma di fiorini trecento sexanta larghi, perda quello segli appartenessi del guadagno gli toccassi.

Et più sono d'acordo che ' primi danari si ritrarranno di decti volumi si paghi el sopradecto Bernardo di tanto quanto servito havessi per decta opera et ogni et qualunche spesa facta si fussi in decti volumi, così di fogli chome d'impressura et storie, e ogni altro resto et quantità[13] di danari si ritrarrà di decti volumi si debba partire per terzo, che a dDio piaccia sia buono guadagno, et che el terzo si dia a messer Christofano, el terzo a Bernardo, l'altro terzo a maestro Nicolò.

E più sono d'acordo che el primo volume di decta somma si debba dare per l'amore di Dio alle donne et monistero delle Murate leghato alle spese di decta compagnia.

E più sono d'achordo che quando e' trovassino di fare mercato della somma di decti mille cento venticinque volumi o quello riusciranno/o di qualunche parte d'essi, sono chontenti et vogliono e sopradecti messer Christofano, Bernardo et Nicolò che quando dua di loro d'acordo saranno, possino sanza alchuno progiudicio fare decto mercato o vero vendita o vero mercati et vendite, sempre com buona sicurtà et prima faccendo di ciò noto al terzo chompagno et assicurarlo per sufficiente mallevadore della terza parte che toccassi.

E più sono d'accordo che el sopradecto maestro Nicolò non possa né debba lavorare né fare lavorare in altri volumi che nel sopradecto fino a tanta che decti volumi harà finiti, et se pure lavorare volessi col quarto strectoio, sia tenuto et debba lavorare o lavorare fare nella sopradecta opera et ne' sopradecti volumi sopra nominati et per decta chompagnia, et chontrafaccendo s'intenda el sopradecto maestro Nicolò havere perduto quanto di guadagno pervenire segli potessi, e per observanza delle infrascripte cose s'oblighano e sopradecti messer Christofano, Bernardo et maestro Nicolò l'uno all'altro et gli altri all'uno loro et loro eredi et beni presenti et futuri et rinuntiano a ogni beneficio, leggie, statuto che contra a cciò facessi et sottomettonsi a ogni corte dove ragione si tenessi così in Firenze chome in qualunche altra città come Pisa, Siena, Bologna et Perugia, et maxime alla Mercatantia della ciptà di Firenze, e per vigore di decta scripta vogliono potere essere chonvenuti in havere et in persona l'uno dall'altro che non observassi quanto in essa si contiene, et per fede di ciò et a preghiera delle sopradecte parti et da lloro richiesto di chomune consentimento, io ser Piero di Francescho da Pratovecchio ho facta la sopradecta scripta di mia propria mano in Firenze, anno et mese et dì decto di sopra, alla quale per observanza delle infrascripte cose in essa chontente gl'infrascripti messer Christofano di Bartholomeo Landini et Bernardo d'Antonio di Ricciardo et maestro Nicholò di Lorenzo si soscriveranno di loro propria mano et obligheransi a quanto di sopra è decto. /

E perchè di sopra per inavvertenza lo dimentichai, agiungho chol consentimento delle sopradecte parti che se el sopradecto Bernardo dessi copia della decta opera o di parte di quella ad alcuno altro o prestassila, incorre nella medesima pena che è posta di sopra a messer Christofano et maestro Nicholò sopradecti.

Io messer Christoforo Landino sopradecto sono contento a quanto di sopra si contiene et chosì m'obligho d'osservare et a fede di ciò mi sono sobscripto di mia propria mano anno et dì sopradecti.

Io Bernardo d'Antonio di Ricciardo degli Alberti m'obligho a quanto in questa si chontiene e per ciò observare mi sono soscripto di mia propia mano anno et mese et dì decto di sopra.

Io Nicholò di Lorenzo sopradecto sono contento a quanto di sopra si contiene et chosì m'obligho d'osservare et per fede di ciò mi sono soscripto di mia propria mano anno, mese et dì di sopra.

5.   ASF, Mercanzia, 7263 (Sentenze, 1 December 1480–17 February 1481); 7264 (Sentenze, 2 January–27 February 1481), both without foliation, under the day.

Die XVII februarii 1480.

Ad petitione del detto maestro Lodovicho di maestro Piero medicho cittadino fiorentino, Giuliano d'Antonio messo di decta corte rapportò al decto messer ufficiale et corte et a me notaio infrascripto se di licentia di decto messer ufficiale havere richiesto il decto

Nicholo di Lorenzo scriptore del popolo di Santo Anbruogio di Firenze per questo dì et hora et prehemptorie ad vedere et udire la infrascripta sententia, condemnatione et tassatione di spese et ciò che in essa si contiene et a dire contra et opporre alias etc., et la detta richiesta avere fatta in persona al decto Nicholo con dimissione di cedola a dì tre di febbraio 1480.

Al nome di Dio amen, noi Vandino de' Vandini da Faenza uffitiale suprascripto, sedente pro tribunali utsupra, insieme di volere, consiglio et deliberatione de' nobili huomini

Antonio di Lorenzo Buondelmonti

Averardo d'Antonio Serristori

Gino di Francesco Ginori

Francesco di Zanobi Lapaccini

Simone d'Amerigho Zati et

Ser Nicolò di Michele Fedini,} gli Signori sei consiglieri collegialmente ragunati et sedenti pro tribunali ne' luogho della nostra usata residentia, et

veduta et considerata una petitione et domanda data et fatta in detta corte per lo detto maestro Lodovicho adi XVIIII del mese di gennaio proximo passato 1480 o altro più vero tempo, per la quale in effecto domandò al decto Nicolo fiorini quattordici larghi per tanti a llui prestati et per lui gli ebbe ricevute da Nicholo di Bartolomeo del Troscia et Baldino Cambi et compagni, come appare al libro d'essi Nicolo et Baldino et compagni, segnato . . . , c. . . . , et veduto ciò che in detta petitione et domanda si contiene e con la productione del decto libro e con le debite richieste, et veduto el decto libro, et finalmente vedute le infrascripte richieste et la forma delle ragioni et delli statuti, il nome di Dio invocato, sedente pro tribunali ut supra, prima fatto et messo et celebrato tra detti nostri consiglieri solempne et secreto squittino a fave nere et bianche et obtenuto el partito tra loro secondo gl'ordini,

pronumptiamo, sententiamo et dichiaramo il decto Nicholo essere stato et essere vero et legiptimo debitore del decto maestro Lodovicho per le soprascripte ragioni et cagioni della detta soprascripta quantità di fiorini quattordici larghi, et condempniamo il decto Nicholo a pagare al decto maestro Lodovicho i detti fiorini quattordici larghi prestati, et lire quattro soldi XII denari X per le spese della corte, le quali così et tanto tassiamo in questa scriptura sententialmente condempnati.

Lata, decta et lecta et in questi scripti sententialmente pronumptiata et promulgata fu la decta sententia, condempnatione et tassatione di spese et tute le
decte chose facte furono per decto messer ufficiale et Sei sedenti pro tribunali
ut supra, dell'anno del Signore 1480, indictione XIIII, et a dì 17 di febraio, presentibus testibus, cioè Giovanni di Biagio et Francesco di Giovanni donzelli di
decta chorte.

> 6.   ASF, Mercanzia, 7271 (Sentenze, 21 February–24 April 1482), no
>   foliation, under the day 24 April 1482.

Ad[14] petitione di detto Giovanni di Bartholomeo di Montino [*sic*] pigicag-
nolo, Colombino messo di detta corte rapportò al detto m. uficiale et corte et a
me notaio infrascritto se essere ito et di licentia di detto m. uficiale et corte avere
richiesto il detto

Nicholo di Lorenzo impressore per questo dì et hora et prehentorie ad vedere et udire la infrascritta sententia, condannagione et tassagione di spese et
tutte le infrascritte chose et ciaschuna di esse a dire opporre alias etc., et detta
richiesta rapportò detto messo avere fatto[15] in presentia al detto reo con cedola
a dì XXII del presente mese d'aprile 1482.

Al nome di Dio amen. Noi Simone de' Simonelli da Orvieto giudice et uficiale
predetto pro tribunali sedente ut supra, veduta una petitione et domanda data et
fatta in detta corte a dì XVI del presente mese d'aprile o altro più vero dì per detto
attore contra al detto reo, al quale il detto attore domanda li. 18 p. per resto di
pigione chome apparisce[16] per una scripta privata di mano del detto Nicholo
sotto dì XXIII del presente mese, colla produtione di detta scripta et richiesta de
l'attore fatta che detto reo a quella vedere, et veduta la detta scripta et ragione ben
calculata, et veduta la scripta ultimamente fatta di detto reo, et la forma delle
ragioni, statuti et ordini et tutto ciò che intorno a cciò fu et è stato da vedere et
considerare, il nome di Dio repetuto, pro tribunali sedente ut supra, pronuntiamo,
sententiamo et dichiariamo et così pronuntiato per questa nostra sententia
condanniamo il detto reo a dare et paghare al detto attore la detta quantità di
li. 18 p. per parte et più li. . . . per le spese, le quali tassiamo et dichiariamo etc.

Lata[17] /[18] a dì XXIIII d'aprile[19] 1482, presentibus ser Baptista di Bartholomeo et ser Vivaldo di Conte notariis in dicta corte testibus etc.

> 7.   ASF, Mercanzia, 7286 (Sentenze, 30 April–22 August 1485), no
>   foliation, under the day.

Die VI augusti.

Ad[20] pititione di detto Francesco di Giovanni di Matteo Cappelli legnaiuolo per se et frategli compagni legnaiuoli, Frate Bogio messo di detta corte rapportò al detto messer ufficiale et corte et a me notario infrascripto se de licentia
de detto messer uficiale essere ito et havere richiesto detti

Francesco d'Andrea calzolaio in Por Sam Piero principale, et maestro Nicholo di . . . tedesco getta e libri in forma de persona et loro donne, figliuoli et famigli et ciascuno di loro per questo dì et hora et per ultimo termine ad vedere et udire questa presente sententia, confermatione di tenuta et comandamento di sgonbro, condapnagione et tassagione di spese, et sua contra et contradire etc., altrimenti [etc.], et dette richieste rapportò detto messo havere facte di detti Francesco im persona et maestro Nicholo alla casa di sua usata habitatione et persona di donna, et tutto con cedola secondo gli ordini a dì XXVIIII di luglio 1485.

Al[21] nome di Dio amen. Noy Andrea de' Recuperati da Faenza giudice e uficiale predetto, sedente pro tribunali ut supra, veduta una pronumptia et commissione di tenuta data et fatta sotto dì 6 di luglio 1485 o in altro più vero dì in favore et ad pititione di detto Francisco ne' beni, de' beni et sopra a' beni, et per le ragioni et cagioni, cose et quantità nella decta pronumptia et commissione contenute etc., et veduto la immissione dipoi facta per messo di detta corte del detto Francesco in tenuta et corporale possessione degli infrascripti beni di sotto et nel rapporto di decta tenuta, confinati in questo modo, cioè:

Una casa con palchi, sale, camere et altri suoi habitationi poste in Firenze et nel populo di Sancto Anbruogio et nella via che si chiama Via Ghibellina, che da primo decta via, a II° Donato Benci, a III° beni del munistero delle Murate di Firenze, a IIII° beni del munistero di Santa Verdiana di Firenze infra predetti confini o vero altri se più ve ne fussi, come beni et de' beni in detta pronumptia et commissione di tenuta contente, et veduto el rapporto di detta tenuta dipoi fatto del detto mese di luglio per parte et comandamento del detto messer uficiale et corte ad petitione di detto Francesco a' detti Francesco et maestro Nicholo et loro donne, figli et famigli di votare et disgombrare et pacificamente rilassare al detto Francesco detti beni et altre cose fare comandati et mandati / et loro commessi et rapporto scripto, et veduto la decta commissione et rapporto, et veduto una comparigione e iustificagione di detta tenuta et productione di ragioni dipoi data per detto Francesco co' lla tenuta [?] et rapporto di tenuta di detti Francesco et maestro Nicholo, et veduto la decta sententia per cui vigore fu pronumptiata la d[ett]a tenuta, et tutti gli atti fatti in decta corte, et la soprascripta richiesta, et gli statuti et ordini, et ciò che fu et è stato da vedere et considerare, il nome di Dio repetito, sedente pro tribunali ut supra, pronumptiamo, sententiamo et dichiariamo et così dichiarati per questa nostra sententia[22] confermiamo et aproviamo detta sententia et pronumptia di tenuta et tutti acti intorno a cciò facti, et condempniamo detto Francesco calzolaio et maestro Nicholo et loro donne, figli [et] famigli et ciaschuno di loro ad rilassare detti beni al detto Francesco, et più condempniamo detti Francesco et maestro Nicholo et ciascuno di loro in tutto nelle spese in detta corte fatte, le quali tassiamo essere stati et essere li. . . .

Lata,[23] data et in questa scripta sententialmente pronumptiata et promulgata fu la decta sententia, confermatione di tenuta, condempnagione, tassazione di spese et suprascripte [?] per lo decto messer uficiale sedente pro tribunale ut supra, socto gli anni del Nostro Signore Iesu Christo 1485, indictione tertia, et a dì . . . d'agosto presente.

Data die VI augusti 1485, presentibus ser Baptista Bartholomei et ser Iohanne de Ghirardinis notariis in detta corte, testibus etc.

8. ASF, Mercanzia, 4503 (Cause straordinarie, 26 April–19 October 1485), fols. 266r–267r, under the day.

Die XX augusti 1485.

Comparì dinanzi al detto uficiale

Messer Batista di Antonio di Sicilia componitore di lettere al presente abitatore in Firenze / e disse et dice che gli è vera cosa che insino del mese di marzo proximo passato o altro più vero tempo, trovandosi nella città di Siena dove esso lavorava della detta sua arte, et quivi etiamdio in detto tempo trovandosi Domenicho di . . . Doni cittadino fiorentino factore di Nicolo di . . . per adrieto donzello della presente corte et de' suoi compagni ne l'arte et exercitio di fare libri in forma nella città di Firenze, el quale Domeniche richiese el detto messer Batista che dovesse venire et lavorare con detto Nicolo et compagni in detto exercitio et che gli darebbe da lavorare per mesi quatro continuamente con salario di fiorini V larghi d'oro in oro il mese. Et finalmente venneno in Firenze in casa el detto Nicolo et compagni et quivi el detto messer Batista cominciò a llavorare, et di[24] novo per detto Nicolo et Domenicho gli fu fatto il salario di fiorini 5 larghi, et così aspettando detto messer Batista in Firenze et allora è stato per insino che sono passati detti quattro messi che esso se ne venne con detto Domenicho fori, et domandandoli sem. pre el suo salario et etiamdio domandandoli lictera di partirsi della città di Firenze e sempre detti Lorenzo [sic] et Domenicho gli ànno promesso di farli el suo dovere et pregatolo che non si parta et che non lasci l'opere imperfecte. Et mai questo suo salario avuto etc., richiede et interpelle el detto Domenicho Doni et detto Nicolo che infra quatro dì proximi futuri gli dieno et debbono aver dato et pagato fiorini dieci larghi d'oro in oro per parte di magior somma etc., altrimenti passato el detto termine detto messer Batista gli domandarà loro detti fiorini dieci larghi d'oro in oro et contro di loro procederà al gravamento reale et personale, in tuto et per tuto, come per li statuti et ordini gli sarà permesso, et protesta loro d'ogni suo danno, spese et interesse. Et richiede el detto messer uficiale che per uno de' suoi messi tutte le sopradette cose si notifichano al detto Domeniche et Nicolo, et questo aciò che delle predecte cosse non possa pretendere né allegare ignorantia alcuna etc. /

Et produsse il diritto pagato, item tutti statuti etc.

Et el detto messer Batista voleva essere e se stava alla p[erson]a o casa di ser Guiglelmo di Filippo etc.

Ad petitione del detto messer Batista il detto messer uficiale commisse a' messo di detta corte che richegha el detto Domeniche et Niccolo ad vedere la suprascripta comparitione, requisitione etc. et protesto, et più gli notifichi in

tuto et per tuto come per lo decto messer Batista fu et è stato domandato, e
questo aciò che delle predette cose non possino pretendere ignorantia etc.

Ad petitione del detto messer Batista, Bartolomeo d'Antonio messo di detta
corte raportò aver richiesto e detti Nicolo di Lorenzo et Domenicho Doni ad vedere la suprascripta comparizione et requisitione et protesto et ciò che in essa si
contiene, e se avergli notificato etc. in tuto et per tuto e tute et singule cose in
detta comissione contente etc., alle case d'essi Nicolo et Domenicho et di ciascuno di loro con cedula secondo gl'ordini etc.

   9. ASF, Mercanzia, 326 (Deliberazioni, 1 March 1486–2 July 1487),
      fol. 16r, under the day.

   Die XII aprilis 1486.

   Ad[25] petitionem Iohannis ser Pieri de Braccinis et sociorum lanaiuolorum,
supradicti Sex etc., servatis etc., assignaverunt terminum XX dierum
Cipriano Iacopi Antonii de Oricellariis ad luendum
libros 14 di più sorte, legati,
190 Donadei sciolti,
I.a Secunda di San Tommaso, et
uno vilume di Buonaventura sciolto,
8 Danti,
4 Giugurtini,
5 vite d'imperadori sciolti, dimissos in pignore pro florenis 20 larghis pro
partita, et commiserunt notificari.

Pistoriensis nuntius retulit se dicto notificasse domui die 14 presentis.

   10. Archivio della Curia Arcivescovile, Firenze, N 360 (Atti civili, ser
        Giuntino di Lorenzo Giuntini, 1471–95), without foliation and
        in chronological disorder[26]

   Item postea dictis anno, indictione et die [iovis VII februarii] et loco et
presentibus ser Piero Pacini notario, ser Benedicto Mathei et ser Sinibaldo Iohannis de Monaldis clerico florentino et aliis presentibus.

   Venerabilis vir ser Iacobus olim Caroli presbiter florentinus per se et suos
heredes ex una, et

   Iohannes Pieri de Alamania stampator librarum populi Sancti Ambroxii
florentini per se et suos heredes pro[27] partibus ex alia, devenerunt ad infrascriptam compositionem, pactum et concordiam, videlicet:

   Quod dictus ser Iacobus teneatur prestare operas suas in exercitio compositionis et[28] stampatoris librorum[29] prefato Iohanni Pieri de Alamania donec
et quousque dictus Iohannes dictum exercitium[30] exercuisset, videlicet[31] usque
quod dictus Iohannes in exercitio predicto vicem suam exercuisset ad ponem
[?] per quindicem dies, cum pacto quod elapsis XV diebus, prefatus ser Iacobus
possit artem suam exercere[32] cum quocumque, cum pacto etiam quod dictus

ser Iacobus teneatur redire ad prestandum operas suas dicto Iohanni quotiens-
cumque per dictum Iohannem requiritur finire [?] infra octo dies. Dictus vero
Iohannes teneatur dare dicto presbitero Iacobo pro forma foliorum mille solidos
X et quando[33] excederet mille folios, solidos 14 p[icciolis] pro forma ut supra./ . . .

    11.   ASF, Notarile antecosimiano, 20496 (ser Niccolò di Guido del
           Trincia, 1487–1490), fols. 170r–171r.

Item[34] postea dictis anno [1490], indictione et die quinta predicta [mensis
novembris], actum in curia Mercantie de Florentia, presentibus ser Michaele
olim ser Nicholai de Catignano et ser Monte Bonaventure Francisci civibus et
notariis florentiniis testibus,

    Tomas olim Luce Betti aromatarius pro se et suis sociis aromatariis ad
Sanctum Polinarem de Florentia et pro quilibet suis sotiis ad cautelam de nat.
et nat. habitis, promisit se facturum alias etc., et Antonius eius frater carnalis
pro omni suo interesse si quod haberet, et quilibet dictorum Tomasii dictis nominibus et Antonii insimul, in solidum et de per se et cum meliori modo etc.,
attendentes ad quandam assertam comparitionem et assertam protestationem,
que dicitur facta in curia Mercantie civitatis Florentiae predicta et intenta in ea
sub die tertia pascatis mensis novembris seu alio veriori die per Rainaldum Petri
de Fabriano assertis modis et nominibus in dicta asserta protestatione contentis,
et attendentes etiam ad quandam aliam procurationem et mandatum per eos
factam in dictos Rainaldum et Baptistam eius fratrem seu in alterum ex eis,
de quo seu qua rogatus fuit ser Pierus ser Mariani Cechi notarius florentinus,
et volentes omnem contumaciam et moram evitare ut ne in aliquam incu[r]rint
vel incurri possint quominus [?] credenti [?] possit incorre, tamen ad omnem
habundantiorem cautelam et ad omnem meliorem iuris effectum et ad omnem
alium meliorem modum, non revocando etc., denuo fecerunt et constituerunt
eorum dictis nominibus procuratores dictum Rainaldum dictis nominibus et
dictum Batistam eius fratrem et quemlibet eorum in solidum, licet absentem,
nominatim ad exigendum et finiendum omnes et ab omnibus debitoribus dicto
Rainaldo dictis nominibus alias quandocumque et quocumque modo assign-
atis per eos seu alterum ex eis, et presertim ab infrascriptis infrascriptas quan-
titates, licet a

    Felice cartolario . . . li. 5 s. 4
    Francisco Dominici cartolario . . . li. 26 s. 5
    Filippo Dominici cartolario . . . li. 79 s. 14
    Dominico Bartolomei . . . li. 5 s. 4
    Francisco Andree . . . li. 14 s. 15
    Angelo de Puppio . . . li. 3 s. 10
    Dominico Parigi . . . li. 68 s. 10
    Iohanne Nicholai . . . li. 9 s. 2
    Heredibus Bartolomei Tucci . . . li. 61
    Heredibus Angeli Iohannis . . . li. 37 s. 13

Iacobo Masii . . . li. 8

Guidone Francisci de Mannellis . . . li. 23 s. 6

Cappone Bartolomei de Capponibus . . . li. 4 s. 6

Heredibus Laurentii Peri . . . li. 46 s. 16 d. 6 /

Nicholao Laurentii inpresore li. quingentas nonaginta unam s. XVI d. 4 . . . li. 591 s. 16 d. 4

Domino Christofero de Pratoveteri li. quadringentas sexaginta nonas s. VIIII d. VIII . . . li. 469 s. 9 d. 8

Heredibus Bartolomei Antonii . . . li. 2

Iohanne Luce . . . li. 7 s. 13

Bartolomeo Dominici . . . li. 17 d. 14

Iohanne Dominici . . . li. 10

Antonio Nicholai . . . li. 3. 3.

Bartolomeo Iohannis li. LXXXVI. 15 . . . li. 86 s. 15

Francisco Berlinghieri . . . li. 6 s. 5

Et etiam [?] ad omnem habundatiorem cautelam et casu quo opus sit, prefati Antonius et Tomas dictis nominibus constituerunt eorum procuratorem ut supra prefatos Fa[b]rianenses ad exigendum in alia parte seu in alia manu a dicto Nicholao Laurentii teutonicho inpressore pro computo Moralium Sancti Gregorii libras[35] tremila quingentis octuaginta tres, licet libras 3583, et propterea et pro predictis omnibus ad agendum etc., item ad faciendum capi et tangi et staggiri et tactum sive capturam et staggite licentiam, item ad intrandum in tenutam et petendum in solutionem etc., item ad revocandum et revocari petendum et faciendum bullectinum et salvumconductum et securitatem quascumque, item ad substituendum et ad exigendum et exigi faciendum ut supra, et ad faciendum contra predicta vel aliquod predictorum omnia necessaria et opportuna. Et hoc ideo inter alia fecerunt et fecisse dixerunt quia debitores prefati a dictis de Fabriano neutra [?] expectant quia occasione mercantiarum illorum de Fabriano eisdem debitoribus per dictos Tomasium et socios sive per dictum Tomasium datarum et venditarum debitores a[s]sisterint prefati omnes ut supra descript[um], que omnia etc., pro quibus omnibus etc., rogantes.

12. ASF, Notarile antecosimiano, 9992 (ser Giuntino di Lorenzo
      Giuntini, 1493), fol. 55r.

1493.[36]

Item postea dictis anno, indictione et die martis XIII[37] augusti, actum Florentie in archiepiscopali palatio florentino, presentibus domino Bartolomeo de Redditis et Luca de Buonaccursis et ser Antonio Dominici de Tubinis et aliis.[38]

Cum sit quod magister Nicolaus Laurentii stampator librorum vendiderit ser Francisco Honofrii de Buonaccursis clerico florentino ibidem presenti etc.[39]

duo torcularia et quasdam "madre[s] di stampa" pro stampariolo, libras VII stanni [?] et guisas pro pretio florenorum sexdecim cum dimidio larghorum, prout de predicta constat scripta privata[40], et cum sit quod dictus ser Franciscus asserat dictas madres non esse iustas et bonas, eapropter dictus ser Franciscus ex una [parte] et dictus Nicolaus ex alia [parte], omni modo per se et eorum et cuiuslibet eorum fratrum [heredes] etc., devenerunt ad infrascriptam concordiam, videlicet quod dicte madre[s] videantur [?] per Iohannem de Maguntia et magistrum Antonium de Mosominis [sic] de Mutina, [?] et declaretur per eos an dicte madre[s] sint iusta et bona et vera, et si ab eis [?] declaratum quod dicte madre[s] non essent bona et iusta, ex tunc dictus magister Nicolaus promisit dicto ser Francisco presenti eas [?] reactare et bonas facere ...

NOTES

INTRODUCTION

1. Scapecchi (2014).
2. Füssel (2013); Haebler (1924).
3. Baurmeister (1990); Romani (1982); Rouse and Rouse (1986).
4. Richardson (2004), p. XI.
5. Goldthwaite (2009), pp. 298–299.
6. Trovato (1998), p. 58.
7. Richardson (2004), pp. 41–42; see also Mattone and Olivari (2006), pp. 706–707.
8. Richardson (2004), pp. 41–42.
9. Harris (2008), especially pp. 487–488; Lowry (1991).
10. Ridolfi (1965), p. 144, n. 2.
11. Some stationers, like Vespasiano da Bisticci, also became members of the Arte dei galigai, the guild of leather workers, especially if they worked with parchment.
12. Ciasca (1922), p. 452 (commissions for the professional brokers, the *sensali*, for the different types of paper from Colle Valdelsa or Fabriano, 1436); see Ciasca (1927), pp. 371, 377. The products traded by the *speziali* were also listed in the custom rules (BNCF, II.IX.154, fols. 39v–44v). Some material on the druggist Federico di Stefano Porcellini, "speziale al Porcellino," with the inventory of his shop and the prices for paper, can also be found in ASF, Ospedale di Santa Maria Nuova, 1234, fols. 117v–118r (2 May 1491). Good introductions into the apothecaries' profession are Astorri (1989) and Shaw and Welch (2011).
13. ASF, Manoscritti, 539. The consuls were elected every four months, but in these elections the guild "subjects" certainly did not have the same voting rights as the full members.
14. ASF, Arte dei medici e speziali, 49, under the date March 1458: one apothecary was counted among the five consuls, and at least another three among the twenty-five members of the general council. Members had to pay to pay their fees every three months; otherwise they were inscribed in the book of the debtors (*specchio*); see Chellini da San Miniato (1984), pp. 201–202.

15. On the earliest religious confraternity of the Florentine stationers, see Fumagalli (2019), pp. 159–160, 245–246.
16. Ciasca (1922), p. 410 ("Niuno sottoposto possi porre querela in alcuna corte," 1414).
17. Bertoli (1992).
18. My sincere thanks to Robert D. Black for this information.
19. See, for example, ASF, Mercanzia, 311, fol. 48r.
20. Böninger (2017b).
21. De la Mare (1985), pp. 412–413.
22. Dallai Belgrano (1989), pp. 11, 40.
23. Conway (1999); on this edition, see Harris (2001).
24. Noakes (1981), p. 24; see also Rouse and Rouse (1988), pp. 40–44.
25. Edler de Roover (1953), p. 229.
26. Ganda (2002), pp. 308, 311.
27. Borraccini et al. (2013).
28. Burkart (2019), p. 35.
29. Burkart (2019), pp. 36, 43.
30. Burkart (2019), p. 45.
31. Burkart (2019), p. 46.
32. McLean and Gondal (2014).
33. For a similar case and a recent discussion on the personnel employed in a printer's workshop, see Gatti (2018), pp. 115–136.
34. Kent (2002), p. 16.
35. Ridolfi (1968).
36. Bühler (1970); Pollard (1905).
37. Böninger (2002).
38. Many of these "official" compromises were copied in the Mercanzia acts, but the registers from 1464 to 1531 are unfortunately missing; see ASF, Mercanzia, 10785–10786.
39. Brucker (2005), pp. 107–108.
40. Some of the other archival series of the Mercanzia are the "Deliberazioni," "Sentenze e tenute," "Ricorsi," "Accomandigie," "Pegni," and "Depositi."
41. Böninger and Procaccioli (2016); see also Harris (2019).

CHAPTER 1. BERNARDO CENNINI AND HIS FAMILY ENTERPRISE, 1471–1472

1. For a discussion of goldsmiths employed by early printers in Rome, see Modigliani (1989), pp. 62–63.
2. Ganda (2006a), pp. 60–66; Hirsch (1967), p. 19; Veneziani (2004), pp. 18–19 (in 1471 Jenson himself was called the "artis librariae mirabilis inventor").
3. *ISTC* is00481000.

4. "Expressis ante calibe caracteribus, ac deinde fusis literis volumen hoc primum impresserunt." Recently, the first part of this work containing this colophon has been reprinted and translated in Servio (2011).

5. Santi (1997).

6. Palma (1979).

7. Fonzio annotated his copy of the Cennini-Servius, today in the British Library, I C 27010, with many comments. On Fonzio and Cennini, see, for example, Caroti and Zamponi (1974); and Fonzio (2011).

8. Guidetti (2014), p. 162: "riveduto et corretto."

9. Albanese and Bessi (2000), p. 215; see also pp. 215–217, on Cennini's editorial method. On his manuscripts, see De la Mare (1985), pp. 445, 526–529.

10. All the older literature is mentioned in Santi (1997).

11. *Le feste del IV centenario cenniniano* (1871).

12. Manzoni (1882), pp. 241–294. Manzoni, a patriotic aristocrat and scholar from Lugo in Romagna (1816–1889), added in his rather detailed critique that in the very same year (1471), in Bologna, the printer Baldassare Azzoguidi had been described as "in sua civitate artis impressoriae inventor" (p. 280).

13. "Dalla prassi di imprimere sul conio d'accaio i ferri recanti i singoli particolari che, una volta composti insieme, concorrevano a riprodurre una figura o una scritta, gli dovette venire l'idea di velocizzare la scrittura di libri mediante caratteri mobili. Non è da escludere che avesse già avuto sentore dell'invenzione di Johann Gutenberg e degli altri stampatori tedeschi che lo hanno preceduto o affiancato, senza tuttavia conoscerne l'applicazione, che con ogni probabilità inventò autonomamente, contando sul proprio intuito." Liscia Bemporad (2014), p. 68.

14. If the Roman edition of Ulrich Han was previous, Cennini's edition was actually the fourth.

15. Bianca (2015); Cesarini Martinelli (2016).

16. "Emendatiores et pulchrioribus litterarum caracteribus insculptos." Rinuccini (1953), p. 134. On the term *emendare,* see Grafton (2011), p. 41; and Grafton (2020), pp. 48–50.

17. Bernocchi (1974), pp. CIII–CVIII (with reference to ASF, Ufficiali della moneta poi Maestri di zecca, 65, fols. 2r-v, 13v, 64r). Cennini was called a "intagliator ferrorum" or "intagliatore delle stampe pro monetando."

18. The date as referred to in Bernocchi (1974), p. CVII ("die 18 ianuarii 1473") is not correct; ASF, Ufficiali della moneta poi Maestri di zecca, 65, fol. 64r, actually reads "die XVIIII ianuarii 1474" (i.e., 1475 in the modern style). For Domenico's early annual contracts, see ASF, Ufficiali della moneta poi Maestri di zecca, 65, fol. 72v (1 March 1475[1476]). Around 1481 he married, and in 1502 reworked the book cover of the New Testament employed for the Priors' oath; ASF, Notarile antecosimiano, 4834, fol. 24r-v;

Donato and Parenti (2013), p. 230. In 1504 he was in Venice trying to sell jewelry for the Medici (Domenico Cennini to Francesco Fortunati, ASF, Mediceo avanti il Principato, LXIX, 37, and LXXI, 80, 82).

19. ASF, Ufficiali della moneta poi Maestri di zecca, 66, fols. 2v, 15r, 95r–138v.

20. See Bernocchi (1974), pp. 411–412.

21. Liscia Bemporad (2006); on Cennini as a silversmith, see also Caglioti (2001).

22. Carl (1984). Both Betto di Francesco's and Piero di Bartolomeo di Sali's workshops were in Via di Vaccereccia; Romby (1976), p. 70.

23. ASF, Signori e Collegi. Deliberazioni di autorità ordinaria, 88, fol. 64r; this type of document was called a *bullettinum securitatis*.

24. ASF, Mercanzia, 10700, fols. 6r–18r, 30v, 112v–113r; see also ASF, Notarile antecosimiano, 16368, fol. 309r and ASF, Mercanzia, 1478, fols. 418v–419r, and 1479, fols 505v, 510r, for some attempts of Piero Sali to cash in some of his credits. Previously Sali was not only in partnerships with artists such as Maso d'Antonio Finiguerra and Antonio del Pollaiuolo, but had also worked for the Florentine mint from at least 1457 on, as "sententiator et assagiator et extimator"; ASF, Notarile antecosimiano, 20705, fol. 50v.

25. ASF, Catasto, 923, fol. 349r–v. A final setting with Betto di Francesco seems to have been reached only in 1475, see ASF, Notarile antecosimiano, 1199, fols. 136v, 145r, 150r, 156v, 164v; ASF, Notarile antecosimiano, 12758, fols. 52v, 60r, 68v.

26. ASF, Notarile antecosimiano, 4824, fol. 27r; on the other daughter, Lucrezia, who died at the age of thirteen in 1477, see ASF, Monte comune o delle Graticole, Parte II, 3744, fol. 191r. Bernardo Cennini was also a member of the religious confraternity of San Zanobi in the cathedral; ASF, Notarile antecosimiano, 2367, fols. 27v–28r.

27. Guidi Bruscoli (1997), pp. 384, 392.

28. ASF, Signori e Collegi. Duplicati delle deliberazioni in forza di ordinaria autorità, 20, fols. 482r, 502r.

29. ASF, Notarile antecosimiano, 6240, fol. 42r–v. There is no evidence that Cennini's workshop was in the premises of the convent of San Iacopo di Ripoli in Via della Scala, as proposed by Liscia Bemporad (2006), p. 235, and (2014), p. 68. Braccio di Filippo died in September 1479 and, according to his heirs, had been a "rigattiere minuto di farsetti e chalze vechie et simili in Merchato vechio"; ASF, Monte comune o delle Graticole, Copie del Catasto, 82, fol. 697r.

30. "Quattuor et quadraginta volumina Servorum grammaticorum impressa, non manu scripta, super expositione operum Virgilii Eineidos, Bucolicorum et Georgiarum"; ASF, Notarile antecosimiano, 2308, fols. 217v, 218r–v, quoted in Böninger (2003), p. 226, n. 4.

31. Ulivi (2002), pp. 25–26, 101.
32. ASF, Notarile antecosimiano, 16266, fol. 4r–v. Agostino left Florence in company of a weaver from Trento who later returned to Florence; ASF, Notarile antecosimiano, 4829, fol. 107r.
33. ASF, Mercanzia, 314, fols. 47r (23 August 1474) and 100r (18 November 1474).

CHAPTER 2. GIORGIO DI NICCOLÒ BALDESI, GIOVANNI DI PIERO DA MAGONZA, AND PARTNERS, 1470–1473

1. *ISTC* ip01032780, ib00739000, id000496000, and ip00393300; see Rhodes (1998), nn. 534, 130, 249, 492.
2. Pietrobon (2018), p. 64, counts ten editions until around 1520.
3. See Bühler (1960), p. 40, and plate IIIa.
4. Kirkham (2001), pp. 14–20; see also Semenzato (2013), pp. 49–50, 53–54, on the curious fact that the Venetian edition of 1472 claims to have come out only one week after Giovanni di Piero's. In 1479 the Venetian edition of the *Filocolo,* imported by Giovanni da Colonia and to be sold by the stationer Zanobi di Mariano, was valued at four *lire;* Archivio degli Innocenti, Florence, 11655, Badia di Fiesole, Libro di debitori e creditori, 1456–1484, fol. 197, left.
5. Bertolini (1982, 1985, 1988). Still other manuscripts are mentioned in Bertolini (1984).
6. Bertolini (1982), pp. 691–692, 694–696; Bertolini (1985), pp. 902–910; Bertolini (1988), pp. 419–455, 505–509, 509–513, 516–521.
7. Amelung (1986).
8. Harris (2007), p. 27; the study refers not only to the author's earlier publications on the "survival" of incunabula, and in particular chivalric romances, but contains critical annotations on Hirsch (1967) and other publications.
9. *ISTC* ib00725200, ie00091200, and it00064300; see Rhodes (1988), pp. 15–16, nn. 127, 275, 750. For the first attribution of these editions to Florence, see Scapecchi (1984).
10. Trovato (1998), pp. 55–57.
11. Branca and Nadin (1974). Nevertheless, the *Deo gratias* is still often given to Naples, despite its relation with the codex Hamilton 90—for example, in R. Daniels (2009), pp. 101–103, 120, 187–188, 202.
12. Armando Petrucci (1974).
13. Böninger (2003), pp. 231–233, 241–242.
14. Böninger (2003), p. 233; ASF, Mercanzia, 1476, fol. 69r, for his credit with Giovanni di Domenico ("debitore di lire 30 per libri a lui venduti," 20 October 1472); Mercanzia, 312, fol. 115v (4 November 1472).

15. The Mercanzia acts do not actually identify this edition as the one contended between Florence and Naples and known as *Deo gratias*. In a similar case, however, the Venetian sale of eighteen copies of the Italian translation of Aurelius Augustinus, *De civitate Dei*, in an edition *sine notis* and contended between Florence and Venice (*ISTC* ia01248000), has been used as an argument to strengthen the hypothesis that this edition was in fact of Venetian origin; Dondi and Harris (2016), p. 260, n. 38.

16. Scapecchi (2007); Scapecchi (2013). See also Scapecchi (2017), p. 142, for BNCF 542: "[Firenze?: Tip. del Terentius, Pr. 6748, (Niccolò di Lorenzo per Antonio di Guido?), ca. 1470-1471?], 2°, rom."; p. 396, for BNCF 2757: "[Firenze?: Tip. del Terentius, Pr. 6748, Lorenzo di Niccolò per Antonio di Guido, ca. 1470-1471]. 4°, rom." (*sic*).

17. Montecchi (2015), p. 215: "Lorenzo di Niccolò della Magna" (*sic*).

18. Recently it has been argued that Giovanni di Piero da Magonza was identical to a well-known printer in Basel, Johannes Petri from Langendorf (1441-1511), but this hypothesis must be sternly refuted; Bernacchioni (2009). I find this *lapsus calami* already in Steinberg (1996), p. 21.

19. ASF, Notarile antecosimiano, 15668, fol. 77r (the identification of the protagonists is difficult because the printer in this document was named only as "Iohannes Pieri teutonichus" and in Florence there were many individuals with this name). Consiglio di Paolo d'Andrea's Catasto returns from 1469 and 1480, in the latter case without any mention of Lisabetta and his son-in-law, can be found in ASF, Monte del Comune, Copie del Catasto, 11, fol. 175r; ASF, Monte del Comune, Copie del Catasto, 12, fol. 209r. He was present at his parish meetings in 1480 and 1483; ASF, Notarile antecosimiano, 4029, fols. 309r-310r, 344v-345r; ASF, Notarile antecosimiano, 4030, fol. 168r-v.

20. Archivio dell'Opera del Duomo, Florence, Atti battesimali, 1, fol. 214. My sincere thanks to Karl Schlebusch for this reference.

21. Conway (1999), pp. 141, 230; Böninger (2019), p. 62.

22. He was no relative of the prominent family of the same name from the quarter of Santa Maria Novella, which until the 1450s held patronage rights over the facade of the church of Santa Maria Novella and ran an important trading company in Venice.

23. ASF, Catasto, 785, fols. 563r-564r.

24. ASF, Arte dei maestri di pietra e legname, 4, fol. 135v.

25. ASF, Ufficiali della moneta poi Maestri di zecca, 65, fol. 10v.: "Georgius Nicolai cartolarius populi Sancti Georgii." In the same year he was also in conflict with the merchant Domenico di Francesco Naldini; ASF, Notarile antecosimiano, 77, fol. 84r. Unfortunately, no account book of Domenico has been preserved in the Naldini family archive, today part of the private Archivio Niccolini.

26. ASF, Catasto, 905, ca. 367r. Later this house was rented out, as a court case from 1487 shows; ASF, Mercanzia, 1531, fol. 113r.

27. ASF, Notarile antecosimiano, 16202, fols. 97r-98r; see also Newbigin (1996), s.v. "Giorgio di Niccolò, *cartolaio.*"

28. ASF, Mercanzia, 4496, fol. 452r-v (the so-called edificio della Nunptiata). See also Henderson (1997), pp. 462-463; ASF, Notarile antecosimiano, 4025, fols. 59r, 104r-v, ad dies 28 novembris 1468, 29 iunii 1469; ASF, Notarile antecosimiano, 13142, fol. 83r; and ASF, Notarile antecosimiano, 13143, fol. 83r. In another meeting of the Annunciation confraternity in November 1470, Baldesi was noted as absent; ASF, Notarile antecosimiano, 13144, fol. 77r.

29. Whereas not very much is known about the banker Salvestro Ceffini, Piero del Massaio's life and work is discussed in Kent and Elam (2015). None of the protagonists has been studied for his role in early printing.

30. Although his birth year is traditionally given as 1440, in the 1469/1470 Catasto he declared himself to be twenty-eight years old (ASF, Catasto, 912, fol. 352).

31. On his biography, see Codazzi (1967); and Roberts (2013), pp. 47-49.

32. ASF, Mercanzia, 1473, fol. 126v: "Die XXII mensis februarii 1471. Dinanzi a vvui messer ufficiale et vostra corte expone [et] dice prefato [?] ser Giovanni di Iacopo Migliorelli notario fiorentino et procuratorio nomine di Francesco di Nicolò Berlinghieri [e] di Piero del Massaio di Iacopo dipintore che egli è certa cossa che insino XX del mese di ottobre dell'anno 1470 o altro più vero tempo decto Francesco et Giorgio di Nicholò cartolaio et decto Piero del Massaro di Iacopo dipintore et Salvestro Ceffini feciono et formarono insieme una compagnia, conventione et pacto, cioè che 'l decto Giorgio fusse tenutto et dovesse cum ogni suo 'ngegno operare sì et in tal modo che condurrebbe a perfectione l'arte di far le scripture formate, et promesso che al tempo che durasse dicta compagnia non darebbe et insegnerebbe decto misterio ad altra persona né parte [?] ad altra persona la vorrebbe, per che dicti compagni e decti Francesco, Piero et Salvestro per la remuneratione di decto Giorgio vellono che la rata [?] di decto Giorgio." The whole document, hastily copied by a notary from Imola, is very difficult to read; unfortunately, this makes its full transcription or edition impossible. In the case of "scripture formare" one could also read "scripture fermare," as the notary often wrote an *e* for an *o*.

33. ASF, Mercanzia, 1473, fol. 127r: "le lectere nette et bene composte et buone tanto [?] in modo che i volumi et libri non arebbono rifiuto [?] per manchamento del compon[i]tore et maestro, et in casso che al decto tempo non si facessi o fusse seghuito quanto è detto, tutti rimassono d'acordo che non s'andassi più inanzi con decta arte, ma fusse [?] et sia finito."

34. Ciasca (1922), p. 170: "Di punire chi farà immagina gittata in forma."

35. On the terminology, see Schröter (1998), p. 98.

36. ASF, Mercanzia, 1473, fol. 127r: "et che la verità fu et è che 'l dicto Giorgio cartolaio non tirò inanzi decta arte né dette la sua perfectione in dicto tempo come di sopra si nomina [?], cioè insino a dì primo di setembre, et in quella non misse alchuna industria che dicta arte si condusse in dicto tempo a perfectione, et aver ciò fato expressamente negò et nega dicto ser Iohanni [Migliorelli] dicti nomi, il perchè vene et si[a] venuto el casso che quella è finita et doversi et debbassi finire con più vantagio si potesse."

37. ASF, Notarile antecosimiano, 9488, fol. 13v, quoted in Böninger (2003), p. 237, n. 54.

38. ASF, Mercanzia, 1473, fol. 127vr.

39. ASF, Mercanzia, 1473, fols. 181r-182v.

40. ASF, Notarile antecosimiano, 19003, fol. 48r. In this document Baldesi was described as living in the parish of San Leonardo (di Arcetri).

41. ASF, Mercanzia, 310, fol. 56v, quoted in Böninger (2003), p. 238, n. 55.

42. ASF, Mercanzia, 1473, fols. 274r-275r: "con questo salvo et limitato che la caxa di decto Zorso tolse a pixone per fare lo exercicio fuor de la porta, ne la qual habita dicto Zorzo familiarmente, che dicto Zorzo abii per atenere et abitare per insino a tutto de mense de octobre futuro senza prezo abii a pagare alcuna cosa a Francesco [Berlinghieri] o altri" (fol. 275r).

43. ASF, Notarile antecosimiano, 4026, ad diem.

44. It is presently not possible to determine the exact location of the house; for the many peasants residing in this neighborhood, see ASF, Catasto, 1108, fols. 288r-344r (1487-1491); for the parish church and its two adjoining houses see ASF, Catasto, 989, fol. 383r (1478). Then, as now, numerous Florentine families possessed farms and villas on Via San Leonardo.

45. "Cumque ipse Iohannes Gulielmus repertus fuerit non solum esse magister sed nec etiam laborator in ipsa arte stampandi ut supra, nec esse ipse Iohannes Gulielmus in ipsa arte expertus prout si expedieret probabitur"; Ganda (2006), p. 75.

46. Böninger (2003), pp. 236-237, 246-248. On this company, which was also run by Piero di Giovanni Capponi, see Buonguglielmi's declaration to the Catasto in 1469; ASF, Catasto, 915, fol. 477r. His testament in Antonio Manetti's hand is in ASF, Notarile antecosimiano, 1795, fols. 48bisr-50r; cf. ASF, Notarile antecosimiano, 16368, fols. 89r-94v.

47. ASF, Mercanzia, 4470, fol. 270r-v: "per pigione di casa."

48. Böninger (2003), p. 246 and n. XX ("scritta overo obregho").

49. ASF, Mercanzia, 1476, fol. 552r: "per panno dato più tempo fa"; see also the final sentence on 18 February 1473 in Böninger (2003), pp. 247.

50. ISTC ip00393300: "MAGISTER:IHOANNES:PETRI://DEMAGONTIA :SCRIPSIT:HOC://OPUS:DIE:XXII:FEBRUARII."

51. BMC, p. 618.

52. ASF, Mercanzia, 4470, fol. 24r ("Dui libri: una Spera e Trionfi del Petrarcha"). The confiscation was ordered on the grounds of a previous sentence of the silk merchants' guild, the Arte di Por Santa Maria. The copy of the *Trionfi* preserved in the British Library was once owned by a certain ser Iacopo di Luca Migliorelli (*BMC*, p. 618), a notary of the Mercanzia who has left five registers (ASF, Notarile antecosimiano, 14187-14192).

53. On Vagnucci, who was also in relations with the Ripoli press, see Conway (1999), pp. 105, 108, 110, 146; and Sebregondi (2005), pp. 73-77.

54. "I° Valerio Maximo, e Trionfi del Petrarcha, et la Spera, et la Rettorica de Tulio volgare, et Sermoni de Sancto Agostino et e Trenta gradi tamquam bona Banchi Filippi Banchi aurificis datis in pignus dicto domino Matteo pro florenis quinque larghis"; ASF, Mercanzia, 313, fol. 8r. Two official valuers of the Mercanzia were called to estimate the prize of these books, which were curiously counted as only four; maybe some of them were bound together.

55. See Cambi (2015). Saint Augustin's *Sermones duo de resurrectione mortuorum* had been printed in Cologne around 1470-1471, but the reference is too general to identify the edition.

56. ASF, Catasto, 822, fols. 119r-120r: "e tutti siamo sanza aviamentto, tutte le fanciulle sono sanza dotta." For Banco's tax declaration in the Catasto of 1469, see ASF, Monte comune o delle Graticole, Copie del Catasto, 81, fol. 335r. For chronological reasons he cannot be the "Bancho orafo" quoted in a document from 1449; Poggi (1988), vol. 2, p. 91.

57. ASF, Signori e Collegi. Deliberazioni di ordinaria autorità, 20, fols. 300v, 301v.

58. ASF, Monte Comune o delle Graticole, Copie del Catasto, 84, fol. 117r; ASF, Notarile antecosimiano, 4829, fols. 55r-v, 106r-107r, 127v-128r, 139r; 4831, under the day 17 March 1479(80). For his shop see Romby (1976), p. 70.

59. Liscia Bemporad (2002), p. 195, n. 27; Draper (1983).

60. ASF, Arte dei giudici e notai o Proconsolo, 215, fol. 22r: "per lavoro."

61. ASF, Mercanzia, 1483, fol. 98v; ASF, Mercanzia, 7236, fols.130v-131r; ASF, Mercanzia, 4473, fol. 290r-v.

62. ASF, Notarile antecosimiano, 2308, fol. 245v: "actum Venetiis in populo Sancti Salvatoris et in domo magistri Niccolai impressoris librorum." On the question of Jenson's workshop, see Dondi (2016), pp. 11-13.

63. Conway (1999), p. 215: "cento lettere per mini picini et tre grandi et tre piastruccie di fogliame per istampare." See also Olocco (2017), p. 55. ASF, Notarile antecosimiano, 4355, under the date 5 December 1482.

64. ASF, Mercanzia, 1527, fol. 95v.

65. By early 1476 Baldesi had certainly left his house on the Costa di San Giorgio, of which an inventory was drawn up; all objects were deposited with a certain silk weaver named Bartolomeo di Guasparre, who had been

Baldesi's procurator from late 1472 onward. The inventory listed, apart from several pieces of art, also a wooden chest which contained parts or drawings of his constructions: "I° casone a due serami d'albero grande finito chonfito, dentrovi fatture e più chosse di 'difici e maserizie di chosse d'inportanza'"; ASF, Notarile antecosimiano, 4028, fol. 113r.

66. At the beginning of the fourteenth century, at Poggiosecco alone, eight mills were active; Valenti (1999), p. 179. On Poggiosecco, see Dini (1897), pp. 18–19, n. 1. A century later, Mona Bartolomea di messer Antonio degli Alberti produced paper at Poggibonsi for the Florentine monastery of Santa Brigida del Paradiso (ASF, Monastero di S. Brigida detto del Paradiso, 277, fol. 81v), and later her family donated the property with an "edificio atto a macinare e al gualcare panni e da carte" at Poggiosecco to the monastery itself; ASF, Notarile antecosimiano, 18510, fols. 221r–222v: "unam domum cum edifitiis aptam ad faciendum foleos et cartas de papiro," 13 July 1420; ASF, Podestà, 4392, final sentence, 1428; Pirillo (2015), p. 275. In the 1427 Catasto, at least one "chartaio a Poggiosecho chomune di Poggibonsi" can be identified; ASF, Catasto, 104, fol. fol 434r.

67. Zaccaria (2015), pp. 496–498. A new mill for Santa Brigida was also planned (or built) in the location of Pian di Campi; ASF, Diplomatico, 16 July 1446 (Normali, San Bonifazio); see also Valenti (1999), pp. 330, 348, 351. According to the 1478 Catasto, the monastery of San Michele di Marturi possessed only one mill, but it remains dubious as to whether it also produced paper; ASF, Catasto, 989, fols. 159v–160v.

68. ASF, Notarile antecosimiano, 9172, under the date 6 May 1476 (but in a fascicle that contains acts from 1470): "libras viginti accie albe in matassis et gomitolis et libras quatuor accie crude etiam in matassis et gomitolis." Another notarial act from 1474 recorded Baldesi as obliged to pay for some metalwork for the religious oratory of Santa Maria outside the city walls of Poggibonsi; ASF, Notarile antecosimiano, 16845, ca. 134v.

69. For its use in pillows, see, for example, the letter of Antonio di Niccolò Mazzanti to Lorenzo de' Medici, 6 February 1473(1474), in ASF, Mediceo avanti il Principato, XXV, 237.

70. ASF, Signori e Collegi. Deliberazioni in forza di ordinaria autorità, 93, fol. 209v: "31 martii 1475. Pro domina Lisabetta filia Consilii Pauli et uxore Iohannis Pieri de Maghanza ut supra, Damiano Mattei Cionisi, et facta fuit commissio notarii Zenobio Simonis mazerio dominorum qui retulit se die prima aprilis notum eidem dom(o sua) etc." The acts of the court of the Podestà for this year are incomplete, and his "Atti civili" for the quarters of Santa Croce and Santo Spirito are missing. A month later, Damiano di Matteo di Cione was elected one of the spies of the Zecca ("explorator et minister secretus in dicta zecca"); ASF, Ufficiali della moneta poi Maestri di zecca, 65, fol. 66r, 27 April.

71. This crisis is generally attributed to an overproduction of titles; for a refutation of this thesis, see, for example, Monfasani (1994).

72. Palmieri (1982), p. 43: "Per certo è vero che chi non cerca non truova, e quando le cose sono trovate ognuno n'era maestro."

CHAPTER 3. WOOL TRADE AND PRINTING

1. ASF, Mercanzia, 1503, fols. 375v–376r, 411v, 437v. The case is interesting for the scribe's position; he felt defrauded by the price, considered far too low; on him, see De la Mare (1985), pp. 425, 494; ASF, Notarile antecosimiano, 2075, fol. 42r–v (ser Francesco's election as notary in 1465). On Zanobi di Mariano, see Levi d'Ancona (1962), pp. 270–274.

2. ASF, Mercanzia, 1507, fol. 220v; ASF, Mercanzia, 1507, 7261, ad diem 10 iulii (the final sentence).

3. Bec (1984), pp. 110, 186–187; Verde (1987), pp. 60–61.

4. ASF, Mercanzia, 7304, ad diem 14 decembris 1489: "uno breviario scripto di penne di charta pechora."

5. Allaire (1990–1991); around 1511 / 1512 he also copied a Florentine "priorista"—now BNCF, Conventi soppressi da ordinare, Badia, ms. 3 (striscia 2). For Giorgio's other son "Pierus Georgii Niccolai Guidonis Baldesi cartolarius et miniator," see Levi d'Ancona (1962), pp. 224–226; Bertoli (1992), p. 139, n. 17.

6. Hoshino (1980), pp. 231–303; see also Munro (2012), pp. 123–124.

7. Hoshino (1980), p. 256; De' Medici (2010), p. 187. Although forbidden, the "truck system"—that is, that of paying the wool workers' wages in kind (wool)—was very common in Florence; De Roover (1968), pp. 284, 304–305.

8. ASF, Notarile antecosimiano, 2201, fol. 89r.

9. Marchetto (2011), pp. 57–58; for another example from Vicenza, see Pinto (2019), p. 230.

10. Padgett and McLean (2002), p. 18, n. 53.

11. Cotrugli Raguseo (1990), pp. 150–156.

12. Boschetto (2005), pp. 701–702.

13. See, in general, Astorri (1988); and Legnani Annichini (2013).

14. *Statuti* (1934), pp. 637–639 (for the law of December 1470).

15. ASF, Mercanzia, 310, fol. 31r; ASF, Mercanzia, 313, fols. 97r–98v. In the 1480s, no fewer then twelve marriage brokers received public approval; ASF, Mercanzia, 323, fol. 118r; ASF, Mercanzia, 324, fol. 62r; ASF, Mercanzia, 328, fol. 42r.

16. ASF, Provvisioni. Registri, 167, fols. 225v–229r. In the fourteenth century, the number of the wool brokers was considerably higher; Atwell (2006), p. 184.

17. Monducci and Canova (2004), p. 14: "Sembra insomma che qui sia effettuata una parte del pagamento allo stampatore per l'*Algorismo;* infatti seconda una prassi ben diffusa ai tempi i tessuti potevano essere usati in luogo del denaro contante."

18. Ganda (2017), pp. 2, 63, 186–187 (doc. 22).

19. See Van der Haegen (2001), p. 66, on the "Große Handelsgesellschaft."

20. This was, of course, already true for handwritten books; see Pinelli (2020).

21. *ISTC* ip00420000. On this text, see Pseudo-Petrarch (2015).

22. ASF, S. Jacopo di Ripoli, 4, no. 17, cited in Nesi (1903), pp. 61–62 (see also p. 20). Flannery (1989), p. 126, misunderstands this document as a printing contract for a hypothetical second edition.

23. Conway (1999), p. 38, n. 105, correctly writes that "there would have been no reason to record" the production of the 1478 Sallustius in the "diary" because it was probably registered in the account book of the stationer Bartolo di Domenico. One of Bartolo's partners could have been Giraldo di Francesco d'Antonio Giraldi, who was a close friend of Bartolomeo Fonzio and himself wrote in a humanist hand; ASF, Mediceo avanti il Principato, XV, 80. He also collected and copied humanist manuscripts; De Robertis and Miriello (1997), pp. 18, n. 7, and 30–31, n. 43. In the 1480 Catasto his father declared that he had no occupation ("Giraldo suo figluolo d'età d'anni 25, sanza exercitio"); ASF, Monte comune o delle Graticole, Copie del Catasto, 102, fol. 145r. In 1496 he became one of the officials of the Florentine University.

24. *ISTC* ib01288250.

25. Rustichi and Giraldi were *lanaiuoli* in the San Martino convent: Archivio Michon Pecori (Villa Calavria, Comeana), Fondo Giraldi, n.s. 350, Debitori e creditori di Francesco di Antonio Giraldi, 1476–1485, fols. 51, 76, 77, 113 (always left and right); on their partnership, see also ASF, Monte comune o delle Graticole, Copie del Catasto, 102, fol. 144v.

26. Some information on him is in Passerini (1861), table 11 (where the date of his death is wrongly given as 1491, though he was still mentioned in 1496). His father's house was originally on the back of the later Palazzo Rucellai before being incorporated into the new building; Mack (1974). In 1476 Cipriano lived on the Canto de' Tornaquinci on the corner of Via Tornabuoni and Via Strozzi when he ordered a painted tabernacle; Ciampaglia (2009), pp. 165–166. He also possessed the "tavern of the Oak" in Pinzidimonte, close to Prato; ASF, Notarile antecosimiano, 4828, fol. 55r.

27. ASF, Monte comune o delle Graticole, Copie del Catasto, 66, fol. 196r–v.

28. ASF, Mercanzia, 10216, fols. 183v, 185v.

29. ASF, Mercanzia, 7298, under the dates and 7 July and 10 July 1488.

30. ASF, Mercanzia, 1506, fol. 468v; see Cipriano's reply on fol. 508v.

31. ASF, Mercanzia, 326, fol. 16v.

32. ASF, Mercanzia, 1531, fols. 573v-574r. Various other debts had to be settled in 1488 and 1489 when Cipriano was still adressed as a "prudens vir"; ASF, Notarile antecosimiano, 7221, fasc. V-VI. In 1491 he had to face a confiscation in court (ASF, Mercanzia, 329, fol.182r), and until the summer of 1494 had to sell real estate to pay his debts (ASF, Ospedale di Santa Maria Nuova, 5637, fols. 260v-261). In his *ricordanze,* Rucellai (2013) mentions Cipriano only very briefly on p. 10.

33. Cagni (1969), p. 133, n. 1; Manetti (1983), ad indices. In 1445 Tani had been Giannozzo Manetti's procurator at the *Monte comune;* ASF, Notarile antecosimiano, 9700, fol. 67r.

34. Their partnership did, however, end in a long and bitter lawsuit.

35. Boschetto (2004), p. 194, n. 37.

CHAPTER 4. IN THE SERVICE OF THE
MERCANZIA, 1464-1475

1. This was his signature in the *volgare* translation of Petrus de Crescentiis known as *Il libro della agricultura* (15 July 1478; *ISTC* ic00973000).

2. Orlandi (1722), pp. 131-132. A modern reprint of this edition was published (with an introduction by Paolo Tinti) by Forni in 2005.

3. In a recent overview on early Florentine printing, however, "Nicolaus Laurentii, Alamanus" and "Nicolò di Lorenzo" have still been considered as two different typographers; Bonifati (2008), table A.4.

4. Rother (1921), pp. 78-80.

5. *BMC,* pp. 624-631.

6. Rhodes (1988), ad indices. Both the *GW* and the *ISTC* can be consulted online; their data are subject to constant modification.

7. Bettarini (2015); Myśliwski (2015). There were also direct contacts between both towns; in early 1440, for instance, the city of Breslau warned the Florentines of the arrival of four counterfeiters of coins (BNCF, Ms. Panciatichi, 148, fol. 122r).

8. On 26 January 1475 and for certain private reasons ("ex certa eius scientia et non per errorem"), "Nicolaus Laurenzii teutonichus domicellus" renounced his post in favor of his successor, a man from Verona (ASF, Notarile antecosimiano, 4358, fascicle 6, ad diem).

9. On their dress, see ASF, Mercanzia, 280, ad diem 8 iulii 1448.

10. ASF, Mercanzia, 261, fol. 23r ("Quod domicelli eligendi sint periti in licteris et sciant legere"). From 1435 on, the same abilities were also required, for example, from the messengers of the wool guild; ASF, Arte della lana, 51, fol. 92r-v.

11. For his last mission, see ASF, Mercanzia, 312, fol. 80v (25 September 1472).

12. In the second part of the fifteenth century, foreigners and "miserables" were often exempt from the Catasto assessments if they "composed" their tax payments with the Ufficiali del Monte.

13. ASF, Notarile antecosimiano, 8873, fols. 159v–160r.

14. ASF, Notarile antecosimiano, 2609, ad diem 16 aprilis 1472. It was quite common for German immigrants to acquire their first real estate with dowry funds. Niccolò's close relation with two woodworkers from the same parish of Sant'Ambrogio, Giovanni and Bartolomeo d'Ulivante di Bartolomeo, after 1471 might in fact derive from parental links; Böninger (2003), p. 230. A later claim, from 9 October 1481, that Niccolò's house lay in the neighboring parish of San Pier Maggiore is certainly an error; see Böninger (2016), p. 114.

15. ASF, Mercanzia, 1476, fol. 233r–v (against Casino di Stagio *filatoiaio,* "lire 4 per pigione d'una casa").

16. See Böninger (2002), p. 104. The last name and origin of Mona Domitilla are unknown.

17. On this monastery, see Lowe (2003).

18. It cost ninety florins and was described as a "domus cum curia, puteo, orto, cella, salis et cameris posita in civitate Florentie et in Via Ghibellina et in populo Sancti Ambrosii"; ASF, Notarile antecosimiano, 2344, fol. 65r.

19. For Andrea's Catasto returns in 1470 and 1480, see ASF, Catasto, 915, fol. 103r (where he still named the Benci as his neighbors); and ASF, Monte Comune o delle Graticole, Copie del Catasto, 45, fol. 65r (where the former Benci property was already given to the Murate).

20. ASF, Catasto, 929, fol. 280r (1470); ASF, Monte comune o delle Graticole, Copie del Catasto, 110, fol. 372r (1480, with the testamentary obligations of the Benci toward the Murate); ASF, Notarile antecosimiano, 21022, fols. 15r–16v (a certain priest, ser Piero, was living in the house in 1489 and maybe it was already at the Murate's disposal). Another small Murate property in Via Ghibellina was rented out from 1 November 1486, and this could indeed have been Donato Benci's former house; ASF, Notarile antecosimiano, 14748, fol. 86v. On the general contest, see also Holmes (2000).

21. ASF, Mercanzia, 1476, fols. 462r–v; ASF, Mercanzia, 4470, fols. 216r, 531v–532r; ASF, Mercanzia, 4472, fols. 138v–139v; ASF, Mercanzia, 7233, fol. 383; ASF, Mercanzia, 7234, fol. 2v–3r, 8v–9v, 52r–v; ASF, Mercanzia, 7235, fol. 190r.

22. Brown (2002), pp. 367–368. Giovanni di Filippo's residence in the early 1470s is not clear.

23. ASF, Mercanzia, 1477, fols. 79v–80r, 81r, 492r–49r; ASF, Mercanzia, 7233, fol. 304r–v. Giovanni di Matteo Benizi's two brothers worked as apothecaries ("speziali") in Prato; ASF, Mercanzia, 1483, fol. 190v.

24. ASF, Otto di Guardia e Balìa della Repubblica, 224, fol. 84r; ASF, Giudice degli appelli e nullità, 84, fols. 297r–298v; ASF, Balie, 29, fol. 96r.

25. Mallett (1967), pp. 71, 171; for the correct name see ASF, Notarile antecosimiano, 15035, fol. 31v; 13954, 30v. Following in his father's footsteps, in March 1470 he entered the Cloth Merchants' Guild, the Arte di Calimala; ASF, Manoscritti, 542, ad diem 19 martii 1469. In early 1472 he sent a private envoy to Ragusa (Dubrovnik) to claim some credits with a local merchant; BNCF, Palatino, 1103, fol. 140r.

26. Dei (1985), p. 86; for Benizi's relations with Bernardo di Niccolò Capponi, see ASF, Notarile antecosimiano, 3333, fol. 178r; ASF, Mercanzia, 1475, fols. 108v–110r; and ASF, Corporazioni religiose soppresse dal governo francese, 83, 114, fol. 13r. For the restitution of this credit, see ASF, Notarile antecosimiano, 7556, ad diem 13 septembris 1475. Capponi intervened as Benizi's agent also in the Mercanzia; see ASF, Mercanzia, 11796, fol. 73r.

27. From April until the summer of 1478 he was in prison for debts originating from his father-in-law, whose heir Giovanni was; see the "justification" for this imprisonment in ASF, Mercanzia, 10208, fol. 2r–v). See also ASF, Mercanzia, 1502, fols. 75v–76v; and ASF, Mercanzia, 4483, n.s 254, 256, 257. In 1480 Benizi was again shortly imprisoned; see ASF, Mercanzia, 7262, ad diem 16 octobris 1480.

28. ASF, Mercanzia, 1537, fol. 138r. In 1488 Benizi's wife claimed to be her husband's creditor of about six thousand florins; ASF, Mercanzia, 1534, ad diem 19 iunii.

29. ASF, Notarile antecosimiano, 16755, fol. 157v.

30. ASF, Catasto, 994, fols. 396r–397r; ASF, Otto di Guardia e Balia della Repubblica, 61, fol. 99r (unfortunately, the preceding n. 60, regarding November 1481, is missing).

31. ASF, Notarile antecosimiano, 15040, fols. 41r–43v.

32. For his contributions to the public debates in 1495 / 1496, see Fachard (2002), pp. 23, 32, 36, 41, 46, 100, 111.

33. ASF, Soprastanti alle Stinche, 117, fol. 7r.

34. Guidetti (2014), pp. 154–155; his house, Palazzo Benizi, was adjacent to that of the Guicciardini family, and in 1515 was actually sold to them; see Guicciardini and Dori (1952), pp. 35–36.

35. The exact date of this election is unknown, but Domizi was removed from this post before 1 August 1486 (ASF, Notarile antecosimiano, 9986, fol. 55r), only a few months before losing his teaching job at the Florentine university; see Black (2015a), pp. 435–436.

36. Conway (1999), pp. 116–117; see also Rouse and Rouse (1988), p. 38, n. 42. On 26 August 1477 the Otto di Guardia e Balìa of Florence convoked Giovanni di Piero da Magonza under the threat of handing over to Giovanni Benizi a certain contract and a hammer; the fact that this office was involved in such an atypical case seems to suggest that it was not

a purely economic question; for the whole document, see Böninger (2003), p. 231, n. 21.

37. Until 24 January 1475 Niccolò was very frequently mentioned as a legal witness to the decisions of the court; see ASF, Mercanzia, 7238, fols. 2v, 3r, 4r, 7r, 38v, 39r.

38. Tedeschi (1991).

39. Böninger (2006b), pp. 332–333; Böninger (2017a), pp. 23–25; see also ASF, Notarile antecosimiano, 12699, fol. 144v.

CHAPTER 5. THE COLLABORATION WITH GIOVANNI DI PIERO DA MAGONZA, AND MARSILIO FICINO'S *DE CHRISTIANA RELIGIONE*, CA. 1474–1476

1. *GW* 09878.

2. *BMC*, p. 624; but, see also the Staatsbibliothek zu Berlin's "Typenrepertorium der Wiegendrucke" online, https://tw.staatsbibliothek-berlin.de/ma08676.

3. *ISTC* if00150000. In contemporary Florentine collections the Latin and the *volgare* editions were not clearly distinguished; see Alessandrini (2018), pp. 233–234.

4. Ficino (2019), p. 85; Rhodes (1988), p. 62, n. 295; Ridolfi (1968), p. 50; Scapecchi (2017), p. 213. From 1980 on, Ridolfi owned a copy himself, now in his collection at the Fondazione Biblioteche della Cassa di Risparmio in Florence with the signature RID A-A 20. It contains his handwritten note that Della Torre (1902) and Kristeller in his *Supplementum Ficinianum* (vol. 1, pp. LVIII–LIX) had dated this book 1474 instead of 1476, and that this copy is on "carta buona (lo spessore è maggiore di quello degli esemplari comuni). Leg[atura] orig[inale] integra." Ridolfi's copy is furthermore interesting for the bad, nearly diagonal mise-en-page of the dedication letter to Bernardo del Nero; its many print errors; and the watermark, a cardinal's hat.

5. Della Torre (1902), p. 602, n. 2; Kristeller (1937), vol. 1, pp. LVIII–LIX; Ficino (1984), p. 83, n. 64; Verde (1985), part 1, pp. 125–127.

6. On Giovan Battista Nelli, see Verde (2010), ad indices. When he got married in September 1477 in the palace of Lorenzo de' Medici, one of the witnesses was the former printer Bernardo Cennini; ASF, Notarile antecosimiano, 14099, fol. 61v; on the dowry, see ASF, Notarile antecosimiano, 15037, fol. 262v. On Antonio Nelli, see Böninger (2019), pp. 57, 59.

7. Kristeller (1937), vol. 1, pp. 10–12. On this patrician from the Oltrarno region, beheaded in 1497 for his Medicean sympathies, see Arrighi (1990).

8. Ficino (2019), pp. 34–52, 145, especially p. 35, n. 61; Vasoli (1999).

9. Ficino (2019), p. 24, n. 30.

10. Ficino (2019), pp. 52-56; see also p. 68: "L'impressione, rafforzata anche dalla data di una delle lettere unite a un esemplare con correzioni, conservato alla Huntington Library (1477), è che il Ficino abbia corretto quasi subito i passi che abbiamo qui analizzato."

11. Vasoli (2007), p. 405.

12. *BMC*, p. XIV.

13. Olocco (2017), p. 66; Olocco (2019), pp. 121-123. Olocco's description is based on Scholderer's: his 115ra and 115rb is the "Type 4: 114R" in *GW,* used presumably for the first time in the edition of Aristotle's *Ethics.*

14. Conway (1999), pp. 35-36, 108, 110-111, 119; see also Olocco (2017), pp. 66-67. This "Cassino" was the weaver "Casinus olim Michaelis Casini textor drapporum," who worked as a real estate agent of San Iacopo di Ripoli from 1478 on; ASF, Notarile antecosimiano, 16783, fols. 78v, 184r. In the convent diary he was mentioned again in October 1479 and March 1483 when he received printed books but sent them back after one month; Conway (1999), pp. 126, 250. Until at least 1490 he also worked as an agent of the nearby hospital of Santa Maria della Scala; ASF, Notarile antecosimiano, 9911, fol. 9v; ASF, Mercanzia, 1506, fol. 339r-v; ASF, Mercanzia, 4515, r. 314.

15. Haebler (1924), p. 159.

16. A recent description of the thirty-seven known copies of this book is contained in Ficino (2019), pp. 75-84.

17. Gentile (2006), especially pp. 148-156.

18. Bühler (1973).

19. Roberts (2013), pp. 50, 121, erroneously attributes such a role to Francesco di Niccolò Berlinghieri. On the crucial role of correctors or "print professionals" in the printer's shop, see Grafton (2011); and Grafton (2020).

20. Fabbri and Tacconi (1997), p. 172. When Cavalcanti had married in 1469, Ficino was counted among the witnesses (ASF, Notarile antecosimiano, 7554, fols. 165r, 167r-168r). In January 1476 Cavalcanti was recorded as the author of a "protesto di giustizia" (ASF, Signori e Collegi. Duplicati delle deliberazioni in forza di autorità ordinaria, 16, fol. 221r), and later served as one of the "Ufficiali dello Studio" (Verde [2010], ad indices).

CHAPTER 6. CAPPONE CAPPONI AND HIS CIRCLE, 1475-1480

1. Böninger (2002), p. 104. Haebler (1921) interpreted the obligation to present to the printer and/or corrector single copies of a newly printed book as a sort of implicit license to later use these copies as models for further print runs. In the case of the publishers' copies, however, the obligation was also the expression of their pride in having financed these works; the most famous case in this sense is presumably that of Peter Ugelheimer from Frankfurt and his illuminated books set on vellum.

2. "Cappone filius Bartolomei Pieri Bartolomei de Capponibus populi Sancti Frediani de Florentia, quia dictus eius [?] pater pro eo iuravit pro magistro secundum formam statutorum dicte artis die XVII iunii anno Domini millesimo CCCC°XLIIII°, indictione VII.a, existentibus consulibus dicte artis Tommaso Laurentii de Soderinis et eorum collegiis, et quia habet benefitium ex persona dicti sui patris in matricula dicte artis pro magistro matriculati"; ASF, Arte della Seta (Por S. Maria), 8, fol. 47r. In 1473 he was one of the consuls of the guild; ASF, Mercanzia, 311, fol. 31r.

3. The matrimonial contract was signed in the Palazzo Medici on 31 March 1461 and the amount of the dowry was decided by Piero di Cosimo de' Medici; ASF, Notarile antecosimiano, 1742, fol. 121r. For its payment on 17 February 1462, see ASF, Notarile antecosimiano, 21064, fol. 93r.

4. ASF, Notarile antecosimiano, 20097, fol. 99r-v.

5. Several of Capponi's letters to Bastiano di Gentile Guidi in Volterra between 1477 and 1495 can be found in ASF, Guidi, Filze e registri 553. These letters speak of his various economic interests in the zone—for example, mining but not printing.

6. ASF, Mediceo avanti il Principato, XXV, 52 (3 May 1471).

7. Böninger (2002), p. 97. In the Valdelsa, Capponi also dealt with grain; see ASF, Mercanzia, 4468, fol. 3v.

8. Lazzareschi (1942); Tazartes (2007), pp. 136–166.

9. ASF, Podestà, 5235, fols. 468r–470r, 605r–v. For Capponi later selling wine from Lucca, see ASF, Notarile antecosimiano, 7785, fol. 54r.

10. ASF, Catasto, 1001, fols. 217r–218r.

11. ASF, Mediceo avanti il Principato, XXVIII, 446.

12. ASF, Mediceo avanti il Principato, LI, 296 (ser Giovanni Antonio d'Arezzo and ser Niccolò Michelozzi to Lorenzo de' Medici, 9 March 1485 [1486]). Capponi was evidently one of Lorenzo's intermediaries for his dealings with the head of the Altopascio hospital, messer Guglielmo di Niccolò Capponi, who in 1486 conceded him the estates of Agnano and Spedaletto.

13. See Salvestrini (2017), p. 483, where "Capone" clearly stands for Cappone Capponi; see also pp. 178–179 for the historical context. It has to be noted, however, that there were also other family members with the same first name.

14. BNCF, Passerini, 186 (Capponi), fols. 280r–287r. On this text, see Kent (1977), p. 56.

15. Neri di Bicci (1976), p. 243. His full name was Antonio di Mariano di Antonio Ticci; in 1464, after the death of his business partner Nuccio di Luca Buonamici, he had taken over his shop in San Frediano; see ASF, Notarile antecosimiano, 19080, fols. 158r–161v.

16. ASF, Mercanzia, 4469, fols. 8r, 42v, 81r–82v; ASF, Mercanzia, 7224, fols. 21v–22r, 52r–v, 175v–176r. This house lay on the so-called Canto della Cuculia in the parish of San Frediano.

17. Böninger (2002), pp. 105–106 (documents 4 and 5). See also ASF, Mercanzia, 4482, n.s 160, 174 (14 and 18 February 1478): "Antonio di Mariano già spetiale, cessante et fuggitivo colle robe altrui."

18. Sorbelli (2004), p. 268: "mercator in artifitio seu exercitio faciendi et vendendi et alias tractandi super libris ac opere librorum et voluminum librorum."

19. Maybe he can be identified with the "Pittore Compitese," Antonio Corsi; see Tazartes (2007), pp. 99–102.

20. Conway (1999), pp. 162, 200, and p. 52, n. 14, for the proposal to identify "ser Meo prete m'aiuta al torchio" with Bartolomeo de' Libri.

21. ASF, Notarile antecosimiano, 13505, fol. 259r.

CHAPTER 7. PRINTING FOR THE CONVENT OF SANTO SPIRITO, CA. 1476–1477

1. Hirsch (1967), p. 19. The dialectic between printer and publisher has been observed also in other towns—as, for example, in Nuremberg from 1470; Hase (1886).

2. Böninger (2002), pp. 104–105.

3. After receiving his doctorate in Siena (1460), Trotti had been a master at Santo Spirito as early as 1466 (ASF, Notarile antecosimiano, 11653, fol. 210r) and had become prior by 1471. In July 1470 he was listed as one of the members of the Florentine faculty of theology (ASF, Notarile antecosimiano, 15656, fols. 156v–157r). In early 1473 he was involved in a dubious real estate deal with Lorenzo de' Medici (Donato Ugolini to Lorenzo de' Medici, 25 February 1473, ASF, Mediceo avanti il Principato, XXIX, 126), but shortly after was exiled together with two of his colleagues by the Florentine office of the Otto di Guardia e Balìa before eventually returning to Santo Spirito. There he was also a member of the religious confraternity of the Holy Spirit (ASF, Notarile antecosimiano, 19228, fol. 107r). He died after a long career in 1496; see Piana (1977), pp. 181–183; Verde (1985), part 1, p. 28; ASF, Mediceo avanti il Principato, XXIX, 772; and ASF, Mediceo avanti il Principato, XLVI, 237 and 278.

4. Böninger (2002), pp. 99, 105–106. From the notarial acts and the fragmentary documentation in the court of the Podestà a reconstruction of this case is impossible.

5. Caby (2014); Fabbri and Tacconi (1997), ad indices.

6. *ISTC* ia00084000.

7. "Nicolò tedescho scriptore . . . de' dare el detto [dì, at an unspecified date in early 1482], come appare scriptura di sua mano la quale à maestro Andrea [Trotti] d'Allexandria, furono danari prestati per gittare libri in forma d'un certo compatto tra maestro Bernardo da Vulterra et maestro Andrea d'Allexandria con detto maestro Nicolò sopradecto, siché el detto maestro

Nicolò rimane debitore al contrario in fiorini d'oro larghi venticinque: fl. 25 l"; ASF, Corporazioni religiose soppresse dal governo francese, 122, 1, fol. 94, on the left; the whole quotation is also in Böninger (2002), p. 99.

8. For the houses and farms owned by Santo Spirito in December 1478, see ASF, Catasto, 989, fols. 790r-793v (where Niccolò di Lorenzo is not mentioned). It must not be forgotten, however, that Capponi had his family chapel in Santo Spirito, dedicated to San Niccolò, where he ordered that he be buried in 1508 (ASF, Notarile antecosimiano, 20097, fol. 99r-v). Before 1481 Niccolò di Lorenzo was "present" in the Oltrarno region on other occasions, also—for example, in 1479 as a witness to the testament of Guido di Pierpaolo Machiavelli in the parish of Santa Maria sopr'Arno (ASF, Notarile antecosimiano, 2441, fols. 82r-83r).

9. The *incipit* exists in two variants; see *BMC*, p. 626.

10. Bakker and Van den Bercken (2010).

11. Again, it cannot be ruled out that the printer's copy originally came from Guglielmo Becchi. Commonly, the belongings of the deceased Augustinian friars or *conversi* were offered at internal auctions in the convent of Santo Spirito. On these occasions Andrea de' Trotti often acquired, at rather low prices, Aristotelian works or commentaries like that of Walter Burley on the *Ethics;* ASF, Corporazioni religiose soppresse dal governo francese, 122, 61, fols. 181-196; ASF, Corporazioni religiose soppresse dal governo francese, 122, 1, fol. 24, on the left. On the teaching of this text by Guglielmo Becchi and at Santo Spirito, see Lines (2002), pp. 190-191.

12. Bühler (1963), p. 102; Hirsch (1967), p. 114.

13. Ridolfi (1968), pp. 49-50; Bastianoni and Catoni (1988), pp. 22-25.

CHAPTER 8. INSTITUTIONAL AND PRIVATE COMMISSIONS, CA. 1476-1480

1. In *ISTC* ia00214400 this title is attributed to the Ripoli press ("c. 1475-77"); for the traditional attribution to Niccolò di Lorenzo, see Cartei (2017), vol. 2, pp. 801-802.

2. That is, "Type 4*" of the "Typenrepertorium" of the *GW;* "114R" of the *BMC.*

3. *GW:* "Type 4: 114R"; *BMC:* "115Ra."

4. *ISTC* ie00091200; *GW* M34162 (with the attribution to Niccolò di Lorenzo, "um 1480"). See also Amelung (1986), pp. 261, 264; and Rhodes (1988), n. 275.

5. See Emison (2006), p. 434, on Giorgio Vasari's claim that the Florentines invented the technique of engraving.

6. *Claudius Ptolemaeus* (1963), p. V. On the first German engravings, see Stijnman and Upper (2014), p. 96. See also Armstrong (2015); Needham (2009); and Roberts (2019).

7. Gray (2012), vol. 1, pp. 157–181; Zucker (2002).

8. BNCF, Magl. E.2.35 (già Pal. E.6.1.55); see also Scapecchi (2017), p. 104.

9. As much as this may sound like a commonplace, it certainly reflected the reading experience of late fourteenth merchants—for example, Francesco Datini; see Brambilla (2007), especially pp. 192–193, 206.

10. Cf. Corbellini, Hoogvliet, and Ramakers (2015).

11. Gray (2012), vol. 1, pp. 173–174; on Feo Belcari and printing, see also Newbigin (2014), p. 2. One of the reasons why a sponsorship of Belcari of the 1477 edition seems improbable is that he was no merchant; at the time of the printing he was sixty-seven years old. In the year 1476 he had been one of the secretaries of the *Monte comune* ("scribani Montis"); ASF, Notarile antecosimiano, 5029, fol. 108r. It is also unclear why he should have maintained his original dedication from 1449 to Giovanni di Cosimo de' Medici instead of updating it.

12. Dufner (1964) quotes a later copy of the will; see also Gray (2012), vol. 1, pp. 172–173. A first draft of his testament was drawn up on 11 June 1480, after Bettini had received a papal bull that allowed him to do so; see Archivio di Stato, Siena, Notarile antecosimiano, 529, fol. 17v; my sincere thanks to Philippa Jackson, who gave me a reproduction of this document.

13. In a copy of the *Monte sancto* preserved in the British Library, one reads that it was sold by a "fra' Iacopo da Radea" for the considerable price of five lire and some soldi (*BMC*, p. 626).

14. Traditionally the date of 1438 or 1439 is given as that of the move; see Uccelli (1865), pp. 48–50. Pope Eugene's bull is, however, dated five years earlier; ASF, Notarile antecosimiano, 3374, fol. 140r-v; see also ASF, Notarile antecosimiano, 13503, fol. 211r (7 February 1434); and ASF, Notarile antecosimiano, 7362, fol. 19r (12 February 1435).

15. Dufner (1975), p. 302; Gagliardi (2004), p. 366; De Robertis and Miriello (2006), p. 27, n. 55, and table 63.

16. ASF, Notarile antecosimiano, 2344, fols. 63r–64v (1467); general chapter meetings were held every two years. On the 1485 reform, see Gagliardi (2004), p. 462.

17. Neri di Bicci (1976), pp. 317–318; see also Bensi (1980). On the genealogy of Fra Antonio, see Litta (1839), table 11, where he is recorded as "Dell'ordine de' Gesuati nel 1468," with a possible reference to this source.

18. Gagliardi (2004), p. 459, n. 1; ASF, Notarile antecosimiano, 2486, fol. 73r.

19. ASF, Mediceo avanti il Principato, XXV, 360 (18 October 1474); an edited version is in Uccelli (1865), pp. 121–122. On the letter by "Antonio veschovo di Fuligno povero di virtudi" from 1462, see Dufner (1964), p. 408.

20. Lowe (1996), p. 25; Medici (1998), p. 347.

21. ASF, Notarile antecosimiano, 16755, fol. 60r (7 September 1476); ASF, Notarile antecosimiano, 13448, fols. 104v–105v (2 February 1478). In September 1477 "fratte Antonio deli Strozi fratte deli Gesuatti" was recorded as a business partner of the painter Bernardo di Stefano Rosselli; Ciampaglia (2009), p. 209. In June 1479 San Giusto claimed a financial credit with the painter Alessio Baldovinetti, presumably for color, and by then the prior's name had changed again; ASF, Notarile antecosimiano, 10085, fol. 359r (with the names of all friars). Later lists of names of priors and friars from 1482 and 1486 can be found in ASF, Notarile antecosimiano, 12024, fols. 45v–46r; and ASF, Notarile antecosimiano, 12861, fol. 124v.

22. ASF, Provvisioni Registri, 167, fol. 242r-v; ASF, Camera del Comune, Massai di Camera, Debitori e Creditori, 13, fols. 4 (left), 9 (right).

23. In a similar case in the early sixteenth century, the Jesuate convent of Ferrara sponsored the print edition of San Bernardo's *volgare* sermons; see Guerrieri (2015), p. 230 n. 40.

24. For the San Giusto altarpiece and its possible date, see Cadogan (2000), pp. 250–252.

25. Biblioteca Riccardiana, Florence, Riccardiano 3575, pp. 4, 5 (Ricc. 419), 21r (Ricc. 1792, the manuscript used in Uccelli's edition of the rule's order). On the MSS Ricc. 1299, 1342, 1394, possibly 1421 and 1597, see also De Robertis and Miriello (2006), p. 27.

26. Canonici (1995), especially pp. 121–122; Rusconi (1980). On an early manuscript of the *Regola della vita spirituale* from the Franciscan convent of Giaccherino, close to Pistoia, see Zamponi (1988), p. 20.

27. For his presence in Florence in 1466, see ASF, Notarile antecosimiano, 388, fol. 435r; on the Monte di pietà in Prato, see Menning (1993), pp. 51–52.

28. "Ho auto aviso dal padre frate Cherubino predichatore el quale ha predichato qui questa quaresima ed è stato di tanto efichace la sua dottrina che non c'è huomo che no' gl'abia posto singhulare amore, e io chome ignota persona e bisongnoso della sua virtù presi dimestichezza cholla sua paternità, e quanto è 'l bisongnio de l'anima dal chanto suo à sodisfetto ottomamente cholla sua disciprinabile dottrina, pure ch'io la metta preseverando inn opera; et per lla sua innata bontà, non per alchuno mio merito verso di lui né per chomessione gli dessi, vegho la sua charità l'à fatto parlare a Vostra Mangnificenza e circha al mio esulio rachomandatomi a quella, [et] della grata e benigna risposta fatto alla sua paternità ed ezia[n] a Pandolfo Rucellai, della quale quanto più so e posso ringrazio la Magnificenza Vostra" (Giandonato Barbadori to Lorenzo de' Medici, 11 May 1472, ASF, Mediceo avanti il Principato, XXVIII, 90).

29. Verde and Giaconi (2003), pp. 1–5.

30. Petrucci (1977), pp. 108–109; De Robertis and Miriello (2013), p. 30, n. 52, and table 61.

31. Cardini (1970); Verde (2010), ad indices.

32. ASF, Notarile antecosimiano, 4828, fol. 182v: "iuvenis, institor et negotiorum gestor et gubernator." Giovanni di Paolo Rucellai's collaboration with Iacopo di Borgianni had begun prior to 1470; see ASF, Notarile antecosimiano, 21176, fol. 2r; 2200, ad diem 1 martii 1469(70).

33. ASF, Notarile antecosimiano 4836, fol. 6v. Iacopo was the financial guarantor ("fideiussor") of the *signore* of Bologna Giovanni Bentivoglio in 1478 (ASF, Mercanzia, 319, fol. 101r), and also served as the legal representative of university professors from San Gimignano and Bologna (ASF, Notarile antecosimiano, 12022, fol. 66v; ibid., 5029, fol. 129r–v). He furthermore knew Bernardo Pulci, whom he appointed as his own procurator in January 1477 (ASF, Notarile antecosimiano, 4828, fol. 99r). In 1481 Iacopo was among the partners of his family's dying business (ASF, Mercanzia, 7270, ad diem 5 dicembris 1481) and in 1498 acted as Taddeo di Piero Gaddi's procurator selling armor and arms in the Casentino region (ASF, Mediceo avanti il Principato, LXXXIV, 38).

34. As early as 1475 he was one of the legal procurators of the convent; ASF, Notarile antecosimiano, 4028, fols. 62v–63r.

35. Kent (1983); Strocchia (2016). In one of his last occupations in 1500, he served as a scribe for the Monte della pietà (ASF, Monte della Pietà, 724).

36. Guidetti (2014), p. 182: "uno Cherubino legato di quelli di Iacopo di Borganni" (and see p. LXIX, n. 281).

37. ASF, Mercanzia, 1502, fols. 576r–v ("Niccolò di Lorenzo fu donzello della Merchatantia").

38. ASF, Mercanzia, 7253, under the date 7 October 1478.

39. Brown (1979), p. 159.

40. On the first two texts, see Scala (1997), pp. 199–202; Poliziano-Becchi (2012); Tobias Daniels (2013), who demonstrates the posterity of the *Florentina Synodus* with respect to the *Excusatio Florentinorum*. For a review of this work by Daniels, see Simonetta (2015).

41. Celati (2013); Poliziano (2015).

42. Conway (1999), p. 204; for copies in contemporary Florentine libraries, see Alessandrini (2018), p. 250.

43. Murano (2009), pp. 793–794, 826; Vaccaro (2017), p. 250, n. 18. On the reception, see Taurino (2006).

44. On Fonzio's life, see Zaccaria (1988).

45. Sabbadini (1971); Sabbadini (1996), p. 207.

46. Guidetti (2014), pp. LXVI, n. 271, and pp. 21, 49, 95, 181. The first manuscript copy was valued at twenty-five lire.

47. Conway (1999), pp. 144–145; Takács and Tuhári (2015). For a review of this work by Takács and Tuhári, see Muecke (2017).

48. "Summis itaque laudibus in primis inventores litterarum sunt prosequendi, deinde etiam librorum impressores non negligendi. Nam cum

sua industria et labore antiquis ac novis scriptoribus aeternitatem concedant, studiosisque viris in magna librorum copiam non parvam ferant, meritam laudem referre debent." The original spelling has been modernized very cautiously; on this dedication letter, see also Verde (1985), part 1, p. 310.

49. *BMC*, p. 627.

50. De la Mare (1976), p. 170 and n. 88.

51. On this manuscript, see Farbaky et al. (2013), pp. 298–299. See also Verde (1985), part 2, p. 841, on Fonzio's critical attitude toward careless printers in 1489.

52. De la Mare (1976), p. 169.

53. Fiaschi (2015).

54. For Fonzio's "relatively accurate" edition, see, however, Bausi (2011), p. 305.

55. The humanist Giorgio Antonio Vespucci possessed even two copies; see Van Binnebeke (2016), pp. 238–239. On copies in contemporary Florentine libraries, see Alessandrini (2018), pp. 156–157.

56. Orvieto (2017), pp. 60–64.

57. Degl'Innocenti (2010), p. 87.

58. *ISTC* ip01109000. A sixth copy, once in the collection of Giuseppe Martini, in which the missing dedication letter is added in the form of a nineteenth-century reprint, was recently offered on the antiquarian book market; on the manuscripts, see Tavernati (1985).

59. Vecce (2017), p. 198; see also Alessandrini (2018), p. 260.

60. The best biography of Luca Pulci is Decaria (2016).

61. The *ante quem* date of printing derives from the owner's note "1479," i.e., "before 25 March 1480," in the copy of Francesco da Castiglione, canon of San Lorenzo, which is now kept in the Beinecke Rare Book and Manuscript Library at Yale University; see Rao (2006). On the other hand, Donato Acciaiuoli in his earlier *Expositio* twice refers to the "nova traductio" of Argyropoulos, and this convinced the catalogers of the Beinecke Library that he was actually referring to a printed copy of the *Ethics*, and they thus dated their copy to "[c. 1477]."

62. *BMC*, p. 627 ("115a"); *ISTC* ia00981000; *GW* 2361 ("type 4: 114R").

63. ASF, Corporazioni religiose soppresse dal governo francese, 119, 246, fol. 220r; ASF, Corporazioni religiose soppresse dal governo francese, 119, 1048, fol. 159r. My sincere thanks to Robert D. Black for both references.

64. Bigi (1962); Giorgetti (2017), with further references; Lines (2002), pp. 487–489; Verde (1985), part 1, pp. 253, 273–274, and passim.

65. Conway (1999), p. 144; Nesi (1903); Scapecchi (1993); see also Böninger (2003), p. 240, n. 62 (on the possible role of Pierfilippo Pandolfini in its publication); and Lines (2018), pp. 283–286.

66. Davies (2007), pp. 66, 72; on the distribution of the text in contemporary Florentine libraries, see Alessandrini (2018), p. 172. See also Lines (2002), p. 51: "The latter redaction, completed by 1478, was the most popular one. It was printed at least seven times in the fifteenth century, and at least eighty-one times in the sixteenth century. It also continued to be printed in the seventeenth and eighteenth centuries."

67. ASF, Notarile antecosimiano, 7527, fol. 200v; one of the witnesses present at this act was the priest Sebastiano Salvini. For an earlier act from January 1479, regarding Isaac's benefices in the diocese of Pistoia, see ASF, Notarile antecosimiano, 10085, fol. 218v. See also Luzzati (1976) on two later acts of Isaac Argyropoulos for Capponi regarding the priory in Pisa; and Verde (1973), p. 321.

68. Kristeller (1993b), p. 193; on p. 201, Kristeller furthermore recognizes Salvini's hand in the marginal notes to the *Epistola*'s copy in the National Central Library of Florence, now BNCF, Magl. B.5.20 (Scapecchi [2017], p. 364). See also Limor (1996); Vasoli (1994), especially pp. 125–126; and Verde (2010), ad indices.

69. Böninger (2006a).

70. In January 1479, Salvini, then still a modest "presbiter et cappellanus Sancti Laurentii," had claimed a credit of fifteen gold florins with the heir of Antonio degli Agli, the deceased bishop of Volterra; ASF, Notarile antecosimiano, 7527, fol. 163v. On Soderini and the establishment of a Monte di pietà at Volterra, see Lowe (1993), p. 16.

71. ASF, Notarile antecosimiano, 7528, fols. 31v–32r; cf. Kristeller (1993a), p. 179. A different date for the ceremony is given in Licciardello (2015), p. 527.

CHAPTER 9. THE END OF THE COMPANY, 1480–1482

1. Böninger (2002), p. 106.

2. This document and maybe other claims against the printer were presumably contained in ASF, Mercanzia, 1509, which is today lost.

3. Conway (1999), p. 163. Not very much is known about this goldsmith who did not figure in the 1480 Catasto. His full name was "Benvenutus olim Clementis Tommasii Buongiovanni aurifex populi Sancte Trinitatis," and in 1485 he was involved in an arbitration case with Lorenzo de' Medici (ASF, Notarile antecosimiano, 15040, ad diem 27 septembris 1485).

4. Olocco (2017), p. 55; Olocco (2019), p. 107.

5. On the Catasto returns of the family in 1480, see Verde (1977), part 1, pp. 246–247.

6. ASF, Mercanzia, 1510, fol. 319r–v.

7. For the activities of the Marinai and Dal Pozzo Toscanelli families, see Pampaloni (1976), ad indices. In March 1482 Ludovico and his brother

were given a safeguard to defend themselves of some financial charges (ASF, Miscellanea Repubblicana, 73, 1, fol. 104r). By 1488, public syndics had been appointed to satisfy Ludovico's creditors (ASF, Mercanzia, 10728, fols. 44v–46r).

8. These were a "debitori e creditori" (1476–1492) and a "quaderno di cassa" (1486–1492); Archivio dell'Ospedale degli Innocenti, Florence, Estranei, 12975, 12976). Whereas the first actually contains an account of Ludovico di maestro Piero for the years 1478–1480 (fol. 74, left/right), there is no trace of any transaction that could be related to Niccolò di Lorenzo.

9. This company, traditionally known as "heirs of Bartolomeo di Cambio," had, for example, sold spices, candles, and wax to the Mercanzia in 1474 (ASF, Mercanzia, 313, under the dates 22 June and 28 June 1474) and the Ufficiali del Monte (ASF, Monte comune o delle Graticole, parte II, 14, fol. 588); the company's debtors resided as far away as Bologna (ASF, Notarile antecosimiano, 12860, fols. 202v, 288v). For one of the company's minor partners, see Astorri (1989), p. 46.

10. ASF, Mercanzia, 1510, fol. 681r.

11. Burkart (2019), p. 44.

CHAPTER 10. A WORK PROPOSAL FOR THE RIPOLI PRESS, 11 NOVEMBER 1480

1. See Barsacchi (2007), pp. 104–105. Grain mills had been among the main targets in this conflict, and in December 1484 many of the Florentine mills had to be exonerated from communal taxes, as they had not yet been repaired; see ASF, Signori e Collegi, Duplicati delle deliberazioni in forza di ordinaria autorità, 24, fols. 798v–805v.

2. Pettas (1973).

3. Böninger (2019); Needham (1998); Nuovo (2013).

4. A Florentine merchant in Venice, Bernardo di Piero Bini, was, for example, in business relations with the company of "Nicholò Iemson" in 1479 (and presumably before); see ASF, Riccardi, 494, fol. 121v.

5. Böninger (2019), p. 65.

6. "Scripse *De temporibus* Matheo Palmieri, volume perspicuo et molto utile, el quale da gl'impressori con somma ingiuria è stato mutilato"; Landino (2001), vol. 1, p. 238); see also Bertolini (2009), pp. 113–114.

7. Conway (1999), pp. 121–122 (regarding some copies of the Legends of St. Catherine of Siena). Sano di Battista had been working as a "bibliopola" in Venice as early as 1471 (BNCF, Palatino, 1103, fol. 133r). He sent Venetian books to one of his colleagues in Florence, Benedetto di Giovanni (Vannuccio) di Geri; see Sano di Battista to Sandro Paganotti, 14 February 1477 (1478), in ASF, Mediceo avanti il Principato, XXXIV, 52; an edited version is in Schlebusch (2017), pp. 36, 237, n. 60. On Benedetto di

Giovanni, see Levi d'Ancona (1962), pp. 61-63. On Sano, see also ASF, Notarile antecosimiano, 16031, fol. 9r; ASF, Notarile antecosimiano, 14419, fol. 228r; and Dondi (2016), p. 18 ("Sano liberer S. Basso").

8. Sabbatini (2000).

9. See his declaration to the Catasto officials in 1480: "Incharichi. Tencha [!] una botecha da Antonio di Nicho' ch'à a lato al Proconsolo, la quale detto Antonio à da Michele da Rabata, la quale ò per tuto gienaio prossimo a venire e non per più, paghone l'ano f. dicasete di sugielo e una oca"; ASF, Monte comune o delle Graticole, Copie del Catasto, 39, fol. 158r. The often assumed birth year for Bartolo of 1430 is certainly wrong; see Bollati (2004), p. 63; and Levi d'Ancona (1962), pp. 39-41. Probably in 1482 he got married and in the following year was a witness to an act of Bartolomeo Fonzio regarding his teaching job at the university. In 1487 he witnessed another important act regarding Piero Pacini and the printer Francesco di Dino and in 1489 rented a farm from the confraternity of Santa Maria del Tempio; ASF, Notarile antecosimiano, 4836, fols. 68v, 99v; ASF, Notarile antecosimiano, 5029, 196v-197r; ASF, Notarile antecosimiano, 9872, fol. 140v; ASF, Notarile antecosimiano, 16033, fol. 188v.

10. Miniato di Tingo already possessed a shop at the Badia; see Guidotti (1985), p. 482 and n. 44.

11. Miniato had to live in the shop "ut vulgus loquitur 'per garzone' et ministro cum dicto Bartolo et sociis chartolariis hoc modo, videlicet quod dictus Minias teneatur stare in dicta apotheca assidue de die et de nocte in omni exercitio et usu seu utilitate et oportunitate eius, prout convenit solicito et diligenti iuveni et ministro et ad discretionem boni viri"; for this service Bartolo was to pay him one-third of the profits but not less than 120 lire a year; ASF, Notarile antecosimiano, 5029, fols. 144v-145r. One of the witnesses of this act was Giraldo di Francesco Giraldi, presumably as one of the partners; this and the following contract were drafted by the notary of the Florentine university, ser Piero di Bernardo Cennini, one of the silversmith's sons.

12. ASF, Notarile antecosimiano 5029, fols. 146v-147v, published in Marzi (1900), pp. 549-552. See Verde (1973), p. 88, for earlier mentions of the document; see also Scarcia Piacentini (1991).

13. "Unus qui suppleat et attendat dictis libris imprimendis."

14. "Providere eis de exemplaribus librorum et foliis et mercede duorum ministrorum, videlicet unius compositoris et unius impressoris seu tortoris."

15. "Gittinis literarum et puntellis, stannis et quolibet alio instrumento." The term "stannis" is here interpreted as "stagnis," as found in Schröter (1998), pp. 205-206.

16. On the term "mostra"/"monstra," see Schröter (1998), pp. 153-154; on proofreaders, see Grafton (2011); and Grafton (2020).

17. ASF, Corporazioni religiose soppresse dal governo francese, 119, 246, fol. 220r; ASF, Corporazioni religiose soppresse dal governo francese, 119, 1048, fol. 159r; my sincere thanks to Robert D. Black for both references. Another hitherto unknown typesetter, a layman, was a certain Girolamo di Antonio di Niccolò "de Mediolano formator librorum," who got married in the summer of 1482; ASF, Notarile antecosimiano, 9222, fol. 138r.

18. ASF, Mercanzia, 324, fol. 4r.

19. ASF, Podestà, 5263, fol. 582r–v; 5264, fol. 287r–v. The text of the compromise has not survived.

20. "Solo questa perchè avendo io fatto chostì [*in Florence*] uno chompromixo in ser Piero Pacini da Pescia, c[i]oè il chancelieri di m. Luigi [*Guicciardini*], il quale chonpromixo era tra Bartolo di Domenicho chartolaio et me per quelli libri che altre volte inte[n]deste, ché per chontumacie m'ebe chontro la sentenzia all'arte delli ispeziali di Firenze, e benchè qui chon exa non mi poteva far niente, pure per potere bazichar chostì [*in Florence*], mi volxi levar da partito et a stanza di ser Lorenzo mio fratello la rimissi in detto ser Piero perchè è parente di stretto della mogle di detto ser Lorenzo, et venemi fatto male, perchè ò fatto chonpromexo en chi è giudice e parte, perchè ò intexo è chonp[agnio] di detto Bartolo a' detti libri, et avendoli mostro chiaro òne avere et none a dare, parvemi a questo dì quando vi fu che avexi il chapo a non farmi il dovere, pertanto inte[n]dete se à lodato e quanto et avisatemi subito infra termine, perchè ò fatto pensieri quando m'avexi troppo tachato d'apellare, pure quando non pasassi quello avexi fatto, [*chon*] fior. 2 lar[ghi] mi leverò da' partito et pasandoli d'uno quatrino vò [a] apellare, siché vi pregho che cho' presteza io n'abia avixo che non' ma[n]chi aciò possa esser a riparare." For inscrutable reasons, this letter, written in Pistoia on 1 January 1487 and directed to a priest or notary in Florence seemingly named ser Iacopo di Gancia, has found its way into the register of a Florentine notary from quite different years; see ASF, Notarile antecosimiano, 2821. Bartolo di Domenico could indeed have been Pacini's business partner; in April 1487 he was a witness to one of his legal acts; Böninger (2017b), p. 230. On the relation between Pacini and Luigi Guicciardini, see Caby (2017), p. 194.

21. ASF, Mercanzia, 1531, fols. 262v; 303v–304r; 369v, 387r ("perché non doveva dare libri se non haveva el prezo etc., et in preiuditio di esso Bartholo").

CHAPTER 11. CRISTOFORO LANDINO'S COMMENTED EDITION OF DANTE'S *DIVINE COMEDY* (1481)

1. On the date of the writing, see Landino (2001), vol. 1, pp. 69–70.

2. See, for example, Gilson (2005), pp. 163–230; Korman (2000); McNair (2019), pp. 166–200; and Verde (1985), part 1, pp. 411–414.

3. Marcelli (2011), pp. 156-157 (referring to the *Comento*, Landino's comment on Horace and his translation of Giovanni Simonetta's *Sforziade*); on the context of these translations, see also Rizzi (2017).

4. Böninger (2015), pp. 116, 120.

5. The document has also been published in Böninger (2016), pp. 110-113.

6. Böninger (2016), p. 104.

7. Boschetto (2016b).

8. See the tax return of Giovanni di Bartolomeo di Rutino *pizzicagnolo* in early 1480: "Sustanze. Una chasa posta nel popolo di Sancto Anbruogio in via Pietrapiana che da primo via, da 2° e 3° Domenicho di Nicholo di Giovannozzo, a 4° Franciescho di Pagholo vochato Pachiante abita a Ppisa, chonperòlla ser Agniolo mio fratello prete, chonperòlla dal munistero di Sancto Anbruogio, chonperòlla [per] fiorini ciento di sugiello, cioè f. 100 di suggiello, ònne di pigione lire trentasei, cioè li. 36"; ASF, Monte comune o delle Graticole, Copie del Catasto, 102, fol. 362r. The rent sum had obviously been lowered for Niccolò di Lorenzo; on the other premises of the convent of Sant'Ambrogio in Via Pietrapiana, see ASF, Catasto, 989, fols. 50r-51r.

9. "Giovanni di Bartholomeo di Rontino pizichagnolo [dice et espone] che Nicholo di Lorenzo impressore fu et è suo vero et legiptimo debitore di lire XVIII picioli per resto di pigione d'una casa conducta et tenuta per detto Nicholo per suoi garzoni da detto actore per tempo d'uno anno a ragione di lire XXIIII picioli per detto tempo, come apparisce per una scripta di mano propria di detto Nicholo"; ASF, Mercanzia, 1514, fol. 536r, 16 April 1482.

10. ASF, Estimo, 87, fol. 36r (in Landino's hand); see also Böninger (2015), p. 111.

11. ASF, Compagnie religiose soppresse da Pietro Leopoldo, 1654, III, fol. 52r. The quotation here is from Black (2007), p. 457; see also p. 735.

12. ASF, Notarile antecosimiano, 12023, fols. 6v-7r; ASF, Notarile antecosimiano, 16266, fols. 78v, 95v; ASF, Notarile antecosimiano, 16267, fol. 26r. Ser Piero even went to court against the church's debtors (ASF, Mercanzia, 319, fol. 139r; ASF, Mercanzia, 4485, n. 448, 16 December 1479), and in 1483 a compromise regarding his administration became necessary (ASF, Notarile antecosimiano, 13447, fols. 501r, 510v).

13. ASF, Notarile antecosimiano, 16266, fols. 91v, 111r-v, 114v-115r. On the question of the name Landino versus Landini, see Landino (2001), vol. 1, p. 148, n. 37.

14. ASF, Notarile antecosimiano, 3334, fol. 68r; on Altoviti, see Böninger (2015), pp. 113-114.

15. ASF, Notarile antecosimiano, 14184, fol. 87r; ASF, Notarile antecosimiano, 9429, ad diem 28 aprilis 1480; ASF, Notarile antecosimiano,

9430, fol. 23r. The last two acts were both registered in the palace of the Parte Guelfa, where Landino was chancellor.

16. ASF, Notarile antecosimiano, 9430, fol. 189v.

17. ASF, Catasto, 1005, fol. 709r–v. On Landino's adoption of Taddeo di Giovanni Casini, in presence of Taddeo's father and that of the Florentine Podestà, see ASF, Notarile antecosimiano, 3333, fol. 63v (31 January 1475). In 1483 Taddeo was named as Landino's agent for his legal affairs in Pratovecchio; ASF, Notarile antecosimiano, 9430, fols. 51v, 87v.

18. See Gentile (2016), p. 395, with further literature; Fabiani was made a notary in August 1487 and drew up a final balance after staying with Ficino for twenty-four years in 1496; see ASF, Notarile antecosimiano, 13535, fol. 186v; and ASF, Notarile antecosimiano, 7530, fol. 161r–v.

19. For identification purposes, family names could even be used for domestic slaves; Kent (2002), p. 42.

20. Antonazzo (2018), pp. 119–142, he concludes "qui importa solo osservare che questo ignoto correttore dovette senz'altro avere accesso ai materiali di Landino, se molti dei suoi interventi trovano rispondenza nella stampa ancora di là da venire. Dovette cioè accadere che l'umanista, in lotta contro il tempo, a un certo punto del processo di revisione—ossia a partire dagli ultimi fogli del libro XXII—si fece affiancare da un collaboratore che agì sotto sua stretta sorveglianza o almeno secondo sue precise direttive" (pp. 141–142).

21. See Harris (2019).

22. *ISTC* id00029000; *BMC*, p. 628; *GW* 7966 (where a slightly smaller 114R has been identified); Olocco (2019), p. 123, n. 134.

23. *BMC*, pp. 628–629.

24. Landino (2001), vol. 1, p. 154.

25. Procaccioli (2016), p. 145. In 1969, Berta Maracchi Biagiarelli had proposed the name of Bartolomeo Fonzio as one of the proof correctors for the *Comento*, p. 216.

26. Procaccioli (2011).

27. When the contract was signed, the work on one printing press had already begun: "più giorni fa s'imposono a uno strectoio"; Böninger (2016), p. 112.

28. Alfredo Petrucci (1963). For the opinion that the illustrations "were made by more than one person, probably working collaboratively together within a workshop," see Gray (2012), vol. 1, pp. 32–34; for other discussions, see Baroni (2016), 169–171; and Roberts (2019), pp. 228–229.

29. The illustrations taken from the copy of the *Comento* in the Biblioteca Riccardiana, Edizioni Rare, 691, are reproduced in Landino (2001), vol. 1, between pp. 216 and 217; one plate exists in two different states.

30. Proccacioli (2019).

31. *ISTC* id00030000; see also Dondi and Harris (2013), pp. 384–385.

32. Tordi (1909-1910), p. 188: "el Dante col comento opera di messer Christofano da Pratovechio."

33. Petrella (2013). On Miniato del Sera, see Böninger (2016), p. 109; and Ganda (2018).

34. Böninger (2016), p. 117; for the price of eighteen lire and twelve soldi for a "Dante chol chomento," probably a bound and possibly illuminated copy, see Guidetti (2014), p. 182; for a bound copy that sold for three ducats in 1528, see Scapecchi (2017), p. 194.

35. ASF, Mercanzia, 1518, fol. 139r.

36. ASF, Mercanzia, 7277, ad diem 4 augusti 1483.

37. ASF, Mercanzia, 10216, fols. 168v-169r (26 September), 182v-183r (16 October, with the list of the properties), 221v (3 December, Landino and all his tenants or workers were ordered to leave their houses). Not included in this list was, interestingly, the tower in Borgo alla Collina in the Casentino region, which Landino had received around 1482 in exchange for his dedication copy of the *Comento;* see Boschetto (2016a), pp. 128-131.

38. ASF, Mercanzia, 1520, fol. 163v; ASF, Mercanzia, 4501, fols. 95v-96v.

39. ASF, Notarile antecosimiano, 7529, fols. 179v-180r; the sums had to be paid in live stock by Landino's land worker at San Miniato al Monte.

40. ASF, Podestà, 5190, fols. 67r-v, 77r-78r; ASF, Podestà, 5191, ad diem.

41. ASF, Notarile antecosimiano, 7528, fol. 18r; ASF, Notarile antecosimiano, 4831, ad diem 20 augusti 1480. The extraordinary nature of Altoviti's purchases is confirmed by the fact that they were recorded by notaries and not by brokers (*sensali*). Together Altoviti and Landino confessed to owing Antonio Francesco Scali on 23 June 1482 more than eighty-four gold florins for a richly furnished wooden room which had to be paid after one year; they also owed the wool merchant Simone di Piero Guiducci ninety-three florins *di suggello* for two pieces of cloth, to be paid in the same way; ASF, Notarile antecosimiano, 3335, fols. 27v-28v, 28v-29r. On 12 July Altoviti and Landino together bought clothes from Giovanni di Francesco Cavalcanti for forty gold florins which they promised to pay after one year; ASF, Notarile antecosimiano, 10086, fol. 243v). At the end of 1482, Landino acted as Altoviti's agent when he bought clothes worth 118 gold florins from the heirs of Bartolomeo Martelli, promising payment after one year; ASF, Notarile antecosimiano, 3335, fols. 62v-63r). On 5 April 1483 Landino was the debtor to the notary ser Battista Bartolomei of thirty gold florins for a white damask vest, bought again for Altoviti, which he promised to pay after ten months; ASF, Notarile antecosimiano, 20612, fascicle III, fol. 211r. On 15 June 1485 the Mercanzia commanded Landino to pay this debt; ASF, Mercanzia, 7286, ad diem.

42. Carlo di Simone Altoviti certainly knew Leon Battista Alberti from 1468 on; Alberti (2007), p. 312.

CHAPTER 12. FROM CRISTOFORO LANDINO'S *DISPUTATIONES CAMALDULENSES* (1480?) TO FRANCESCO BERLINGHIERI'S *GEOGRAPHIA* (1481-1482)

1. Fubini (1996); see also McNair (2019), pp. 94-146.
2. *ISTC* il00037000; *BMC*, pp. 627-628 (115Ra); *GW* M16839 ("Type 4: 114R").
3. Rhodes (1982), pp. 205-206, n. 1075.
4. ASF, Notarile antecosimiano, 9429, ad diem. The two brothers, with no clear profession, were then twenty-five and nineteen years old; ASF, Monte Comune o delle Graticole, Copie del Catasto, 73, fols. 328r-329r. Apparently, they had received from Landino objects to sell, possibly books. The Lapaccini were one of the most important families of the guild of doctors and apothecaries, in which many of them served as "console" in the fifteenth century.
5. On the Horace, see Verde (1985), part 1, pp. 448-450; Black (2016).
6. ASF, Mediceo avanti il Principato, LXXXII, 74, fol. 245; on Pagagnotti, see Boschetto (2003), pp. 251-253.
7. See Procaccioli (2016), p. 139. For some years, Lorenzo di Pierfrancesco had also been in business relations with the aforementioned bookseller in Venice, Sano di Battista.
8. On this edition, see Verde (1985), part 2, pp. 766-768. On its as yet nameless printer and his use of typographical material coming from Niccolò di Lorenzo's shop, see Ridolfi (1968), pp. 95-111; and Tura (2001), p. 19.
9. ASF, Notarile antecosimiano, 3335, fols. 245v-246r; ASF, Notarile antecosimiano, 17163, fols. 132r-133v.
10. ASF, Notarile antecosimiano, 9430, fol. 84r. In June 1483 a part of the dowry of fifteen hundred gold florins had already been paid by the officials of the "Monte delle doti"; Landino's remainder of six hundred florins of "res mobiles" may partly have been paid in books; ASF, Notarile antecosimiano, 4836, fol. 109r.
11. On Scala's oration, see Maxson (2015), p. 122; and Scala (1997), pp. 215-223.
12. Roberts (2013), p. 20.
13. Opinions on the literary qualities of this poem, with its lengthy lists and digressions, are quite discordant; see Roberts (2013), p. 10.
14. On the possible author(s) of the engravings, see Roberts (2011). It may be noted that Francesco Berlinghieri's relation with the Massaio family continued even after the painter's death, when he acted as arbiter for his widow and her sister (June 1485); see ASF, Podestà, 5222, fols. 201r-202v, 215r-216r, 525r-v, 613r-614v.
15. Roberts (2013), p. 82.
16. ASF, Notarile antecosimiano, 9634, fols. 223r-227v.

17. ASF, Notarile antecosimiano, 16756, fol. 79r. For full payment the stationer was given four years; the first thirty gold florins had to be given in fine wool cloth of either San Martino or San Matteo quality.

18. ASF, Mercanzia, 1518, fols. 294v, 303r. Folco's shop lay on the Piazza del Grano; ASF, Mercanzia, 1514, fol. 561v. In November 1482 Berlinghieri together with Antonio di Iacopo Berlinghieri had been commanded to pay the wool merchant Bernardo di Giovanni Rustichi more than ten gold florins "for woolen cloth sold to them"; ASF, Mercanzia, 7274, ad diem 23 novembris.

19. On Filippo Valori, see, for example, Böninger (2019), pp. 60–61 and n. 28; Jurdjevic (2008), pp. 47–48; and Verde (2010), ad indices. On his matrimony in 1477, see ASF, Notarile antecosimiano, 8015, fol. 97v.

20. Conway (1999), pp. 17, 46, 268–275; Conway (2000); Kristeller (1993a).

21. Taucci (1967); see also Roberts (2013), pp. 33, 201, n. 109.

22. ASF, Notarile antecosimiano, 13959, fol. 199r; both the ordinary and the extraordinary acts of the Mercanzia between summer 1492 and spring 1493 are missing. Other members of the Parigi family had worked with Piero del Massaio on maps; on Domenico's bookshop at the Badia fiorentina, see Bertoli (1992), p. 146, n. 48.

23. *BMC*, p. 629; Veneziani (1982).

24. "I caratteri che Niccolò Tedesco impiegò per la stampa della *Geografia* furono dunque tre: R 115-A che non risulta essere mai stato impiegato dopo il 1480; R 115-B che è una rifusione del precedente, con lievi modifiche, fatta presumibilmente proprio per la stampa del Dante del 1481 e mai impiegato altrove, a parte ovviamente la *Geografia;* R 111-A che è un'ulteriore modifica dei precedenti e che fu in uso a partire dal 1482"; Veneziani (1982), p. 201. The first of these is identical with the "Type 4: 114R" of the *GW,* already used for Aristotle's *Ethics* and Landino's *Comento* (see note 2 in this chapter). For further considerations of Veneziani's critique, see Roberts (2013), pp. 92–95.

25. Veneziani (1982), pp. 202–203.

26. Veneziani (1982), pp. 206–207: "Quello che mi sembra singolare in questa operazione di ringiovimento editoriale è il fatto che nel colophon aggiunto non appaia il nome dei Giunti bensì quello del tipografo che effettivamente aveva stampato la *Geografia,* Niccolò Tedesco che nel 1486 aveva interrotto la sua attività, pochi anni dopo la stampa dell'opera del Berlinghieri, probabilmente proprio a cagione dell'arcaicità dei suoi caratteri e del suo 'stile' tipografico. Evidentemente ben quarant'anni dopo aver cessato l'attività, il nome del tipografo della *Commedia* era ancora così vivo nel ricordo del pubblico che accorti commercianti come i Giunti potevano ritenere che costituisse un buon incentivo commerciale nel rilancio di una edizione sontuosa, ma in realtà di scarso successo."

CHAPTER 13. FROM NICCOLÒ PEROTTI'S *RUDIMENTA GRAMMATICES* (1483) TO SAINT GREGORY'S *MORALI* (1483-1486)

1. "Niccolò tedescho che gitta e libri in forma"; ASF, Mercanzia, 7275, ad diem.

2. The book was sold at the moderate price of two lire; Verde (1985), part 2, p. 857.

3. Scapecchi (2016), p. 49, n. 100; Villoresi (2014), pp. 23-29.

4. Dutton (2001). On the distribution of this text in contemporary Florentine libraries, see Alessandrini (2018), p. 187.

5. Black (2007), pp. 144, n. 487; 402, n. 333; Kristeller (1993b), p. 205. Further information on Gaspare can be found in ASF, Ospedale di Santa Maria Nuova, 5636, fol. 11v ("prete e maestro di gramaticha sta alla Piazza di Madonna", 1482; ASF, Corporazioni religiose soppresse dal governo francese, 113, 87, fol. 85r; ASF, Corporazioni religiose soppresse dal governo francese, 113, 149, fol. 110r; ASF, Notarile antecosimiano, 14200, fols. 235r-236v; ASF, Notarile antecosimiano, 10085, fol. 351v; ASF, Notarile antecosimiano, 3333, fol. 192r; ASF, Notarile antecosimiano, 2913, fol. 13r-v.

6. *BMC*, p. 631.

7. Dufner (1958); Zanobi da Strada and Giovanni da San Miniato (2005), pp. 784-785.

8. And, of course, also among private citizens: in 1478 a certain Niccolò di Iacopo Orlandi was called to redeem from his creditors "uno libro di Morali di San Ghirigoro sopra Iob di carta bambagina, legato in asse, di coverta rosso" which he had left as collateral together with a copy of Francesco da Barberino's *Documenti d'amore* for twenty lire; ASF, Mercanzia, 319, fol. 172r.

9. Vespasiano da Bisticci (1976), vol. 2, p. 195; see also Cortesi (2014), p. 581.

10. Verde (1977), part 1, p. 144. The edition in question was that printed in Rome by Vitus Puecher in 1475 (*ISTC* ig00428000).

11. Dufner (1958), pp. 71-72; Zanobi da Strada and Giovanni da San Miniato (2005), p. XVI, n. 3.

12. Dondi (2016), pp. 310-312, which notes that it was printed with "Fabriano paper watermarked with a prelate hat"; one wonders if this was already the paper imported by the Peterlini family (see the Epilogue).

13. This was the first time that the term "stampatore di forma" was used for Niccolò, to distinguish him from other "stampatori" who applied their stamps on cloth or leather; for the earliest examples of this new usage of the term, see Schröter (1998), pp. 228-233.

14. ASF, S. Maria Regina Coeli detta del Chiarito, 158bis, fol. 200r-v (and fol. 202r-v, for another *volgare* contract for Tommaso di Luca di Betto Bernardi). Molletti's official Latin documents for the brothers are in ASF, Notarile antecosimiano, 14418, fols. 263v, 280v, 286v, 290v, 297v, 330v,

417r; ASF, Notarile antecosimiano, 14419, fols. 40r, 54r, 93v–94r, 172r, 278v, 282v–283r, 462v (edited versions of both can be found in Böninger [2002], pp. 106–107); ASF, Notarile antecosimiano, 14420, fols. 8r, 22r–v (also in Böninger [2002], pp. 108–109), 44r, 63r, 79v (the last power of attorney, 13 April 1486, in the presence of the *cartaio* Battista di Piero [Peterlini] da Fabriano).

15. ASF, Mercanzia, 10831, fol. 90r. For the edition of the contract, see Ridolfi (1965); the documents had been discovered by Gino Corti.

16. On Bencivenni's office in 1479, see the list regarding the *Arte dei medici e speziali in* ASF, Manoscritti, 539, no pagination. He also had a discreet political career: in 1470 he had served as the Podestà of Galluzzo; ASF, Notarile antecosimiano, 4026, fols. 65r–66r, 68v–69r.

17. See Goldthwaite (2009), pp. 67, 438, 466–467. Many other scholars have used the single Mercanzia register ASF, Mercanzia, 10831, for their studies on the *accomandite* contracts.

18. ASF, Catasto, 76, fols. 11r–15v (the *portata* of their grandfather Betto di Luca Bernardi in 1427); ASF, Catasto 925, fol. 227r–v (the *portata* of the three brothers Piero, Tommaso, and Antonio and their mother in 1469); ASF, Notarile antecosimiano, 6240, fol. 64v (the compromise of the three brothers with their mother in 1474).

19. ASF, Notarile antecosimiano, 14419, fols. 93v–94r ("unam apotecham cum coquina, puteo et fundachetto et aliis suis habituris pertinentis").

20. ASF, S. Maria Regina Coeli detta del Chiarito, 158bis, fol. 95r–v.

21. "Piero di Luca a S. Polinari"; Romby (1976), p. 67.

22. "Faciamo un pocho di bottegha d'artte di spezialle in sul chanto di San Pulinari in detto popolo ..., e in detta bottegha abiamo maserizie a detto asiercizio, e pe' tenporalli chativi fac[i]amo pocho e quelo fa[i]amo, fac[i]amo chol ch[r]editto"; ASF, Monte Comune o delle Graticole, Copie del Catasto, 93, fols. 395r–396r. Many of their clients came from the upper Arno River valley, the Casentino and Mugello areas, as the Mercanzia registers show.

23. In May 1482 the brothers received part of the sum of 474 lire which the cleric and stationer Francesco di Benedetto di Giovanni di Geri owed them on account of his deceased father, almost certainly for paper; ASF, Notarile antecosimiano, 16756, fol. 79r; 12024, fol. 120r–v. Some of the payments in wool went directly to a paper merchant from Fabriano, Battista di Piero (Peterlini).

24. Böninger (2002), p. 106.

25. ASF, Notarile antecosimiano, 4351, penultimate fascicle, ad diem 18 maii 1485.

26. ASF, Mercanzia, 1521, fol. 36r (5 May 1484). On his family, see, for example, Verde (1977), part 1, p. 280; in 1469 Cei had been one of the Priors of Liberty.

27. ASF, Manoscritti, 539, under the dates; in 1477/1478, he also acted as the guild's procurator in the Mercanzia; ASF, Mercanzia, 10206, fols. 134v-135r; 10207, fol. 78r. Already in 1486, however, he was forced to open his account books there (ASF, Mercanzia, 11759, fol. 87r), and in 1497 died a poor man, as recorded by his nephew Galeotto di Giovanbattista Cei; his records are now in BNCF, II. IV, 14, fols. 1v-2v; and BNCF II. IV. 380, fols. 3-5.

28. Galeotto di Francesco Cei was also a friend of Vespasiano da Bisticci; see Cagni (1969), p. 180.

29. *ISTC* ig00435000; *GW* 11438: "Type 6: 111r""for quires a-gg, with the exception of folio ff3; "Type 7: 113R" (folio ff3, quires hh-Ss).

30. *BMC,* p. 631 (111rb).

31. Böninger (2002), p. 107.

32. Antonio di Filippo di Ventura was a less prominent stationer active from the late 1460s onward.

33. "Ser Lorenzo di Girolamo suprascripto è prete, non ha a l'anno adviamento fermo, uficia al presente per I° capellano in San Biagio, d'età d'anni 22"; ASF, Monte comune o delle Graticole, Copie del Catasto, 67, fol. 125r-v. His brother, the notary ser Mariotto Tinghi, served in the chancery of the Mercanzia and in 1490 was accused of malpractice, but was later readmitted; (ASF, Mercanzia, 329, fols. 45v-46v, 66r); in 1486 an economic agreement was reached between the Tinghi brothers (ASF, Notarile antecosimiano, 4359, fascicle 3, ad diem 2 martii 1485[6]). On the youngest brother, Girolamo di Girolamo Tinghi, OP, see Verde (1994), p. 525.

34. ASF, Ospedale di Santa Maria Nuova, 5635, fol. 214v; for an earlier deposit by his mother, see fol. 209v. For Lorenzo's relation with Marsilio Ficino's bother, the *speziale* Arcangelo di maestro Ficino, see ASF, Ospedale di Santa Maria Nuova, 5636, fol. 65r (March 1484).

35. ASF, Notarile antecosimiano, 12024, fol. 34r; ASF, Notarile antecosimiano, 9986, fols. 54v-55r, 80r; ASF, Notarile antecosimiano, 20612, fasc. IV, fol. 325r. His characterization as a chaplain in the church of San Giovanni Battista (i.e., the Battistero) is certainly wrong (ASF, Notarile antecosimiano, 7646, fol. 23v). At other times he was just called a priest; ASF, Notarile antecosimiano, 4030, fol. 248r-v; ASF, Notarile antecosimiano, fol. 28v.

36. Bertoli (2001).

37. ASF, Notarile antecosimiano, 14184, fols. 87r-88r; on Dell'Azzurro, see Black (2015b), p. 110; and Verde (1973), pp. 390-391. On a chaplain of Orsanmichele in 1484 who was also a "magister organorum," see ASF, Notarile antecosimiano, 9894, fol. 22r-v.

38. ASF, Catasto, 291, fol. 72r-v; see also ASF, Capitani di Orsanmichele, 466, fols. 268r, 278r, where the monthly income of the chaplains was fixed at

seven lire. On the 1415 college ("Collegiata") of ten priests and two clerics, see Richa (1754), pp. 24–25.

39. "Non fiat amplius ibi aliquod manuale opus, aut tradatur eruditio alicuius artis liberalis vel illiberalis seu mechanice, neque illic doceatur aut teneantur schole nisi forte docerentur sacre littere vel misteria divinorum officiorum aut evangelica doctrina traderetur"; ASF, Provvisioni. Registri, 171, fols. 122r–123r.

40. His father in 1471 had been a member of the pro-Medici *Balìa;* Rubinstein (1997), p. 347.

41. ASF, Catasto, 911, fol. 534r (1469); ASF, Catasto, Monte comune o delle Graticole, Copie del Catasto, 34, fols. 279r–280r (1480); ASF, Provvisioni. Registri, 170, fols. 129v–130r; BNCF, Poligrafo Gargani, 588, n. 148.

42. In 1482 his father's credit of six hundred florins in the public debt of Florence, the Monte comune, was registered under his and his brother's name; ASF, Notarile antecosimiano, 17903, fol. 42r.

43. Later the number of copies was actually given as 1,050.

44. Böninger (2002), p. 108. Between September 1484 and March 1485 Ridolfi was actually covering the office of the Podestà in Pistoia and was therefore absent from Florence. After the fall of the Medici, in December 1494, he became one of the syndics of their creditors.

45. Curiously, no documentary evidence regarding this case has been found in the files of the Podestà or the Mercanzia; unfortunately, the year 1485 is also missing in the series ASF, Soprastanti delle Stinche.

46. "Unum torchulum pro imprimendo litteras pro formando cum omnibus suis fulcimentis et libras ducentas litterarum pro imprimendo et formando libros illius qualitatis de qua imprimuntur dicta *Moralia Sancti Gregorii,* que littere et torchulum sunt dicti Nicolai et ad eum pertinent et expettant"; Böninger (2002), p. 108.

47. ASF, Notarile antecosimiano, 9986, fols. 54v–55r; on this shop, see note 19 in this chapter.

48. ASF, Notarile antecosimiano, 9985, fol. 69r; this sale of "brachia 14 1/8 panni monachini" was sealed in the archbishop's court.

49. ASF, Mercanzia, 7287, ad diem 24 octobris (the first charge dated 31 May; none of Ciachi's partners is mentioned by name).

50. ASF, Mercanzia, 1529, fol. 450r–v ("panni perpignani"); ASF, Mercanzia, 7289, ad diem 24 aprilis; ASF, Podestà, 5241, fols. 44r–45v; 240r–v; 5244, fol. 194r–v.

51. ASF, Giudice degli Appelli e Nullità, 132 (Condannati), fol. 211v (commanded to pay two soldi for each lira—i.e., 10 percent—from the original sum of thirty florins; date not given, but possibly after 15 July 1486).

52. ASF, Mercanzia, 1530, fol. 307r; ASF, Mercanzia, 7291, ad diem 16 septembris (final sentence regarding this confiscation).

53. ASF, Mercanzia, 1531, fols. 246v–247r; curiously, the Mercanzia notary from Viterbo copied the profession of "maestro Nicholò di Lorenzo di Nicholò" as that of a "sartore," certainly misreading the term "scriptore" in the original. Rosso da Sommaia worked in the metal trade and his "merchandise" must therefore have consisted in metal used for printing.

54. *BMC*, p. 631; the copy G-223(2) today in the Bodleian Library, University of Oxford, originally comes from the Florentine convent of Santa Chiara and bears two different forms of the woodcut of Saint Gregory together with the title. My sincere thanks to Neil Harris for this information.

CHAPTER 14. BAPTISTA SICULUS AND LEON BATTISTA ALBERTI'S *DE RE AEDIFICATORIA* (1485)

1. Böninger (2007); see also Cartei (2017), vol. 1, pp. 349–363, who proposes the title *De re edificatoria*.

2. Modigliani (2013), p. 99.

3. Cf. Van Binnebeke (2016), p. 242–243, n. 13, on the copy in the Pierpont Morgan Library; and Fossati (2020), p. 128, on the copy in the Biblioteca Braidense in Milan. For copies in contemporary Florentine libraries, see Alessandrini (2018), p. 227. As mentioned before, Vespucci also possessed two copies of Cornelius Celsus' *De medicina*.

4. Poliziano's possible role has especially stimulated widespread curiosity; see Branca (2000); and Patetta (1996).

5. *BMC*, pp. 630–631; Tura (2001), p. 19. In the copy of the Bodleian Library which presents "a third stage," the last gathering is also printed with "Nerlius 110R."

6. As, for example, in the copy once owned by Roberto Ridolfi, now in the Fondazione Biblioteche della Cassa di Risparmio, Florence, RID A-A 74.

7. Martelli (1965), pp. 191–192, n. 53; Ridolfi (1965), pp. 13–14.

8. Fiaschi (2001), especially pp. 275–277; Hellinga (2014), pp. 67–102, and especially 83–84. The manuscript has also been described in Cartei (2005).

9. As has been seen in the case of the confiscation of Cristoforo Landino's houses in 1483, these confiscations did not always have practical consequences.

10. On this confraternity, see Henderson (1997), p. 444; ASF, Notarile antecosimiano, 6087, fol. 177r–v; and ASF, Notarile antecosimiano, 6093, fol. 12r–v.

11. ASF, Mercanzia, 1524, fol. 346r (14 March 1485); ASF, Mercanzia, 1525, fols. 71v–72r (7 July) and 77v–78r (13 July, "ordine di sgombro," first mention of "Nicolò tedescho"). It may be noted that ASF, Mercanzia, 1525, does not pertain to the series of the "cause ordinarie," but to that of the "Sentenze and tenute"; its correct archival registration would therefore

be ASF, Mercanzia, 10219, which is presently recorded in the inventory as "missing."

12. The reference to cash was by no way incidental, as most books were still exchanged on barter; from a contemporary source it is known that *De re aedificatoria* was sold at the price of four lire; see Verde (1985), part 2, p. 858.

13. Honnacker (2005).

14. Sorbelli (2004), pp. 50, 157, 165.

15. See, in general, Baldacchini (1989), p. 683; and Gerulaitis (1976), p. 16.

16. Sorbelli (2004), pp. 229-230.

17. Pettas (1973), pp. 70, 79, 81.

18. On the Dei family, see Guidotti (1988). On Doni's family relations, see BNCF, Poligrafo Gargani, 731, fols. 53, 64; see also ASF, Notarile antecosimiano, 2200, ad diem 21 ianuarii 1470 (1471). In 1476, after the Doni brothers' bankruptcy, Matteo Doni gave a power of attorney to Benedetto Dei's twin brother, Miliano (ASF, Notarile antecosimiano, 14417, fol. 346v), and on 13 November 1477 signed the final agreement regarding his mother's rights (ASF, Notarile antecosimiano, 2203, ad diem).

19. Orvieto (1969), p. 237, cf. pp. 258-260, 265, on his own dealings with him in 1467.

20. BNCF, Poligrafo Gargani, 731, fols. 62-63.

21. ASF, Notarile antecosimiano, 14418, fols. 70r, 199r-v, 204r.

22. ASF, Monte comune o delle graticole, Copie del catasto, 12, fol. 211r.

23. Conway (1999), pp. 274, 277 (where only one commission to Doni is recorded). The two individuals were wrongly identified as the same person in Galli (1942), p. 164, and in Perini (1987), p. 63.

24. Böninger (2002), p. 108; ASF, Notarile antecosimiano, 13294, fol. 9r (the word "Lumia" is not clearly readable). One of the witnesses present was the apothecary Antonio di Luca di Betto Bernardi.

25. ASF, Notarile antecosimiano, 16757, fol. 109v; on Strinato Strinati, see Böninger (2016), p. 104, n. 15.

26. For example, in 1487/1488 for the payment of a saddle; ASF, Mercanzia, 1532, fol. 480r; ASF, Mercanzia, 7297, 8 May 1488.

EPILOGUE

1. Scapecchi (2013).

2. "Non pochi bibliografi asseriscono aver egli cessato di stampare nell'anno 1486, ma mi fu dato vedere un volume da lui stampato nell'anno 1491 insieme con Lorenzo di Matteo Morgiani, di cui ho già tenuto sopra parola, per cui è certo che egli più oltre ha seguitato a stampare"; Ottino (1871), p. 51; earlier, however, Ottino mentioned Morgiani as a partner of Giovanni di Piero da Magonza between 1490 and 1497 (p. 45).

3. ASF, Notarile antecosimiano, 9993, fols. 122v-123r.

4. *BMC,* pp. 680–689; Avigliano (2012); Periti (2003), pp. 296–300; Tura (2001), pp. 23–30.

5. *ISTC* ip00322500; *GW* M31160, six known copies.

6. *ISTC* ic00788300; *GW* 13392, four known copies. On Buonuomini, see Nuovo (2013), ad indices; on the *Libro da compagnia,* see Dondi (2016), pp. 459–460.

7. The date of this contract, however, is uncertain. On 6 October 1488 the office of the Otto di Guardia di Balìa ruled furthermore that "Ioannes de Maganza," presumably the printer, should not be arrested; ASF, Otto di Guardia e Balia della Repubblica, 83, fol. 88v. Nothing more is known about this case.

8. See *BMC,* pp. 669–677.

9. "Clerics, especially those in minor orders, played a great part in early typography all over the West, but they seem unusually numerous at Florence"; Scholderer (1966), p. 208; see also Bevilacqua (1943).

10. Clerical printers were also exempt from the jurisdiction of the Arte dei medici e speziali, which usually had the first word in disputes on printing. The same happened elsewhere, of course—for example, in Bologna with Ugo Ruggeri; see Monducci-Canova (2004), p. 12, n. 6.

11. Bertoli (2001). Other stationers became friars—as, for example, Bastiano di Michele di Giovanni around 1480; see Levi d'Ancona (1962), pp. 50–51.

12. ASF, Mercanzia, 1519, fol. 154r; ASF, Mercanzia, 10217, fols. 148v–149r. On his activity as stationer, see Conway (1999), pp. 245, 258. In 1482 one of Francesco's sisters entered the so-called convent of *Fuligno;* see Böninger (2017b), pp. 232–233, n. 15.

13. ASF, Mercanzia, 7269, ad diem 19 octobris 1482. In this case, the information regarding his clerical status was added by the notary in a second moment.

14. ASF, Notarile antecosimiano, 12024, fol. 120r-v. Many of Francesco's debts were paid with cloth; for the underlying debt of 474 lire; see ASF, Notarile antecosimiano, 16756, fol. 79r.

15. "Et se cento lingue avessi et tutti li fogli di Fabriano"; Medici (1977), p. 21; see also Guidetti (2014), p. LXIX, n. 280.

16. ASF, Mercanzia, 4467, fols. 268v–269v.

17. ASF, Mercanzia, 1537, fol. 491r-v.

18. ASF, Mercanzia, 1537, fols. 504r-v, and 515v: "et però domanda [Tommaso di Luca di Betto] che in caso che a detto Rinaldo s'avesse dare copia o sumpto di detti libri—che dare non si può né debba—si dia et facessi con conditione che si debba fare detta defalchatione et dispentione et non altrimenti etc."

19. ASF, Mercanzia, 1537, fols. 525v–526r, 551v.

20. "Chalculatores et rationerios et revisores"; ASF, Mercanzia, 329, fol. 45v.

21. "Per carta a loro data et venduta et chome appare al libro loro tenuto dell'anno 1480 et dipoi infino nell'anno 1485"; ASF, Mercanzia, 7308, ad diem 13 augusti 1490. In these months Peterlini was repeatedly named as a witness in notarial acts in the Mercanzia; ASF, Notarile antecosimiano, 13959, fols. 6v-7r, 12r-15v, 33v. In November 1490 he appointed a procurator, the stationer Monte di Giovanni di Miniato, to cash in two hundred lire from Tommaso and Antonio di Luca di Betto Bernardi; ASF, Notarile antecosimiano, 13959, fol. 36v. From the canceled name "et a Nicholao Laurentii teutonico" it seems that this first, partial sentence was already related to the printing of Saint Gregory's *Morali*. On 29 April 1491 followed Rinaldo Peterlini's last power of attorney; ASF, Notarile antecosimiano, 13959, fol. 91v.

22. The books were in fact counted as 825; the remaining number had probably been given to Niccolò di Lorenzo's last business partner, Tommaso Ciachi.

23. ASF, Mercanzia, 1538, fols. 9v-10r ("Nicholò di Lorenzo tedescho et compagni impressori").

24. ASF, Mercanzia, 1538, fol. 73r: "Item prima che del mese d'agosto 1483 Antonio di Lucha di Betto spetiale contrasse compagnia con Nicholò di Lorenzo tedescho: Non credit Tomasius. Non credit Antonius. Item che delle predette cose et altre fu fatta scripta tra detti Nicolò et Antonio: Pendet Antonius. Pendet Tomasius. Item che dipoi et del detto mese d'agosto 1483 o altro più vero tempo Batista di Pietro da Fabriano, essendo in Firenze, a richiesta del detto Antonio et di Tomaso fratello del detto Antonio fecie mercato della carta che bisognava per detta opera: Pendet Antonius. Non credit Tomasius."

25. ASF, Mercanzia, 1538, fol. 67r: "Item che il detto Batista da Fabriano fece el detto merchato cho' detto Nicholò tedescho et compagni della detta carta per la detta opera de' *Morali* di San Ghirighoro etc., et per e co' [?] effecti et parole et solicitudine et instigatione d'essi Tommaso et Antonio fu choncluso el detto mercato, el quale esso Batista non avrebbe altrimenti facto perchè non lo cognoscevao detto Nicolò et non sapevao chi si fussino e sua compagni, et [di] detti Tomaso et Antonio si confidavao assai perchè facevao tutti le loro faciende con loro. Et così fu et è la verità. . . . Item che il detto Antonio et Tomaso di Lucha insieme o de per se l'altro di loro hanno, tenghono et posseghono volumi mille venticinque di *Morali* di San Ghirighoro scripti et formati per detto Nicholò tedescho et compagni. Item che di tucte le predette cose fu et è publica voce et fama nella città di Firenze et maxime nel popolo di San Pulinari et di San Firenze di Firenze etc. Sopra i quali capitoli et tutte le dette cose il detto Rinaldo induxe et produxe gli infrascripti testimoni, cioè: X X X, i quali . . ." Rinaldo's deposition was communicated to "Nicholò tedescho et compagni" too.

26. ASF, Mercanzia, 1538, fols. 119v–120r, 123r: "Anchora perchè se alchuni libri de' *Morali* o altri si trovassero apresso a detto Tomaso di detto Nicholò tedescho, non seguiterebbe però che fussero quegli che detto Rinaldo dice essere stati impressi nella carta che dice aver data et venduta a detto Nicholò etc."

27. Needham (2000), p. 6. In 1483 in Brescia, Vernacci had paid ten Venetian ducats (i.e., ten gold florins), for each bale; see Pettas (1973). Different prizes are given in Bonifati (2008), p. 131.

28. In the Mercanzia sentence of 24 September 1490 this time is given as four months: "et finalmente la instantia della detta causa perì pel passamento de' quattro mesi secondo gli ordini"; ASF, Mercanzia, 10770, ad diem); see Boschetto (2016b), p. 190.

29. ASF, Mercanzia, 329, fol. 51r (2 July, "contra Nicholaum Laurenzii et socios impressores et Antonium et Tomasium Luce Betti"); ASF, Mercanzia, 4515, fol. 68v (20 August); ASF, Mercanzia, 329, fol. 70r (11 September).

30. ASF, Mercanzia, 10730, fols. 13v–16r, 17v–19r. Tommaso and Antonio presented their legal guarantees on 11 September; ASF, Mercanzia, 329, fol. 70r.

31. Here their names are omitted; none of them is known to have been directly involved with printing.

32. ASF, Mercanzia, 10730, fol. 23r–v.

33. On this concept, see Kuehn (2011), p. 383.

34. "Appresso et nelle mani d'uno o più cartolai e quali si eleghino et nominino per decto Rinaldo et appresso a' quali cartolai detti *Morali* stieno et stare possino et debbino per tempo di mesi sei proximi da oggi."

35. "Con questo nondimeno che prima che ne venda alchuno debbi notifichare prima a' detti Thommaso et Antonio e prezzi ne truova, a effecto che detti Tommaso et Antonio fra uno mese proximo dal dì di notifichatione abbino electione di dare tale pregio et che tali *Morali* aspettino loro per quanto così paghassino."

36. "XXV volumi di detti *Morali* o quello fussino, e quali detto Antonio et Tommaso dichono havere mandati a Perugia per chonto de' Fabrianesi detti, et detto Rinaldo detti nomi gli niegha."

37. ASF, Mercanzia, 10770, ad diem 24 septembris 1490; ASF, Mercanzia, 329, fols. 88v–90v.

38. ASF, Mercanzia, 4515, fols. 147v–149r (2 October).

39. Obviously Bartolo di Domenico was not only dealing in printed books; on 3 March 1491 he charged, for example, a debtor for "quaderni undici di carta pecora in forma di messale rigati per lire tredici picioli e un libro legato per lire 12"; ASF, Mercanzia, 4515, fol. 413r.

40. ASF, Mercanzia, 4515, fols. 160v–161v.

41. ASF, Mercanzia, 4515, fols. 167v–168r.

42. ASF, Notarile antecosimiano, 4888, fol. 38r-v: "Nicolaum tautonicum [*sic*] habitatorem Florentie olim domicellum Mercantie, stampator[em] di libri in forma."

43. ASF, Mercanzia, 4515, fol. 173r.

44. ASF, Mercanzia, 4515, fols. 196v-197r (29 October); one of the four names was already present in the apothecaries' list of debtors; the other three reguarded smaller debts which did not even arrive at the price of a copy of the *Morali*.

45. ASF, Mercanzia, 4515, fols. 199v-200r.

46. ASF, Mercanzia, 4515, fol. 202r-v: "maxime contradice ad quello che essi Thomaso et Antonio dicono de la consignatione che dicono fare a esso Rinaldo di Nicolò di Lorenzo etc."

47. ASF, Mercanzia, 4516, fols. 64v-65r.

48. ASF, Mercanzia, 10228, fols.51v-54v (29 April), 56r-57v (30 April), 98v-99v (16 May), 101v-102v (18 May).

49. ASF, Mercanzia, 4516, fols. 107r, 157r.

50. ASF, Mercanzia, 10228, fols. 124r-125r.

51. ASF, Mercanzia, 329, fol. 191v.

52. ASF, Mercanzia, 11585, fol. 56v.

53. ASF, Signori e Collegi, Duplicati delle deliberazioni in forza di ordinaria autorità, 26, fol. 185v; ASF, Notarile antecosimiano, 20497, fol. 44v.

54. ASF, Mercanzia, 1537, fol. 55r: "per valuta de uno libro de' *Morali* di San Gregorio in vulgare" (11 August 1489).

55. Ridolfi (1965), p. 9, n. 8.

56. ASF, Decima Repubblicana, 30, fol. 489r.

57. Tura (2001), pp. 16-23.

58. On Buonaccorsi, see, for example, Maracchi Biagiarelli (1972). As Pettas has shown, he had started in 1483-1484 as inker ("battitore") for Antonio Miscomini; Pettas (1973), pp. 71, 80-82.

APPENDIX A. BOOKS PRINTED BY NICCOLÒ DI LORENZO DELLA MAGNA OR ATTRIBUTED TO HIS PRESS

1. *ISTC* if00148000; *GW* 9876; Rhodes (1988), n. 294; Scapecchi (2017), n. 1150.

2. *ISTC* ic00338000; *GW* 6409; Rhodes (1988), n. 171; Scapecchi (2017), n. 789.

3. *ISTC* iv00092000; *GW* M49436; Rhodes (1988), n. 762; Scapecchi (2017), n. 2916.

4. *ISTC* ia00886000; *GW* 2204; Rhodes (1988), n. 54; Scapecchi (2017), n. 217.

5. *ISTC* ic00436000; *GW* 6593; Rhodes (1988), n. 183; Scapecchi (2017), n. 825.

6. *ISTC* ib00298000; *GW* 3798; Rhodes (1988), n. 92; Scapecchi (2017), n. 410.

7. *ISTC* ip00181600; *GW* M30149; Rhodes (1988), n. 481.

8. *ISTC* ie00109600; *GW* 487; Rhodes (1988), n. 281; Scapecchi (2017), n. 1109.

9. *ISTC* ic00973000; *GW* 7826; Rhodes (1988), n. 226; Scapecchi (2017), n. 979.

10. *ISTC* is00300700; *GW* M40748; Rhodes (1988), n. 713; Scapecchi (2017), n. 2622.

11. *ISTC* if00207300; *GW* 10049; Rhodes (1988), n. 746.

12. *ISTC* ip00892500; *GW* M34738; Rhodes (1988), n. 516; Scapecchi (2017), n. 2309.

13. *ISTC* ic00364000; *GW* 6456; Rhodes (1988), n. 179; Scapecchi (2017), n. 813.

14. *ISTC* ip01109000; *GW* M36562; Rhodes (1988), n. 557; Scapecchi (2017), n. 2369.

15. *ISTC* is00117000; *GW* M39854; Rhodes (1988), n. 599; Scapecchi (2017), n. 2485.

16. *ISTC* ia00981000; *GW* 2361; Rhodes (1988), n. 60; Scapecchi (2017), n. 250.

17. *ISTC* ic00155000; *GW* 6105; Rhodes (1988), n. 159; Scapecchi (2017), n. 740.

18. *ISTC* ip00394000; *GW* M31684; Rhodes (1988), n. 87; Scapecchi (2017), n. 2155.

19. *ISTC* ie00092800; *GW* M3416110 (under the title "Plenarium"); Rhodes (1988), n. 276; Scapecchi (2017), n. 1104.

20. *ISTC* if00207450; *GW* 10047; Rhodes (1988), n. 309; Scapecchi (2017), n. 1184.

21. *ISTC* is00581500; *GW* M44490; Rhodes (1988), n. 732; Scapecchi (2017), n. 2683.

22. *ISTC* il00037000; *GW* M16839; Rhodes (1988), n. 394; Scapecchi (2017), n. 1643.

23. *ISTC* is00566400; *GW* 0002520 N; Rhodes (1988), n. 381.

24. *ISTC* is00566300; *GW* 00025; Rhodes (1988), n. 382.

25. *ISTC* ia00712900; *GW* 01922; Rhodes (1988), n. 37; Scapecchi (2017), n. 151.

26. *ISTC* is003303600; *GW* M4075010; Rhodes (1988), n. 715; Scapecchi (2017), n. 2625.

27. *ISTC* ib00342000; *GW* 3870; Rhodes (1988), n. 108; Scapecchi (2017), n. 433.

28. *ISTC* ic0043800; *GW* 6598; Rhodes (1988), n. 184; Scapecchi (2017), n. 828.

29. *ISTC* il00043600; *GW* M16899; Rhodes (1988), n. 402; Scapecchi (2017), n. 1651.

30. *ISTC* il0043300; *GW* M16898; Rhodes (1988), n. 401.

31. *ISTC* ip00318780; *GW* M3115310; Rhodes (1988), n. 487.

32. *ISTC* ih00357750; *GW* 13331; Dondi (1916), pp. 310–312; Rhodes (1988), n. 373.
33. *ISTC* ic00439000; *GW* 6599; Rhodes (1988), n. 185; Scapecchi (2017), n. 829.
34. *ISTC* io00065450; *GW* M2784710; Rhodes (1988), n. 471; Scapecchi (2016), n. 100.
35. *ISTC* ig00304000; *GW* 10921; Rhodes (1988), n. 342; Scapecchi (2017), n. 1275.
36. *ISTC* ip00687000; *GW* M33569; Rhodes (1988), n. 507.
37. *ISTC* im344500; *GW* M21522; Rhodes (1988), n. 434; Scapecchi (2017), n. 1833.
38. *ISTC* ia00926470; *GW* 0228310N; Rhodes (1988), n. 542bis. The only copy of this work, once property of Roberto Ridolfi and with his new binding, is now kept in the Fondazione Biblioteche della Cassa di Risparmio di Firenze, RID A–A 79, with Ridolfi's notes: "Edizione sconosciuta. Esemplare unica. . . . La carta ha la stessa filigrana del Dante del 1481."
39. *BMC*, p. 631 ("The type of this book, which varies between 115 mm. and 117 mm. in height, appears to contain elements from 113 R. as well as 114 R., but the extremely bad presswork renders its classification uncertain. Possibly it is the work of a journeyman using type discarded by Laurentii."); *ISTC* ia00884500; *GW* 0220310N; Rhodes (1988), n. 53.
40. *BMC*, pp. 630–631; *ISTC* ia00215000; *GW* 00579; Cartei (2017), vol. 1, pp. 349–363; Rhodes (1988), n. 17; Scapecchi (2017), p. 84, n. 49.
41. *ISTC* ip0089500; *GW* M34776; Rhodes (1988), n. 520; Scapecchi (2017), n. 2312.
42. *ISTC* is00302300; *GW* M40758; Rhodes (1988), n. 714; Scapecchi (2017), n. 2623.
43. *ISTC* ig00435000; *GW* 11438; Rhodes (1988), n. 355; Scapecchi (2017), n. 1311.

APPENDIX B. DOCUMENTS

1. *On the left margin:* Non paga diritto perchè è protesto, è procuratore ser Santi dal Bagnano.
2. *Follows (canceled):* et
3. *Follows (canceled):* generaliter
4. *Follows (canceled):* et sociis
5. *Follows (canceled):* et generaliter etc.
6. *Added, interlinear: de et super predictis etc.*
7. *Follows (canceled):* se super
8. *On the left margin:* Pagassi di diritto s. 15 a dì primo di dicembre 1480, c. 47, procuratore ser Nicholò da Pistoia

9. *Follows (canceled):* il libro di detta compagnia il detto
10. *Follows (canceled):* per le spese
11. *On the left margin:* Die 15 decembris, presentibus Francisco et Iacopo
12. *Corrected:* avessi *to* avenissi
13. *Corrected:* quantità *to* quantitate
14. *On the left margin:* Retulit ut hic
15. *Follows (canceled):* a dì
16. *Follows (canceled):* a' libro
17. *On the left margin:* Lata
18. From here onward, another notary copied the text.
19. *Follows (canceled):* present.
20. *On the left margin:* Registrata ut hic
21. *On the left margin:* Vidi videnda
22. *Follows (canceled):* condempniamo detti
23. *On the left margin:* lata
24. *Repeated:* di
25. *On the left margin:* Iohannis terminus
26. Both this text and that in no. 11 have been copied by the same notary who only worked in the archbishop's court, ser Giuntino Giuntini, in a hasty and quite superficial hand. His acts in the diocesan archive are in many cases without clear dates and today their once chronological order has been changed. The dating of no. 10 as Thursday, 7 February—necessarily relating to the year 1488—is taken from the preceding act. Both no. 10 and no. 12 are given here in abbreviated forms, with some doubts on the correct transcription.
27. *Of unclear reading:* pro
28. *Added on the left margin:* compositionis et
29. *Follows (canceled):* donec et quousque dicto
30. *Of unclear reading:* exercitium *(exertranum?)*
31. *Follows (canceled):* quomodo dictus
32. *Follows:* p
33. *Follows:* p
34. *On the left margin:* Tomasii aromatarii ad Sanctum Pulinarem procura
35. *Follows (canceled):* trecentos tres
36. *On the left margin:* compromissum
37. *Follows (canceled):* men. (?)
38. *Follows canceled:* Venerabilis vir Franciscus Honofrii de Buon
39. *Follows canceled:* nonnulla
40. *Inserted on the left margin:* prout de predicta constat scripta privata

BIBLIOGRAPHY

Albanese, Gabriella, and Rossella Bessi. 2000. *All'origine della guerra dei trent'anni. Una novella latina di Bartolomeo Facio e il volgarizzamento di Jacopo di Poggio Bracciolini.* Rome: Edizioni di storia e letteratura.

Alberti, Leon Battista. 2007. *Corpus epistolare e documentario di Leon Battista Alberti.* Edited by Paola Benigni, Roberto Cardini, and Mariangela Regoliosi. Florence: Edizioni Polistampa.

Alessandrini, Adriana. 2018. *Il libro a stampa e la cultura del Rinascimento. Un'indagine sulle biblioteche fiorentine negli anni 1470–1520.* Florence: SISMEL / Edizioni del Galluzzo.

Allaire, Gloria. 1990–1991. "Due inediti di Andrea da Barberino nella Biblioteca Palatina di Parma." *Pluteus* 8–9, pp. 19–25.

Amelung, Peter. 1986. "Die Florentiner 'Trionfi'-Ausgaben des 15. Jahrhunderts." In *Ars impressoria. Entstehung und Entwicklung des Buchdrucks. Eine internationale Festgabe für Severin Corsten zum 65. Geburtstag,* edited by Hans Limburg, Hartwig Lohse, and Wolfgang Schmitz, pp. 251–265. Munich: K. G. Saur.

Antonazzo, Antonino. 2018. *Il volgarizzamento pliniano di Cristoforo Landino.* Messina, Italy: Centro internazionale di studi umanistici.

Armstrong, Lilian. 2015. *La xilografia nel libro italiano del Quattrocento.* Milan: EduCatt.

Arrighi, Vanna. 1990. "Del Nero, Bernardo." In *DBI,* vol. 38, pp. 170–173.

Astorri, Antonella. 1988. "Il 'Libro delle senserie' di Girolamo di Agostino Maringhi (1483–1485)." *Archivio Storico Italiano* 146, pp. 389–408.

——. 1989. "Appunti sull'esercizio dello speziale a Firenze nel Quattrocento." *Archivio Storico Italiano* 147, pp. 31–62.

Atwell, Adrienne. 2006. "Ritual Trading at the Florentine Wool-Cloth 'Botteghe.'" In *Renaissance Florence: A Social History,* edited by Roger J. Crum and John T. Paoletti, pp. 182–215. Cambridge: Cambridge University Press.

Avigliano, Pasqualino. 2012. "Morgiani, Lorenzo." In *DBI,* vol. 76, pp. 775–777.

Bakker, Paul J. J. M., and John H. L. van den Bercken. 2010. "The Commentary on Aristotle's 'De anima' by Alphonsus Vargas Toletanus, OESA." *Bulletin de Philosophie Médiévale* 52, pp. 201–234.

Baldacchini, Lorenzo. 1989. "La parola e la cassa. Per una storia del compositore nella tipografia italiana." *Quaderni storici* 72, pp. 679–698.

Baroni, Alessandra. 2016. "L'autore delle incisioni del 'Comento' e la controversa figura di Baccio Baldini." In *Per Cristoforo Landino lettore di Dante. Il contesto civile e culturale, la storia tipografica e la fortuna del Comento sopra la Comedia. Atti del Convegno internazionale Firenze 7–8 novembre 2014,* edited by Lorenz Böninger and Paolo Procaccioli, pp. 155–171. Società Dantesca Italiana, Centro di Studi e Documentazione Dantesca e Medievale, Quaderno 9. Florence: Le Lettere.

Barsacchi, Marco. 2007. *Cacciate Lorenzo! La guerra dei Pazzi e l'assedio di Colle Valdelsa (1478–1479).* Siena, Italy: Protagon Editori.

Bastianoni, Curzio, and Giuliano Catoni. 1988. *Impressum Senis. Storie di tipografi, incunaboli e librai.* Siena, Italy: Accademia Senese degli Intronati.

Baurmeister, Ursula. 1990. "Clément de Padoue, enlumineur et premier imprimeur italien?" *Bulletin du bibliophile* 1, pp. 19–28.

Bausi, Francesco. 2011. *Umanesimo a Firenze nell'età di Lorenzo e Poliziano. Jacopo Bracciolini Bartolomeo Fonzio Francesco da Castiglione.* Rome: Edizioni di storia e letteratura.

Bec, Christian. 1984. *Les livres des Florentins (1413–1608).* Florence: Olschki.

Bensi, Paolo. 1980. "Gli arnesi dell'arte. I gesuati di San Giusto alle mura e la pittura del Rinascimento a Firenze." *Studi di storia delle arti* 3, pp. 33–47.

Bernacchioni, Annamaria. 2009. "Ridolfo del Ghirlandaio: Una pala per 'Johannes Petri italiano.'" *Arte cristiana* 97, pp. 345–350.

Bernocchi, Mario. 1974. *Le monete della Repubblica fiorentina.* Vol. 1, *Il Libro della Zecca.* Florence: Olschki

Bertoli, Gustavo. 1992. "Librai, cartolai e ambulanti immatricolati nell'Arte dei medici e speziali di Firenze dal 1490 al 1600. Parte I." *La Bibliofilía* 94, pp. 125–164.

———. 2001. "Documenti su Bartolomeo de' Libri e i suoi primi discendenti." *Rara volumina* 1–2, pp. 19–56.

Bertolini, Lucia. 1982. "Censimento dei manoscritti della 'Sfera' del Dati. I: I manoscritti della Biblioteca Laurenziana." In *Annali della Scuola Normale Superiore di Pisa. Classe di Lettere e Filosofia,* ser. 3, no. 12, pp. 665–705.

———. 1985. "Censimento dei manoscritti della 'Sfera' del Dati. II: I manoscritti della Biblioteca Riccardiana." In *Annali della Scuola Normale Superiore di Pisa. Classe di Lettere e Filosofia,* ser. 3, no. 15, pp. 889–940.

———. 1988. "Censimento dei manoscritti della 'Sfera' del Dati. III: I manoscritti della Biblioteca Nazionale Centrale di Firenze e dell'Archivio di Stato di Firenze." In *Annali della Scuola Normale Superiore di Pisa. Classe di Lettere e Filosofia,* ser. 3, no. 18, pp. 417–588.

———. 1984. "L'attribuzione della 'Sfera' del Dati nella tradizione manoscritta." In *Studi offerti a Gianfranco Contini dagli allievi pisani,* pp. 33–43. Florence: Le Lettere-Libreria Commissionaria Sansoni.

———. 2009. "Mattia Palmieri e la stampa." *La Bibliofilía* 111, pp. 109–145.

Bettarini, Francesco. 2015. "The New Frontier: Letters and Merchants between Florence and Poland in the Fifteenth Century." *Mélanges de l'École française de Rome—Moyen Âge* 127, pp. 2–16.

Bevilacqua, Mario. 1943. "Tipografi ecclesiastici nel quattrocento." *La Bibliofilía* 45, pp. 1–29.

Bianca, Concetta. 2015. "La diffusione della stampa e la nascita della filologia." In *Acta Conventus Neo-Latini Monasteriensis: Proceedings of the Fifteenth International Congress of Neo-Latin Studies (Münster 2012)*, edited by Astrid Steiner-Weber and Harl A. E. Enenkel, pp. 3–17. Leiden: Brill.

Bigi, Emilio. 1962. "Argiropolo, Giovanni." In *DBI*, vol. 4, pp. 129–131.

Black, Robert. 2007. *Education and Society in Florentine Tuscany: Teachers, Pupils and Schools, c. 1250–1500*. Vol. 1. Leiden: Brill.

———. 2015a. "Machiavelli and the Grammarians: Benedetto Riccardini and Paolo Sassi da Ronciglione." *Archivio Storico Italiano* 173, pp. 427–481.

———. 2015b. "The School of San Lorenzo, Niccolò Machiavelli, Paolo Sassi, and Benedetto Riccardini." In *Essays in Renaissance Thought and Letters in Honor of John Monfasani*, edited by Alison Frazier and Patrick Nold, pp. 107–133. Leiden: Brill.

———. 2016. "Cristoforo Landino, Commentator of Horace's 'Ars Poetica' and the Academic Tradition." In *Per Cristoforo Landino lettore di Dante. Il contesto civile e culturale, la storia tipografica e la fortuna del Comento sopra la Comedia. Atti del Convegno internazionale Firenze 7–8 novembre 2014*, edited by Lorenz Böninger and Paolo Procaccioli, pp. 75–94. Società Dantesca Italiana, Centro di Studi e Documentazione Dantesca e Medievale, Quaderno 9. Florence: Le Lettere.

Black, Robert, Jill Kraye, and Laura Nuvoloni, eds. 2016. *Palaeography, Manuscript Illumination and Humanism in Renaissance Italy: Studies in Memory of A. C. de la Mare*. London: Warburg Institute.

Bonifati, Giovanni. 2008. *Dal libro manoscritto al libro stampato. Sistemi di mercato a Bologna e a Firenze agli albori del capitalismo*. Turin: Rosenberg e Sellier.

Bollati, Milvia, ed. 2004. *Dizionario biografico dei miniatori italiani secoli IX–XVI*. Milan: Edizioni Sylvestre Bonnard.

Böninger, Lorenz. 2002. "Ein deutscher Frühdrucker in Florenz: Nicolaus Laurentii de Alemania (mit einer Notiz zu Antonio Miscomini und Thomas Septemcastrensis)." *Gutenberg-Jahrbuch 2002*, pp. 94–109.

———. 2003. "Ricerche sugli inzi della stampa fiorentina." *La Bibliofilía* 105, pp. 225–248.

———. 2006a. "Das florentinische Kloster Santo Spirito und die deutsche Gemeinschaft im fünfzehnten Jahrhundert." In *Vita communis und ethnische Vielfalt. Multinational zusammengesetzte Klöster im Mittelalter. Akten des internationalen Studientags vom 26. Januar 2005 im Deutschen Historischen Institut in Rom*, edited by Uwe Israel, pp. 73–95. Berlin: Lit Verlag.

———. 2006b. *Die deutsche Einwanderung nach Florenz im Spätmittelalter.* Leiden: Brill.

———. 2007. "Leon Battista Alberti in tipografia: Le stampe del Quattrocento." In *Leon Battista Alberti umanista e scrittore. Filologia, esegesi, tradizione. Atti del Convegno internazionale del Comitato Nazionale VI centenario della nascita di Leon Battista Alberti, Arezzo, 24–25–26 giugno 2004,* vol. 2, edited by Roberto Cardini and Mariangela Regoliosi, pp. 611–630. Florence: Edizioni Polistampa.

———. 2015. "Minima landiniana." In *Il laboratorio del Rinascimento. Studi di storia e cultura per Riccardo Fubini,* edited by Lorenzo Tanzini, pp. 103–119. Florence: Le Lettere.

———. 2016. "Il contratto per la stampa e gli inizi del commercio del 'Comento sopra la Comedia.'" In *Per Cristoforo Landino lettore di Dante. Il contesto civile e culturale, la storia tipografica e la fortuna del Comento sopra la Comedia. Atti del Convegno internazionale Firenze 7–8 novembre 2014,* edited by Lorenz Böninger and Paolo Procaccioli, pp. 97–118. Società Dantesca Italiana, Centro di Studi e Documentazione Dantesca e Medievale, Quaderno 9. Florence: Le Lettere.

———. 2017a. "Die beiden oberdeutschen Kartographen Donnus Nicolaus Germanus und Henricus Martellus—auch eine (späte) Erwiderung auf Luisa Rubini Messerli." In *11. Kartographiehistorisches Colloquium Nürnberg 19–21. September 2002. Vorträge Berichte Posterbeiträge,* edited by Markus Heinz, pp. 17–31. Bonn: Kirschbaum Verlag.

———. 2017b. "Ser Piero Pacini, Francesco di Dino e la prima edizione del 'Formularium diversorum contractuum' (ca. 1484–1486)." *La Bibliofilía* 119, pp. 229–238.

———. 2019. "Venetian Incunabula for Florentine Bookshops (ca. 1473–1483)." In *Buying and Selling: The Business of Books in Early Modern Europe,* edited by Shanti Graheli, pp. 55–71. Leiden: Brill.

Böninger, Lorenz, and Paolo Procaccioli. 2016. *Per Cristoforo Landino lettore di Dante. Il contesto civile e culturale, la storia tipografica e la fortuna del Comento sopra la Comedia. Atti del Convegno internazionale Firenze 7–8 novembre 2014.* Società Dantesca Italiana, Centro di Studi e Documentazione Dantesca e Medievale, Quaderno 9. Florence: Le Lettere.

Borraccini, Rosa Maria, Giuseppe Lipari, Carmela Reale, Marco Santoro, and Giancarlo Volpato, eds. 2013. *Dizionario degli editori, tipografi, librai itineranti in Italia tra Quattrocento e Seicento.* Pisa: Fabrizio Serra.

Boschetto, Luca. 2003. "Incrociare le fonti: Archivi e letteratura. Rileggendo la lettera di Leon Battista Alberti a Giovanni di Cosimo de' Medici, 10 aprile [1456?]." *Medioevo e Rinascimento* 17, n.s., 14, pp. 243–264.

———. 2004. "Una nuova lettera di Giannozzo Manetti a Vespasiano da Bisticci. Con alcune considerazioni sul commercio librario tra Firenze e Napoli a metà Quattrocento." *Medioevo e Rinascimento* 18, n.s., 15, pp. 175–206.

——. 2005. "Tra Firenze e Napoli. Nuove testimonianze sul mercante-umanista Benedetto Cotrugli e sul suo 'Libro dell'arte di mercatura.'" *Archivio Storico Italiano* 163, pp. 687–715.

——. 2016a. "L'ufficio del ricorso presso la Mercanzia fiorentina tra Quattro e Cinquecento." In *Tribunali di mercanti e giustizia mercantile nel tardo medioevo*, edited by Elena Maccioni and Sergio Tognetti, pp. 183–205. Florence: Olschki.

——. 2016b. "Ritratto di Bernardo d'Antonio degli Alberti." In *Per Cristoforo Landino lettore di Dante. Il contesto civile e culturale, la storia tipografica e la fortuna del Comento sopra la Comedia. Atti del Convegno internazionale Firenze 7–8 novembre 2014*, edited by Lorenz Böninger and Paolo Procaccioli, pp. 119–135. Società Dantesca Italiana, Centro di Studi e Documentazione Dantesca e Medievale, Quaderno 9. Florence: Le Lettere.

Brambilla, Simona. 2007. "'Libro di Dio e dell'anima certamente.' Francesco Datini fra spiritualità e commercio librario." In *L'antiche e le moderne carte. Studi in memoria in Giuseppe Billanovich*, edited by Antonio Anfredi and Carla Maria Monti, pp. 189–246. Rome: Editrice Antenore.

Branca, Vittore. 2000. "Angelo Poliziano e Leon Battista Alberti." In *Leon Battista Alberti. Actes du Congrès International de Paris. Sorbonne—Institut de France—Institut culturel italien—Collège de France 10–15 avril 1995*, vol. 2, edited by Francesco Furlan, pp. 865–870. Paris-Turin: J. Vrin-Nino Aragno.

Branca, Vittore, and Lucia Nadin. 1974. "La stampa 'Deo gratias' del 'Decameron' e il suo carattere contaminato." *Studi sul Boccaccio* 8, pp. 1–77.

Brown, Alison. 1979. *Bartolomeo Scala, 1430–1497, Chancellor of Florence: The Humanist as Bureaucrat*. Princeton, NJ: Princeton University Press.

——. 2002. "Insiders and Outsiders: The Changing Boundaries of Exile." In *Society and Individual in Renaissance Florence*, edited by William J. Connell, pp. 337–383. Berkeley: University of California Press.

Brucker, Gene. 2005. *Living on the Edge in Leonardo's Florence: Selected Essays*. Berkeley: University of California Press.

Bühler, Curt F. 1960. *The Fifteenth Century Book: The Scribes, the Printers, the Decorators*. Philadelphia: University of Pennsylvania Press.

——. 1963. "Roman Type and Roman Printing in the Fifteenth Century." In *Bibliotheca Docet. Festgabe für Carl Wehmer*, edited by Siegfried Joost, pp. 101–110. Amsterdam: Erasmus Antiquariaat.

——. 1970. "False Information in the Colophons of Incunabula." *Proceedings of the American Philosophical Society* 114, pp. 398–406.

——. 1973. "The First Edition of Ficino's 'De christiana religione': A Problem in Bibliographical Description." In *Early Books and Manuscripts: Forty Years of Research*, pp. 303–312. New York: Grolier Club / Pierpont Morgan Library.

Burkart, Lucas. 2019. "Early Book Printing and Venture Capital in the Age of Debt: The Case of Michel Wenssler's Basel Printing Shop (1472–1491)." In *Buying and Selling: The Business of Books in Early Modern Europe*, edited by Shanti Graheli, pp. 23–54. Leiden: Brill.

Caby, Cécile. 2014. "Les ermites de saint Augustin et leur livres à l'heure de l'humanisme: Autour de Guglielmo Becchi e Ambrogio Massari." In *Entre stabilité et itinerance. Livres et culture des ordres mendiants XIIIe–XVe siècle*, edited by Nicole Beriou, Martin Morard, and Donatella Nebbiai, pp. 247-286. Turnhout, Belgium: Brepols.

———. 2017. "Histoires de livres, histoires de vies: À propos des manuscrits de Piero Pacini de Pescia." *Medioevo e Rinascimento* 31, n.s., 28, pp. 193-211.

Cadogan, Jean K. 2000. *Domenico Ghirlandaio: Artist and Artisan*. New Haven, CT: Yale University Press.

Caglioti, Francesco. 2001. "Benedetto da Maiano e Bernardo Cennini nel dossale argenteo del Battistero fiorentino." In *Opere e giorni. Studi su mille anni di arte europea dedicati a Max Seidel*, edited by Klaus Bergdolt and Giorgio Bonsanti, pp. 331-348. Venice: Marsilio.

Cagni, Giuseppe B. 1969. *Vespasiano da Bisticci e il suo epistolario*. Rome: Edizioni di storia e letteratura.

Cambi, Matteo. 2015. "Sul più antico volgarizzamento dei 'Gradi' di s. Girolamo (ms. Pisa, Biblioteca Cateriniana, n. 43)." *Medioevi* 1, pp. 141-168.

Canonici, Luciano. 1995. "Fra Cherubino da Spoleto predicatore del secolo XV." *Studi francescani* 92, pp. 107-125.

Cardini, Franco. 1970. "Borgianni, Iacopo." In *DBI*, vol. 12, pp. 743-744.

Cardini, Roberto, ed. 2005. *Leon Battista Alberti. La biblioteca di un umanista. Firenze, Biblioteca Medicea Laurenziana, 8 ottobre 2005-7 gennaio 2006*. Florence: Mandragora.

Carl, Doris. 1984. "Il contratto per una compagnia orafa fra Betto di Francesco di Duccio e Bernardo Cennini." *Rivista d'Arte* 37, pp. 189-202.

Caroti, Stefano, and Stefano Zamponi. 1974. *Lo scrittoio di Bartolomeo Fonzio umanista fiorentino*. Milan: Il Polifilo.

Cartei, Stefano. 2005. "Firenze, Biblioteca Medicea Laurenziana, Pluteo 89 sup. 113." In *Leon Battista Alberti. La biblioteca di un umanista. Firenze, Biblioteca Medicea Laurenziana 8 ottobre 2005-7 gennaio 2006*, edited by Roberto Cardini, pp. 374-376. Firenze: Mandragora.

———. 2017. *La tradizione a stampa delle opere di Leon Battista Alberti*. Florence: Edizioni Polistampa.

Celati, Marta. 2013. "L'Editio princeps fiorentina del 'Coniurationis commentarium' di Angelo Poliziano e il tipografo Niccolò tedesco: Nuove acquisizioni." *Archivum mentis* 2, pp. 169-188.

Cesarini Martinelli, Lucia. 2016. *Umanesimo e filologia*. Edited by Sebastiano Gentile. Pisa: Pacini.

Chellini da San Miniato, Giovanni. 1984. *Le Ricordanze di Giovanni Chellini da San Miniato*. Edited by Maria Teresa Sillano. Milan: Franco Angeli.

Ciampaglia, Margherita. 2009. "Il libro di bottega segnato 'A' di Bernardo di Stefano Rosselli (15 giugno 1475-3 marzo 1500). Pittura a Firenze nel secondo Quattrocento." PhD diss., Università degli Studi Roma Tre.

Ciasca, Raffaele, ed. 1922. *Statuti dell'arte dei medici e speziali*. Firenze: Olschki.

———. 1927. *L'arte dei medici e speziali nella storia e nel commercio fiorentino dal secolo XII al XV*. Florence: Olschki.

Claudius Ptolemaeus. 1963. *Claudius Ptolemaeus Cosmographia Bologna 1477*. Amsterdam: N. Israel/Meridian.

Codazzi, Angela. 1967. "Berlinghieri, Francesco." In *DBI*, vol. 9, pp. 121-124.

Conway, Melissa. 1999. *The "Diario" of the Printing Press of San Jacopo di Ripoli 1476-1484: Commentary and Transcription*. Florence: Olschki.

———. 2000. "The Early Career of Lorenzo de Alopa." *La Bibliofilía* 102, pp. 1-10.

Corbellini, Sabrina, Margriet Hoogvliet, and Bart Ramakers, eds. 2015. *Discovering the Riches of the Word: Religious Reading in Late Medieval and Early Modern Europe*. Leiden: Brill.

Cortesi, Mariarosa. 2014. "Gregorio Magno e gli umanisti." In *Gregorio Magno e le origini dell'Europa. Atti del Convegno internazionale Firenze, 13–17 maggio 2006*, edited by Claudio Leonardi, pp. 577-599. Florence: SISMEL/Edizioni del Galluzzo.

Cotrugli Raguseo, Benedetto. 1990. *Il libro dell'arte di mercatura*. Edited by Ugo Tucci. Venice: Arsenale Editrice.

Dallai Belgrano, Norma. 1989. "L'arte dei librai a Genova tra il 1450 ed il 1546." *La Berio* 29, pp. 5-48.

Daniels, Rhiannon. 2009. *Boccaccio and the Book: Production and Reading in Italy 1340-1520*. London: Legenda/Modern Humanities Research Association/Maney.

Daniels, Tobias. 2013. *La congiura dei Pazzi: I documenti del conflitto fra Lorenzo de' Medici e Sisto IV. Le bolle di scomunica, la "Florentina Synodus," e la "Dissentio" insorta tra la Santità del Papa e i Fiorentini. Edizione critica e commento*. Florence: Edifir.

Davies, Martin. 2007. "'Non ve n'è ignuno a stampa': The Printed Books of Federico da Montefeltro." In *Federico da Montefeltro and His Library*, edited by Marcello Simonetta, pp. 63-78. Milan: Y Press.

De la Mare, Albinia. 1976. "The Library of Francesco Sassetti (1421-90)." In *Cultural Aspects of the Italian Renaissance: Essays in Honour of Paul Oskar Kristeller*, edited by Cecil H. Clough, pp. 160-201. Manchester, UK: Manchester University Press/Alfred F. Zambelli.

———. 1985. "New Research on Humanistic Scribes in Florence." In *Miniatura fiorentina del Rinascimento 1440-1525. Un primo censimento*, vol. 2, edited by Annarosa Garzelli, pp. 393-600. Florence: Giunta Regionale Toscana/La Nuova Italia.

De Robertis, Teresa, and Rosanna Miriello, eds. 1997. *I manoscritti datati della Biblioteca Riccardiana di Firenze I. MSS. 1-1000*. Manoscritti datati d'Italia 2. Florence: SISMEL/Edizioni del Galluzzo.

———, eds. 2006. *I manoscritti datati della Biblioteca Riccardiana di Firenze III. MSS 1401-2000*. Manoscritti datati d'Italia 14. Florence: SISMEL/Edizioni del Galluzzo.

——, eds. 2013. *I manoscritti datati della Biblioteca Riccardiana di Firenze IV. MSS 2001–4270*. Manoscritti datati d'Italia 23. Florence: SISMEL/Edizioni del Galluzzo.

De Roover, Raymond. 1968. "Labour Conditions in Florence around 1400: Theory, Policy and Reality." In *Florentine Studies: Politics and Society in Renaissance Florence*, edited by Nicolai Rubinstein, pp. 277–313. London: Faber and Faber.

Decaria, Alessio. 2016. "Pulci, Luca." In *DBI*, vol. 85, pp. 662–665.

Degl'Innocenti, Luca. 2010. "Il 'Morgante' postillato da Jacobo Corbinelli alla Bibliothèque de l'Arsenal: Un progetto cinquecentesco di edizione." *Rassegna europea di letteratura italiana* 36, pp. 71–97.

Dei, Benedetto. 1985. *La Cronica dall'anno 1400 all'anno 1500*. Edited by Roberto Barducci. Florence: Francesco Papafava.

Della Torre, Arnaldo. 1902. *Storia dell'Accademia platonica di Firenze*. Florence: Carnesecchi.

Dini, Francesco. 1897. "La rocchetta di Poggibonsi e Giovanni Acuto." *Miscellanea storica della Valdelsa* 5, pp. 13–31.

Donato, Maria Monica, and Daniela Parenti, eds. 2013. *Dal Giglio al David. Arte civica a Firenze fra medioevo e rinascimento*. Florence: Giunti.

Dondi, Cristina. 2016. *Printed Books of Hours from Fifteenth-Century Italy: The Texts, the Books, and the Survival of a Long-Lasting Genre*. Florence: Olschki.

Dondi, Cristina, and Neil Harris. 2013. "Green Ginger. The Zornale of the Venetian Bookseller Francesco de Madiis, 1484–1488." In *Documenting the Early Modern Book World: Inventories and Catalogues in Manuscript and Print*, edited by Malcolm Walsby and Natasha Constantinidou, pp. 341–406. Leiden: Brill.

——. 2016. "I romanzi cavallereschi nel 'Zornale' di Francesco de Madiis (1484–88): Profilo merceologico di un genere." In *Carlo Magno in Italia e la fortuna dei libri di cavalleria*, edited by Johannes Bartuschat and Franca Strologo, pp. 251–299. Ravenna, Italy: A. Longo Editore.

Dorini, Umberto, ed. 1934. *Statuti dell'Arte di Por Santa Maria del tempo della repubblica*. Florence: Olschki.

Draper, James David. 1983. "Andrea vocato El Riccio Orafo." *Burlington Magazine* 966, pp. 541–542.

Dufner, Georg. 1958. *Die "Moralia" Gregors des Grossen in ihren italienischen volgarizzamenti*. Padova, Italy: Editrice Antenore.

——. 1964. "Antonio Bettini, Jesuat und Bischof von Foligno." *Rivista di storia della chiesa in Italia* 18, pp. 399–428.

——. 1975. *Geschichte der Jesuaten*. Rome: Edizioni di storia e letteratura.

Dutton, Marsha L. 2001. "The Medici Connection: Gilbert of Hoylant's 'Sermons on the Song of Songs' in Renaissance Italy." *Citeaux: Commentarii cistercienses* 52, pp. 93–119.

Edler de Roover, Florence. 1953. "New Facets on the Financing and Marketing of Early Printed Books." *Bulletin of the Business Historical Society* 27, pp. 222–230.

Emison, Patricia. 2006. "The Replicated Image in Florence, 1300-1600." In *Renaissance Florence: A Social History,* edited by Roger J. Crum and John T. Paoletti, pp. 431-453. Cambridge: Cambridge University Press.

Fabbri, Lorenzo, and Marica Tacconi, eds. 1997. *I libri del Duomo di Firenze. Codici liturgici e biblioteca di Santa Maria del Fiore (secoli XI–XVI).* Florence: Centro Di.

Farbaky, Péter, Dániel Pócs, Magnolia Scudieri, Lia Brunori, Enikö Spekner, and András Végh, eds. 2013. *Mattia Corvino e Firenze. Arte e umanesimo alla corte del re di Ungheria.* Florence: Giunti.

Fachard, Denis, ed. 2002. *Consulte e pratiche della Repubblica fiorentina 1495–1497.* Geneva: Droz.

Fiaschi, Silvia. 2001. "Una copia di tipografia finora sconosciuta: Il Laurenziano Plut. 89 sup. 113 e l'Editio princeps' del De re aedificatoria." *Rinascimento,* ser. 2, no. 41, pp. 267-284.

——. 2015. "Scritti ipocratici per un principe ipocondriaco: Le traduzioni filelfiane del 'De flatibus' e del 'De passionibus.'" In *Il ritorno dei Classici nell'Umanesimo. Studi in memoria di Gianvito Resta,* edited by Gabriella Albanese, Claudio Ciociola, Mariarosa Cortesi, and Claudio Villa, pp. 279-298. Florence: SISMEL / Edizioni del Galluzzo.

Ficino, Marsilio. 2019. *De Christiana religione.* Edited by Guido Bartolucci. Pisa: Scuola Normale Superiore Pisa.

Flannery, Melissa C. 1989. "San Iacopo di Ripoli Imprints at Yale." *Yale University Library Gazette* 63, pp. 114-131.

Fonzio, Bartolomeo. 2011. *Letters to Friends.* Edited by Alessandro Daneloni and translated by Martin Davies. Cambridge, MA: Harvard University Press.

Fossati, Fabrizio, ed. 2020. *Biblioteche riscoperte. "Ab artis inventae origine." Storie di libri, persone e biblioteche milanesi tra le edizioni quattrocentesche della Braidense. Biblioteca Nazionale Braidense, 4 febbraio–28 marzo 2020.* Milan: CRELEB / Edizioni CUSL.

Fubini, Riccardo. 1996. "Cristoforo Landino, le 'Disputationes Camaldulenses' e il volgarizzamento di Plinio: questioni di cronologia e di interpretazione." In *Quattrocento fiorentino. Politica diplomazia cultura,* pp. 303-332. Pisa: Pacini.

Fumagalli, Giuseppe. 2019. *Aneddoti bibliografici.* Edited by Matteo Joja. Milan: La Vita Felice.

Füssel, Stephan. 2013. "Die Ausbreitung des Buchdrucks in Deutschland und durch deutsche Drucker in Europa (ca. 1454-1470)." In *Mobiltà dei mestieri del libro tra Quattrocento e Seicento. Convegno internazionale Roma, 14–16 marzo 2012,* edited by Marco Santoro and Samanta Segatori, pp. 55-76. Pisa: Fabrizio Serra.

Gagliardi, Isabella. 2004. *I "pauperes yesuati" tra esperienze religiose e conflitti istituzionali.* Rome: Herder.

Galli, Giuseppe. 1942. "Gli ultimi mesi di vita della stamperia di Ripoli e la stampa del Platone." In *Studi e ricerche sulla storia della stampa del Quattrocento.*

Omaggio dell'Italia a Giovanni Gutenberg nel V centenario della sua scoperta, pp. 159–184. Milan: Hoepli.

Ganda, Arnaldo. 2002. "Due agenti librari di Giovanni da Colonia a Pavia nel 1474." *Bollettino della Società Pavese di Storia Patria* 102, pp. 303–314.

——. 2006a. *Filippo Cavagni da Lavagna editore, tipografo, commerciante a Milano nel Quattrocento.* Florence: Olschki.

——. 2006b. "Un tipografo millantatore a Milano nel 1471: Giovanni Guglielmo da San Salvatore del Monferrato." In *Arte e storia di Lombardia. Scritti in memoria di Grazioso Sironi*, pp. 69–76. Città di Castello, Italy: Società Editrice Dante Alighieri.

——. 2017. *L'umanesimo in tipografia. Alessandro Minuziano e il genero Leonardo Vegio editori e stampatori (Milano, 1485–1521).* Rome: Edizioni di storia e letteratura.

——. 2018. "'In molti loci grande quantità di libri et debitori.' Accordi tipografici e commerciali di Bonino Bonini e Miniato Delsera con Pietro Antonio Castiglione (Crema, 1491–Milano, 1495)." *Bibliologia* 13, pp. 39–75.

Gatti, Elena. 2018. *Francesco "Platone" de' Benedetti. Il principe dei tipografi bolognesi fra corte e "Studium" (1482–1496).* Udine, Italy: Forum.

Gentile, Sebastiano. 2006. "Nello 'scriptorium' ficiniano: Luca Fabiani, Ficino Ficini, e un inedito." In *Marsilio Ficino. Fonti, testi, fortuna. Atti del Convegno internazionale (Firenze, 1–3 ottobre 1999)*, edited by Sebastiano Gentile and Stéphane Toussaint, pp. 145–182. Rome: Edizioni di Storia e Letteratura.

——. 2016. "Nuove considerazioni sullo 'scrittoio' di Marsilio Ficino: tra paleografia e filologia." In *Palaeography, Manuscript Illumination and Humanism in Renaissance Italy: Studies in Memory of A. C. de la Mare*, edited by Robert Black, Jill Kraye, and Laura Nuvoloni, pp. 385–403. London: Warburg Institute.

Gentile, Sebastiano, Sandra Niccoli, and Paolo Viti, eds. 1984. *Marsilio Ficino e il ritorno di Platone. Manoscritti stampe e documenti 17 maggio–16 giugno 1984.* Florence: Le Lettere.

Gerulaitis, Leonardas Vytautas. 1976. *Printing and Publishing in Fifteenth-Century Venice.* Chicago: American Library Association.

Gilson, Simon. 2005. *Dante and Renaissance Florence.* Cambridge: Cambridge University Press.

Giorgetti, Leonardo. 2017. "Aristotele nel chiostro. Un episodio inedito della ricezione umanistica fiorentina dell'Etica Nicomachea." *Viator* 48, pp. 293–331.

Goldthwaite, Richard A. 2009. *The Economy of Renaissance Florence.* Baltimore: Johns Hopkins University Press.

Grafton, Anthony. 2011. *The Culture of Correction in Renaissance Europe.* Panizzi Lectures 2009. London: British Library.

——. 2020. "Humanists with Inky Fingers: The Corrector in the Printing House." In *Inky Fingers: The Making of Books in Early Modern Europe*, pp. 29–55. Cambridge, MA: Harvard University Press.

Gray, Emily Rosanna. 2012. "Early Florentine Engravings and the Devotional Print: Origins and Transformations, c. 1460–85." 2 vols. PhD diss., Courtauld Institute of Art, University of London.

Guerrieri, Elisabetta. 2015. "Un'antologia di San Bernardo in volgare: Prime note sul ms. Barberiniano latino 4040." *Medioevo e Rinascimento* 29, n.s., 26, pp. 221–242.

Guicciardini, Paolo, and Emilio Dori. 1952. *Le antiche case ed il palazzo dei Guicciardini in Firenze*. Florence: Olschki.

Guidetti, Lorenzo di Francesco. 2014. *Ricordanze*. Edited by Lorenz Böninger. Rome: Edizioni di storia e letteratura.

Guidi Bruscoli, Francesco. 1997. "Politica matrimoniale e matrimoni politici nella Firenze di Lorenzo de' Medici. Uno studio del ms. Notarile antecosimiano 14099." *Archivio Storico Italiano* 155, pp. 347–398.

Guidotti, Alessandro. 1985. "Indagini su botteghe di cartolai e miniatori a Firenze nel XV secolo." In *La miniatura italiana tra gotico e Rinascimento. Atti del II Congresso di storia della miniatura italiana Cortona 24–26 settembre 1982*, vol. 2, pp. 473–507. Florence: Olschki.

———. 1988. "Dei, famiglia." In *DBI*, vol. 37, pp. 243–249.

Haebler, Konrad. 1921. "Vom Nachdruck im 15. Jahrhundert." In *Collectanea variae doctrinae Leoni S. Olschki bibliopolae florentino sexagenario*, pp. 113–120. Munich: Jacques Rosenthal.

———. 1924. *Die deutschen Buchdrucker des XV. Jahrhunderts im Auslande*. Munich: Jacques Rosenthal.

Harris, Neil. 2001. "The Ripoli Diary." *Book Collector* 52, pp. 10–32.

———. 2007. "La sopravvivenza del libro, ossia appunti per una lista della lavandaia." *Ecdotica* 4, pp. 24–65.

———. 2008. "Ombre della storia del libro italiano." In *The Books of Venice: Il libro veneziano*, edited by Lisa Pon and Craig Kallendorf, pp. 454–516. Miscellanea Marciana 20. Venice, Italy, and New Castle, DE: Biblioteca Nazionale Merciana/La Musa Talìa/Oak Knoll.

———. 2019. Review of *Per Cristoforo Landino lettore di Dante. Il contesto civile e culturale, la storia tipografica e la fortuna del Comento sopra la Comedia. Atti del Convegno internazionale Firenze 7–8 novembre 2014*, edited by Lorenz Böninger and Paolo Procaccioli, 2016. *The Library* 20, pp. 246–248.

Hase, Oskar. 1886. "Zum Gesellschaftsbetrieb im Druckgewerbe. Frühestes Nürnberger Beispiel." *Archiv für Geschichte des Deutschen Buchhandels* 10, pp. 5–8.

Hellinga, Lotte. 2014. "List of Printer's Copy Used in the Fifteenth Century." In *Texts in Transit: Manuscript to Proof and Print in the Fifteenth Century*, pp. 67–102. Leiden: Brill.

Henderson, John. 1997. *Piety and Charity in Late Medieval Florence*. Chicago: University of Chicago Press.

Hirsch, Rudolf. 1967. *Printing, Selling and Reading, 1450–1550*. Wiesbaden, Harassowitz.

Holmes, Megan. 2000. "Giovanni Benci's Patronage of the Nunnery, Le Murate." In *Art, Memory, and Family in Renaissance Florence,* edited by Giovanni Ciappelli and Patricia Lee Rubin, pp. 114–134. Cambridge: Cambridge University Press.

Honnacker, Hans. 2005. "Il caso curioso del 'Carmen in persona auctoris' di Bapista siculus nella 'princeps' del 'De re aedificatoria.'" *Albertiana* 8, pp. 239–253.

Hoshino, Hidetoshi. 1980. *L'arte della lana in Firenze nel basso medioevo. Il commercio della lana e il mercato dei panni fiorentini nei secoli XIII–XV.* Florence: Olschki.

Jurdjevic, Mark. 2008. *Guardians of Republicanism: The Valori Family in the Florentine Renaissance.* Oxford: Oxford University Press.

Kent, Francis William. 1977. *Household and Lineage in Renaissance Florence: The Family Life of the Capponi, Ginori, and Rucellai.* Princeton, NJ: Princeton University Press.

———. 1983. "Lorenzo di Credi, His Patron Iacopo Bongianni and Savonarola." *Burlington Magazine* 125, pp. 539–541.

———. 2002. "'Be Rather Loved Than Feared': Class Relations in Quattrocento Florence." In *Society and Individual in Renaissance Florence,* edited by William J. Connell, pp. 13–50. Berkeley: University of California Press.

Kent, Francis William, and Caroline Elam. 2015. "Piero del Massaio: Painter, Mapmaker and Military Surveyor." *Mitteilungen des Kunsthistorischen Institutes in Florenz* 57, pp. 64–89.

Kirkham, Victoria. 2001. *Fabulous Vernacular: Boccaccio's "Filocolo" and the Art of Medieval Fiction.* Ann Arbor: University of Michigan Press.

Korman, Sally. 2000. "'Danthe Alighieri Poeta Fiorentino': Cultural Values in the 1481 Divine Comedy." In *Revaluing Renaissance Art,* edited by Gabriele Neher and Rupert Sheperd, pp. 57–65. Aldershot, UK: Ashgate.

Kristeller, Paul Oskar. 1937. *Supplementum Ficinianum.* 2 vols. Florence: Olschki.

———. 1993a. "The First Printed Edition of Plato's Works and the Date of Its Publication (1484)." In *Studies in Renaissance Thought and Letters,* vol. 3, pp. 135–146. Rome: Edizioni di storia e Letteratura.

———. 1993b. "Sebastiano Salvini, a Florentine Humanist and Theologian, and a Member of Marsilio Ficino's Platonic Academy." In *Studies in Renaissance Thought and Letters,* vol. 3, pp. 175–206. Rome: Edizioni di storia e Letteratura.

Kuehn, Thomas. 2011. "Debt and Bankruptcy in Florence: Statutes and Cases." *Quaderni storici* 46, pp. 355–390.

Landino, Cristoforo. 2001. *Comento sopra la Comedia.* Edited by Paolo Procaccioli. 4 vols. Rome: Salerno.

Lazzareschi, Eugenio. 1942. "Prototipografi lucchesi e germanici." In *Studi e ricerche sulla storia della stampa del Quattrocento. Omaggio dell'Italia a Giovanni Gutenberg nel V centenario della sua scoperta,* pp. 191–196. Milan: Hoepli.

Le feste del IV centenario cenniniano. 1871. *Le feste del IV centenario cenniniano. Relazione di Piero Barbèra. Bernardo Cennini e il suo tempo. Discorso di Andrea Bertolotto. Un pensiero alla stampa. Discorso del Professor Carlo Fontanelli.* Florence: M. Celllini.

Legnani Annichini, Alessia. 2013. *"Proxeneta est in tractando." La professione ingrata del mediatore di commercio (secc. XII–XVI).* Bologna: Bononia University Press.

Levi d'Ancona, Mirella. 1962. *Miniatura e Miniatori a Firenze dal XIV al XVI secolo. Documenti per la storia della miniatura.* Florence: Olschki.

Licciardello, Pierluigi. 2015. "Il testamento e la libreria di Sebastiano Salvini (1512)." *Aevum* 89, pp. 525–560.

Limor, Ora. 1996. "The Epistle of Rabbi Samuel of Morocco: A Best-Seller in the World of Polemics." In *Contra Iudaeos: Ancient and Medieval Polemics between Christians and Jews,* edited by Ora Limor and Guy G. Strousa, pp. 177–194. Tübingen: Germany: Mohr.

Lines, David A. 2002. *Aristotle's "Ethics" in the Italian Renaissance (ca. 1300–1650): The Universities and the Problem of Moral Education.* Leiden: Brill.

——. 2018. "Defining Philosophy in Fifteenth-Century Humanism: Four Case Studies." In *Et Amicorum: Essays in Renaissance Humanism and Philosophy in Honour of Jill Kraye,* edited by Anthony Ossa-Richardson and Margaret Meserve, pp. 281–297. Leiden: Brill.

Liscia Bemporad, Dora. 2002. "Per Andrea del Verrocchio orafo." *Medioevo e Rinascimento* 13, pp. 189–202.

——. 2006. "I punzoni per il fiorino sulla Porta del Paradiso: Michelozzo e Bernardo Cennini." *Medioevo e Rinascimento* 20, n.s., 17, pp. 227–243.

——. 2014. "Nel cantiere del Ghiberti. Un concorso singolare." In *La Porta d'oro del Ghiberti. Atti del ciclo di conferenze Firenze, 20 novembre 2012–4 giugno 2013,* edited by Timothy Verdon, pp. 65–73. Florence: Mandragora.

Litta, Pompeo. 1839. *Famiglie celebri italiane.* Dispensa 71 (Strozzi di Firenze, part 2). Milan: Ferrario.

Lowe, Kate J. P. 1993. *Church and Politics in Renaissance Italy: The Life and Career of Cardinal Francesco Soderini (1453–1524).* Cambridge: Cambridge University Press.

——. 1996. "Lorenzo's 'Presence' at Churches, Convents and Shrines in and outside Florence." In *Lorenzo the Magnificent: Culture and Politics,* edited by Michael Mallett and Nicholas Mann, pp. 23–36. London: Warburg Institute.

——. 2003. *Nuns' Chronicles and Convent Culture in Renaissance and Counter-Reformation Italy.* Cambridge: Cambridge University Press.

Lowry, Martin. 1991. *Nicholas Jenson and the Rise of Venetian Publishing in Renaissance Europe.* Oxford: Basil Blackwell.

Luzzati, Michele. 1976. "Capponi, Guglielmo." In *DBI,* vol. 19, pp. 60–62.

Mack, Charles Randall. 1974. "The Rucellai Palace: Some New Proposals." *Art Bulletin* 56, pp. 517–529.

Mallett, Michael E. 1967. *The Florentine Galleys in the Fifteenth Century: With the Diary of Luca di Maso degli Albizzi, Captain of the Galleys, 1429–1430.* Oxford: Clarendon.

Manetti, Giannozzo. 1983. *Dialogus consolatorius.* Edited by Alfonso De Petris. Rome: Edizioni di Storia e Letteratura.

Manzoni, Giacomo. 1882. *Studii di Bibliografia analitica. Tomo primo che contiene tre studii con dieci tavole.* Bologna: Gaetano Romagnoli.

Maracchi Biagiarelli, Berta. 1969. "Editori di incunaboli fiorentini." In *Contributi alla storia del libro italiano. Miscellanea in onore di Lamberto Donati*, pp. 221–220. Florence: Olschki.

———. 1972. "Buonaccorsi, Francesco." In *DBI*, vol. 15, p. 83.

Marcelli, Nicoletta. 2011. "La 'Naturalis Historia' di Plinio nel volgarizzamento di Cristoforo Landino." *Archives internationales d'histoire des sciences* 61, pp. 137–161.

Marchetto, Giuliano. 2011. "Legge, statuto, diritto comune nei 'consilia' del Quattrocento." In *Challenging Centralism: Decentramento e autonomie nel pensiero politico europeo*, edited by Lea Campos Boralevi, pp. 53–62. Florence: Firenze University Press.

Martelli, Mario. 1965. *Studi laurenziani.* Florence: Olschki.

Marzi, Demetrio. 1900. "I tipografi tedeschi durante il secolo XV." In *Festschrift zum fünfhundertjährigen Geburtstage von Johann Gutenberg*, edited by Otto Hartwig, pp. 505–578. Leipzig: Harassowitz.

Mattone, Antonello, and Tiziana Olivari. 2006. "Dal manoscritto alla stampa. Il libro universitario italiano nel XV secolo." In *Manoscritti, editoria e biblioteche dal medioevo all'età contemporanea. Studi offerti a Domenico Maffei per il suo ottantesimo compleanno*, vol. 1, edited by Mario Ascheri and Gaetano Colli, pp. 679–730. Rome: roma nel rinascimento.

Maxson, Brian Jeffrey. 2015. "Humanism and the Ritual of Command in Fifteenth-Century Florence." In *After Civic Humanism: Learning and Politics in Renaissance Italy*, edited by Nicholas Scott Barker and Brian Jeffrey Maxson, pp. 113–129. Toronto: Centre for Reformation and Renaissance Studies.

McLean, Paul D., and Neha Gondal. 2014. "The Circulation of Interpersonal Credit in Renaissance Florence." *European Journal of Sociology* 55, pp. 135–176.

McNair, Bruce. 2019. *Cristoforo Landino: His Works and Thought.* Leiden: Brill.

Medici, Lorenzo de'. 1977. *Lettere.* Vol. 1, *1460–1474.* Edited by Riccardo Fubini. Florence: Giunti-Barbèra.

———. 1998. *Lettere.* Vol. 2, *1482–1484.* Edited by Michael Mallett. Florence: Giunti-Barbèra.

———. 2010. *Lettere.* Vol. 15, *Marzo–agosto 1489.* Edited by Lorenz Böninger. Florence: Giunti-Barbèra.

Menning, Carol Bresnahan. 1993. *The Monte di Pietà of Florence: Charity and State in Late Renaissance Italy.* Ithaca, NY: Cornell University Press.

Modigliani, Anna. 1989. *Tipografi a Roma prima della stampa. Due società per fare libri con le forme (1466–1470).* Rome: roma nel rinascimento.

———. 2013. "Per la datazione del 'De re aedificatoria.' Il codice e gli archetipi dell'Alberti." *Albertiana* 16, pp. 91–110.

Monducci, Elio, and Andrea Canova. 2004. "Agli inizi della tipografia reggiana: L'Algorismo in volgare (1478)." In *Rhegii Lingobardiae. Studi sulla cultura a Reggio Emilia in età umanistica,* edited by Andrea Canova and Reggio Emilia, pp. 11–29. Reggio Emilia: Aliberti editori.

Monfasani, John. 1994. Review of *Nicholas Jenson and the Rise of Venetian Publishing in Renaissance Europe,* by Martin Lowry, 1991. *Journal of Modern History* 66, pp. 402–404.

Montecchi, Giorgio. 2015. *Storia del libro e della lettura.* Vol. 1, *Dalle origini ad Aldo Manuzio.* Milano: Mimesis.

Muecke, Frances. 2017. Review of *Two Renaissance Commentaries on Persius: Bartholomaeus Fontius' and Ioannes Britannicus' Commentaries on Persius,* edited by László Takács and Attila Tuhári, 2015. *Bryn Mawr Classical Review* 2017.11.09, https://bmcr.brynmawr.edu/2017/2017.11.09/.

Munro, John H. 2012. *The Rise, Expansion, and Decline of the Italian Wool-Based Cloth Industries, 1100–1730: A Study in International Competition, Transaction Costs, and Comparative Advantage. Studies in Medieval and Renaissance History,* 3rd ser., 9, pp. 45–207.

Murano, Giovanna. 2009. "'Memoria e richordo.' I libri di Giordano di Michele Giordani (a. 1508)." *Aevum* 83, pp. 755–826.

Myśliwski, Grzegorz. 2015. "Retail Trade in Wrocław between around the Mid-Thirteenth and the Fifteenth Century." In *Il commercio al minuto. Domanda e offerta tra economia formale e informale secc. XIII–XVIII / Retail Trade: Supply and Demand in the Formal and Informal Economy from the 13th to the 18th Century.* Florence: Firenze University Press, pp. 277–294.

Needham, Paul. 1998. "Venetian Printers and Publishers in the Fifteenth Century." *La Bibliofilía* 100, pp. 157–200.

———. 2000. "Concepts of Paper Study." In *Puzzles in Paper: Concepts in Historical Watermarks,* edited by Daniel W. Mosser, Michael Saffle, and Ernest W. Sullivan III, pp. 1–36. New Castle, DE: Oak Knoll.

———. 2009. "Prints in the Early Printing Shops." In *The Woodcut in Fifteenth-Century Europe,* edited by Peter Parshall, pp. 39–91. Washington, DC, and New Haven, CT: National Gallery of Art / Yale University Press.

Neri di Bicci. 1976. *Le ricordanze (10 marzo 1453–24 aprile 1475).* Edited by Bruno Santi. Pisa: Edizioni Marlin.

Nesi, Emilia. 1903. *Il diario della stamperia di Ripoli.* Florence: Seeber.

Newbigin, Nerida. 1996. *Feste d'Oltrarno: Plays in Churches in Fifteenth-Century Florence.* 2 vols. Florence: Olschki.

———. 2014. "Feo Belcari's Rappresentazione di Abram Offset in Phalaris's Epistolae: Adventures of a Florentine Incunabulum." *Electronic British Library*

Journal 2014, article 14, https://www.bl.uk/eblj/2014articles/pdf/ebljarticle 142014.pdf.

Noakes, Susan. 1981. "The Development of the Book Market in Late Quattrocento Italy: Printers' Failures and the Role of the Middlemen." *Journal of Medieval and Renaissance Studies* 11, pp. 23–55.

Nuovo, Angela. 2013. *The Book Trade in the Italian Renaissance.* Leiden: Brill.

Olocco, Riccardo. 2017. "The Archival Evidence of Type-Making in 15th-Century Italy." *La Bibliofilía* 119, pp. 33–79.

———. 2019. "A New Method of Analysing Printed Type: The Case of 15th-Century Venetian Romans." PhD diss., University of Reading.

Orlandi, Pellegrino Antonio. 1722. *Origine e progressi della stampa o sia dell'arte impressoria e notizie dell'opere stampate dall'anno M.CCCC.LVIII. sino all'anno M.D.* Bologna: Constantinus Pisarius.

Orvieto, Paolo. 1969. "Un esperto orientalista del '400: Benedetto Dei." *Rinascimento,* sec. ser., 10, pp. 205–275.

———. 2017. *Pulci. Luigi e una famiglia di poeti.* Rome: Salerno Editrice.

Ottino, Giuseppe. 1871. *Di Bernardo Cennini e dell'arte della stampa in Firenze nei primi cento anni dall'invenzione di essa.* Florence: Tip. Galileiana di M. Cellini.

Padgett, John, and Paul McLean. 2002. "Economic and Social Exchange in Renaissance Florence." Working Paper 02-07-032, Santa Fe Institute. https://www .santafe.edu/research/results/working-papers/economic-and-social-exchange -in-renaissance-floren.

Palma, Marco. 1979. "Cennini, Piero." In *DBI,* vol. 23, pp. 572–575.

Palmieri, Matteo. 1982. *Vita civile.* Edited by Gino Belloni. Florence: Sansoni.

Pampaloni, Guido. 1976. *La miniera del rame di Montecatini Val di Cecina. La legislazione mineraria di Firenze e i Marinai di Prato, secolo XV, seconda metà.* Prato, Italy: Cassa di risparmi e depositi.

Passerini, Luigi. 1861. *Genealogia e storia della famiglia Rucellai.* Florence: Cellini.

Patetta, Luciano. 1996. "Poliziano e la cultura architettonica alla corte di Lorenzo il Magnifico." In *Poliziano nel suo tempo. Atti del VI Convegno internazionale (Chianciano-Montepulciano 18–21 Iuglio 1994),* edited by Luisa Secchi Tarugi, pp. 239–254. Florence: Franco Cesati.

Perini, Leandro. 1987. "Stamperie quattrocentesche: vocabolario, tecniche e rapporti giuridici." In *Tecnica e società nell'Italia dei secoli XII–XVI. Pistoia, 28–31 ottobre 1984,* pp. 59–70. Pistoia, Italy: Centro italiano di studi di storia e d'arte.

Periti, Simona. 2003. "L'edizione miscominiana della 'Compagnia del Mantellaccio' ed altre 'giunte e correzioni' fiorentine a IGI." *Medioevo e Rinascimento* 17, n.s., 14, pp. 281–306.

Petrella, Giancarlo. 2013. "Dante in tipografia. errori, omissioni e varianti nell'edizione Brescia, Bonino Bonini, 1487." *La Bibliofilía* 115, pp. 167–195.

Petrucci, Alfredo. 1963. "Baldini, Baccio." In *DBI,* vol. 5, pp. 478–481.

Petrucci, Armando. 1974. "Il MS. berlinese Hamiltoniano 90. Note codicologiche e paleografiche." In Giovanni Boccaccio, *Decameron. Edizione diplomatico-*

interpretativa dell'autografo Hamilton 90, edited by Charles S. Singleton, pp. 647–661. Baltimore: Johns Hopkins University Press.

———. 1977. *Catalogo sommario dei manoscritti del Fondo Rossi, Sezione Corsiniana.* Accademia Nazionale dei Lincei, Indici e sussidi bibliografici della Biblioteca 10. Rome: Accademia Nazionale dei Lincei.

Pettas, William A. 1973. "The Cost of Printing a Florentine Incunable." *La Bibliofilía* 75, pp. 67–85.

Piana, Celestino, OFM. 1977. *La facoltà teologica dell'università di Firenze nel Quattro e Cinquecento.* Rome: Collegio S. Bonaventura a Quaracchi.

Pietrobon, Ester. 2018. "Fare penitenza all'ombra di Dante. Questioni di poesia e devozione dei 'Sette salmi.'" *L'Alighieri. Rassegna dantesca* 51, pp. 63–80.

Pinelli, Paola. 2020. "La compravendita di libri nella contabilità dei mercanti fiorentini. Un confronto coi prezzi dei generi di prima necessità nella seconda metà del XV secolo." In *Printing R-Evolution and Society 1450–1500: Fifty Years That Changed Europe,* edited by Cristina Dondi, pp. 495–510. Venice: Edizioni Ca' Foscari.

Pinto, Giuliano. 2019. "'Beneficium civitatis.' Considerazioni sulla funzione economica e sociale dell'arte della lana in Italia (secoli XIII-XV)." *Archivio Storico Italiano* 177, pp. 213–233.

Pirillo, Paolo. 2015. *Forme e strutture del popolamento nel contado fiorentino.* Vol. 3, *Gli insediamenti al tempo del primo catasto (1427–1429).* Florence: Olschki.

Poggi, Giovanni. 1988. *Il Duomo di Firenze. Documenti sulla decorazione della chiesa e del campanile tratti dall'archivio dell'Opera,* edited by Margaret Haines. 2 vols. Florence: Kunsthistorisches Institut in Florenz.

Poliziano, Angelo. 2015. *Coniurationis commentarium.* Edited by Marta Celati. Alessandria, Italy: Edizioni dell'Orso.

Poliziano, Angelo, and Gentile Becchi. 2012. *La congiura della verità.* Edited and translated by Marcello Simonetta. Naples: La scuola di Pitagora.

Pollard, Alfred W. 1905. *An Essay on Colophons, with Specimens and Translations, by Alfred W. Pollard, and an Introduction by Richard Garnett.* Chicago: Caxton Club.

Procaccioli, Paolo. 2011. "Forme aperte: le vite ulteriori del Dante 1481." In *"Books Seem to Be Pestilent Things." Studi in onore di Piero Innocenti per i suoi 65 anni,* vol. 1, pp. 335–353. Manziana, Italy: Vecchiarelli.

———. 2016. "La redazione e la stampa del 'Comento.' Tempi, modi, illazioni e implicazioni." In *Per Cristoforo Landino lettore di Dante. Il contesto civile e culturale, la storia tipografica e la fortuna del Comento sopra la Comedia. Atti del Convegno internazionale Firenze 7–8 novembre 2014,* edited by Lorenz Böninger and Paolo Procaccioli, pp. 137–153. Società Dantesca Italiana, Centro di Studi e Documentazione Dantesca e Medievale, Quaderno 9. Florence: Le Lettere.

———. 2019. "Il 'cosa' della parola e quello dell'immagine. Landino e Baldini nel Dante del 1481." In *Dante visualizzato. Carte ridenti.* Vol. 3, edited by Rossend Arqués Corominas and Sabrina Ferrara, pp. 73–94. Florence: Franco Cesati.

Pseudo-Petrarch. 2015. *The Lives of the Popes and Emperors.* Edited by Aldo S. Bernardo, Reta A. Bernardo, and Tania Zampini. New York: Italica.

Rao, Ida Giovanna. 2006. "Per la biblioteca di Francesco da Castiglione." In *Il Capitolo di San Lorenzo nel Quattrocento. Convegno di studi, Firenze, 28–29 marzo 2003,* edited by Paolo Viti, pp. 131–144. Florence: Olschki.

Rhodes, Dennis E. 1982. *A Catalogue of Incunabula in All the Libraries of Oxford University outside the Bodleian.* Oxford: Clarendon.

———. 1988. *Gli annali tipografici fiorentini del XV secolo.* Florence: Olschki.

Richa, Giuseppe. 1754. *Notizie delle chiese fiorentine divise ne' suoi quartieri.* Vol. 1. Florence: Pietro Gaetano Viviani.

Richardson, Brian. 2004. *Print Culture in Renaissance Italy: The Editor and the Vernacular Text 1470–1600.* 2nd ed. Cambridge: Cambridge University Press.

Ridolfi, Roberto. 1965. "Le ultime imprese tipografiche di Niccolò tedesco." *La Bibliofilía* 67, pp. 143–152.

———. 1968. *La stampa in Firenze nel secolo XV.* Florence: Olschki.

Rinuccini, Alamanno. 1953. *Lettere ed orazioni,* edited by Vito R. Giustiniani. Florence: Olschki.

Rizzi, Andrea. 2017. *Vernacular Translators in Quattrocento Italy: Scribal Culture, Authority, and Agency.* Turnhout, Belgium: Brepols.

Roberts, Sean. 2011. "Francesco Rosselli and Berlinghieri's Geographia Reexamined." *Print Quarterly* 28, pp. 4–17.

———. 2013. *Printing a Mediterranean World: Florence, Constantinople, and the Renaissance of Geography.* Cambridge, MA: Harvard University Press.

———. 2019. "Engravings." In *Book Parts,* edited by Dennis Duncan and Adam Smyth, pp. 223–236. Oxford: Oxford University Press.

Romani, Valentino. 1982. "Clemente da Padova." In *DBI,* vol. 27, pp. 367–369.

Romby, Giuseppina Carla. 1976. *Descrizioni e rappresentazioni della città di Firenze nel XV secolo con la trascrizione inedita dei manoscritti di Benedetto Dei e un indice ragionato dei manoscritti utili per la storia di Firenze.* Florence: Libreria editrice fiorentina.

Rother, C. H. 1921. "Nikolaus Laurentii und seine Danteausgabe vom Jahre 1481." *Zeitschrift für Bücherfreunde* 13, pp. 78–80.

Rouse, Mary A., and Richard H. Rouse. 1986. "Nicolaus Gupalatinus and the Arrival of Print in Italy." *La Bibliofilía* 88, pp. 221–247.

———. 1988. *Cartolai, Illuminators and Printers in Fifteenth-Century Italy: The Evidence of the Ripoli Press.* Los Angeles: Department of Special Collections, University Research Library, University of California.

Rubinstein, Nicolai 1997. *The Government of Florence under the Medici (1434 to 1494).* 2nd ed. Oxford: Clarendon.

Rucellai, Giovanni di Pagolo. 2013. *Zibaldone,* edited by Gabriella Battista. Florence: SISMEL/Edizioni del Galluzzo.

Rusconi, Roberto. 1980. "Cherubino da Spoleto." In *DBI,* vol. 24, pp. 446–453.

Sabbadini, Remigio. 1971. "Sui codici della Medicina di Corn. Celso." In *Storia e critica di testi latini,* 2nd ed., pp. 215–237. Padova: Antenore.

———. 1996. *Le scoperte dei codici latini e greci ne' secoli XIV e XV. Nuove ricerche col riassunto filologico dei due volumi.* Florence: Le Lettere.

Sabbatini, Renzo. 2000. "Cartolai, librai, tipografi ed editori nella Firenze del Quattro-Cinquecento." In *Arti fiorentine. La grande storia dell'Artigianato*, vol. 3, *Il Cinquecento*, edited by Franco Franceschi and Gloria Fossi, pp. 81–105. Florence: Giunti.

Salvestrini, Francesco. 2017. *Il carisma della magnificenza. L'abate vallombrosano Biagio Milanesi e la tradizione benedettina nell'Italia del Rinascimento, con l'edizione critica del "memoriale" dell'abate Biagio Milanesi*. Rome: Viella.

Santi, Bruno. 1997. "Cennini, Bernardo." In *DBI*, vol. 23, pp. 563–565.

Scala, Bartolomeo. 1997. *Bartolomeo Scala: Humanistic and Political Writings*, edited by Alison Brown. Tempe, AZ: Medieval and Renaissance Texts and Studies.

Scapecchi, Piero. 1984. "Scava, scava, vecchia talpa! L'oscuro lavoro dell'incunabolista." *Biblioteche oggi* 2, pp. 37–50.

——. 1993. "New Light on the Ripoli Edition of the 'Expositio' of Donato Acciaioli." In *The Italian Book 1465–1800: Studies Presented to Dennis E. Rhodes on His 70th Birthday*, edited by Denis V. Reidy, pp. 31–33. London: British Library.

——. 2007. "Una dibattuta questione. Da [Napoli, tipografo del Terentius] a [Firenze, Niccolò di Lorenzo per Antonio di Guido]. Sull'identificazione e la localizzazione di una ignota tipografia." *Rara volumina* 2, pp. 5–11.

——. 2013. "Niccolo di Lorenzo." In *DBI*, vol. 78, pp. 414–415.

——. 2014. "Esemplari stampati a caratteri mobili presenti in Italia prima dell'introduzione della stampa. Prospettive di studio." *La Bibliofilía* 116, pp. 9–15.

——. 2015. "Pietro di Salvatore da Pisa." In *DBI*, vol. 83, pp. 549–551.

——. 2016. *Una collezione per una città. Catalogo delle edizioni quattrocentesche della Biblioteca Comunale e dell'Accademia Etrusca di Cortona*, edited by Edoardo Barbieri. Siena, Italy: Società Bibliografica Toscana.

——, ed. 2017. *Catalogo degli incunaboli della Biblioteca Nazionale Centrale*. Florence: Biblioteca Nazionale Centrale di Firenze / Nerbini.

Scarcia Piacentini, Paola. 1991. "Domenico da Pistoia." In *DBI*, vol. 49, pp. 657–659.

Schlebusch, Karl. 2017. *Giorgio Antonio Vespucci 1434–1514. Maestro canonico domenicano*. Florence: Nerbini.

Scholderer, Victor. 1966. "Printers and Readers in Italy in the Fifteenth Century." In *Fifty Essays in Fifteenth- and Sixteenth-Century Bibliography*, edited by Dennis E. Rhodes, pp. 202–215. Amsterdam: Menno Hertzberger.

Schröter, Kirsten. 1998. *Die Terminologie der italienischen Buchdrucker im 15. und 16. Jahrhundert*. Tübingen, Germany: Max Niemeyer Verlag.

Sebregondi, Ludovica. 2005. *San Jacopo in Campo Corbolini a Firenze. Percorsi storici dai templari all'ordine di Malta all'era moderna*. Florence: Edifir.

Semenzato, Francesco. 2013. "La fortuna editoriale del 'Filocolo' nel Cinquecento: il Quarto libro nell'edizione veneziana del 1514." PhD diss., Università Ca' Foscari di Venezia.

Servio, Mauro Onorato. 2011. *Commentario alle Bucoliche di Virgilio nell'incunabolo di Bernardo e Domenico Cennini 7 XI 1471*, edited by Paolo Cantinelli. Florence: Edizioni Polistampa.

Shaw, James, and Evelyn Welch. 2011. *Making and Marketing Medicine in Renaissance Florence.* Amsterdam: Brill.

Simonetta, Marcello. 2015. Review of *La congiura dei Pazzi: I documenti del conflitto fra Lorenzo de' Medici e Sisto IV. Le bolle di scomunica, la "Florentina Synodus," e la "Dissentio" insorta tra la Santità del Papa e i Fiorentini. Edizione critica e commento,* edited by Tobias Daniels, 2013. *Renaissance Quarterly* 68, pp. 674–675.

Sorbelli, Albano. 2004. *Corpus chartarum Italiae ad rem typographicam pertinentium ab arte inventa ad ann. MDL.* Vol. 1, *Bologna,* edited by Maria Gioia Tavoni. Rome: Istitito Poligrafico e Zecca dello Stato / Libreria dello Stato.

Steinberg, Sigfrid Henry. 1996. *Five Hundred Years of Printing.* Rev. ed. Revised by John Trevitt. London: British Library / Oak Knoll.

Stijnman, Ad, and Elizabeth Upper. 2014. "Color Prints before Erhard Ratdold: Engraved Paper Instruments in Lazarus Beham's 'Buch von der Astronomie' (Cologne: Nicolaus Götz, c. 1476)." *Gutenberg-Jahrbuch,* pp. 86–105.

Strocchia, Sharon T. 2016. "Begging for Favours: The 'New' Clares of Santa Chiara Novella and Their Patrons." In *Studies on Florence and the Italian Renaissance in Honour of F. W. Kent,* edited by Peter Howard and Cecilia Hewlett, pp. 277–294. Turnhout, Belgium: Brepols.

Takács, László, and Attila Tuhári, eds. 2015. *Two Renaissance Commentaries on Persius: Bartholomaeus Fontius' and Ioannes Britannicus' Commentaries on Persius.* Budapest: Avicenna Institute of Middle Eastern Studies.

Taucci, Raphaele. 1967. "La 'Geografia' del Berlinghieri della Biblioteca Alessandrina di Roma." *La Bibliofilía* 69, pp. 69–73.

Taurino, Antonio. 2006. "I 'Libri Commodorum Ruralium' di Pietro de Crescenzi, bolognese (1233–1321). Edizioni a stampa e manoscritti." In *Manoscritti, editoria e biblioteche dal medioevo all'età contemporanea. Studi offerti a Domenico Maffei per il suo ottantesimo compleanno,* edited by Mario Ascheri and Gaetano Colli, pp. 1281–1309. Rome: roma nel rinascimento.

Tavernati, Andrea. 1985. "Appunti sulla diffusione quattrocentesca de 'Il Driadeo' di Luca Pulci." *La Bibliofilía* 87, pp. 267–279.

Tazartes, Maurizia. 2007. *Fucina lucchese. Maestri, botteghe, mercanti in una città del Quattrocento.* Pisa: Edizioni ETS.

Tedeschi, Martha. 1991. "Publish and Perish: The Career of Lienhart Holle in Ulm." In *Printing the Written Word: The Social History of Books, circa 1450–1520,* edited by Sandra Hindman, pp. 41–67. Ithaca, NY: Cornell University Press.

Tordi, Domenico. 1909–1910. "Ser Agnolo Ferrini legatore d'incunaboli (1473–1488)." *La Bibliofilía* 11, pp. 182–190.

Trovato, Paolo. 1998. "Il libro in Toscana nell'età di Lorenzo." In *L'ordine dei tipografi. Lettori, stampatori, correttori fra Quattro e Cinquecento,* pp. 49–89. Rome: Bulzoni.

Tura, Adolfo. 2001. "Saggio su alcuni selezionati problemi di bibliografia fiorentina." In *Edizioni fiorentine del Quattrocento e primo Cinquecento in Trivulziana,* edited by Adolfo Tura, pp. 9–65. Milan: Biblioteca Trivulziana.

Uccelli, Giovan Battista. 1865. *Il convento di S. Giusto alle mura e i gesuati. Aggiungonsi i capitoli della loro regola testo di lingua.* Florence: Tipografia delle Murate.

Ulivi, Elisabetta. 2002. *Benedetto da Firenze (1429–1479), un maestro d'abaco del XV secolo. Con documenti inediti e con un'Appendice su abacisti e scuole d'abaco a Firenze nei secoli XIII–XVI.* Pisa: Istituti editoriali e Poligrafici internazionali.

Vaccaro, Giulio. 2017. "Bastiano de' Rossi editore e vocabolarista." *Studi di lessicografia italiana* 34, pp. 243–279.

Valenti, Marco. 1999. *Carta archeologica della provincia di Siena.* Vol. 2, *La Val d'Elsa (Colle di Val d'Elsa e Poggibonsi).* Siena, Italy: Nuova immagine editrice.

Van Binnebeke, Xavier. 2016. "Additions to the Latin Library of Giorgio Antonio Vespucci." In *Palaeography, Manuscript Illumination and Humanism in Renaissance Italy: Studies in Memory of A. C. de la Mare,* edited by Robert Black, Jill Kraye, and Laura Nuvoloni, pp. 231–250. London: Warburg Institute.

Van der Haegen, Pierre L. 2001. *Der frühe Basler Buchdruck.* Basel: Schwabe.

Vasoli, Cesare. 1994. "Brevi considerazioni su Sebastiano Salvini." In *Italia e Ungheria all'epoca dell'umanesimo corviniano,* edited by Sante Graciotti and Cesare Vasoli, pp. 111–133. Florence: Olschki.

———. 1999. "Per le fonti del 'De christiana religione.'" In *Quasi sit Deus. Studi su Marsilio Ficino,* pp. 113–219. Lecce, Italy: Conte Editore.

———. 2007. "Il 'De christiana religione' di Marsilio Ficino. Parole chiave: religione, sapienza, profezia, vita civile, ebrei." *Bruniana et Campanelliana* 13, pp. 403–428.

Vecce, Carlo. 2017. *La biblioteca perduta. I libri di Leonardo.* Rome: Salerno Editrice.

Veneziani, Paolo. 1982. "Vicende tipografiche della Geografia di Francesco Berlinghieri." *La Bibliofilía* 84, pp. 195–208.

———. 2004. "Jenson, Nicolas." In *DBI,* vol. 62, pp. 205–208.

Verde, Armando F., OP. 1973. *Lo Studio fiorentino 1473–1503. Ricerche e documenti. Vol. 2 (Docenti-Dottorati).* Florence: Istituto Nazionale di Studi sul Rinascimento.

———. 1977. *Lo Studio fiorentino 1473–1503. Ricerche e documenti. Vol. 3 (Studenti. "Fanciulli a scuola" nel 1480).* 2 parts. Pistoia: Presso "Memorie domenicane."

———. 1985. *Lo Studio fiorentino 1473–1503. Ricerche e documenti. Vol. 4 (La vita universitaria).* 3 parts. Florence: Olschki.

———. 1987. "Libri tra le pareti domestiche. Una necessaria appendice a 'Lo studio fiorentino 1473-1503.'" *Memorie domenicane,* n.s., 18, pp. 1–225.

———. 1994. *Lo Studio fiorentino 1473–1503. Ricerche e documenti. Vol. 5 (Gli stanziamenti).* Florence: Olschki

———. 2010. *Lo Studio fiorentino 1473–1503. Ricerche e documenti. Vol. 6 (Indici).* Edited by Raffaela Maria Zaccaria. Florence: Olschki.

Verde, Armando F., OP, and Elettra Giaconi, eds. 2003. "Epistolario di fra Santi Rucellai." *Memorie Domenicane,* n.s., 37, pp. III–XLVI, 1–411.

Vespasiano da Bisticci. 1976. *Le vite,* edited by Aulo Greco. 2 vols. Florence: Istituto Nazionale di Studi sul Rinascimento.

Villoresi, Marco. 2014. *Sacrosante parole. Devozione e letteratura nella Toscana del Rinascimento.* Florence: Società Editrice Fiorentina.

Zaccaria, Raffaela Maria. 1988. "Della Fonte, Bartolomeo." In *DBI*, vol. 36, pp. 808–814.

——. 2015. *Il carteggio della Signoria fiorentina all'epoca del cancellierato di Carlo Marsuppini (1444–1453). Inventario e regesti.* Rome: Ministero dei beni e delle attività culturali e del turismo.

Zamponi, Stefano, ed. 1988. *Le devote carte. Esegesi, devozione, culto mariano nei manoscritti di enti ecclesiastici pistoiesi.* Pistoia, Italy: Edizioni del Comune di Pistoia.

Zanobi da Strada and Giovanni da San Miniato. 2005. *Morali di Santo Gregorio Papa sopra il libro di Iob,* edited by Giuseppe Porta. Florence: SISMEL / Edizioni del Galluzzo.

Zucker, Mark. 2002. Review of *Sandro Botticelli: The Drawings for Dante's Divine Comedy,* by Heiner-Th. Schulze Altcappenberg. *Print Quarterly* 19, pp. 81–82.

INDEX